Marine Fish
of the
Channel Islands

Alex Plaster
Paul Chambers

Marine Fish of the Channel Islands

First published in Great Britain
in 2018 by Charonia Media

A catalogue record of this report is available from the British Library

ISBN 978 0 9560655 6 8

Contents

Guide to the Fish Families

Introduction

This book covers all known marine fish species from Jersey, Guernsey, Alderney, Sark, Herm and the other islets and reefs that collectively form the Channel Islands. The authors have combed historical archives, contemporary reports and scientific records to produce a list of 216 fish species that have at least one contemporary or historical report from the Channel Islands.

Situated on the southern edge of the British Isles, the Channel Islands have a notable diversity of fish species, many of which are rare or absent from UK waters. These range from sharks that can reach several metres in length through to gobies of just a few centimetres. There are the everyday fish that we catch and eat regularly, such as mackerel, plaice and seabream, but also bizarre and unexpected species that have strayed into local waters on a handful of occasions such as the Deep-sea Angler, Flying Fish and Bramble Shark.

Written with the angler, naturalist and ichthyologist in mind, this book represents the most comprehensive available guide to the marine fish species of the Channel Islands. The thousands of records gathered by the authors have revealed new information about historical and recent trends within Channel Island fish populations and have brought to light unexpected events and anecdotes relating to local fishing culture. For those fish that are most popular with recreational anglers capture techniques and bait preferences are given. All this is accompanied by several hundred colour illustrations, maps and photographs.

Most of this information is being made available for the first time and it is hoped that, as well as being a useful guide to the islands' naturalists and angling enthusiasts, this book will be of interest to marine biologists, historians and fishery managers.

Whether it is a recently arrived fish from southern Europe or a traditional species seen every day, this book will help to put a perspective on the scope and status of fish species in one of Europe's most important but fragile regional maritime regions.

Alex Plaster and Paul Chambers
October 2018

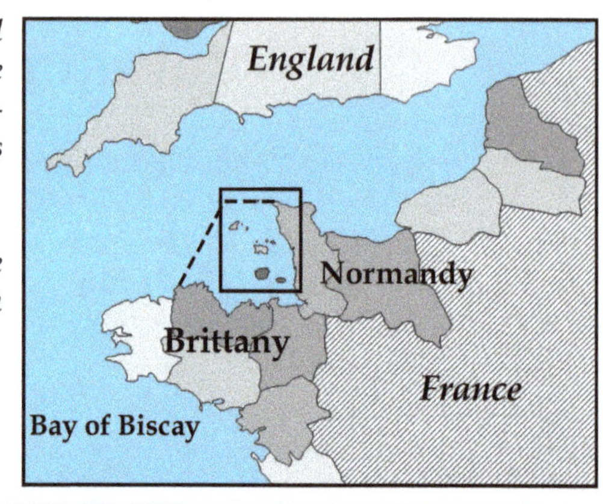

Right: *A map of the English Channel and northern Bay of Biscay. The dashed line indicates the Normano-Breton Gulf. The solid box indicates the extent of the map below.*

Below: *A bathymetric map of the Channel Islands with the main islands, islets and reefs labelled.*

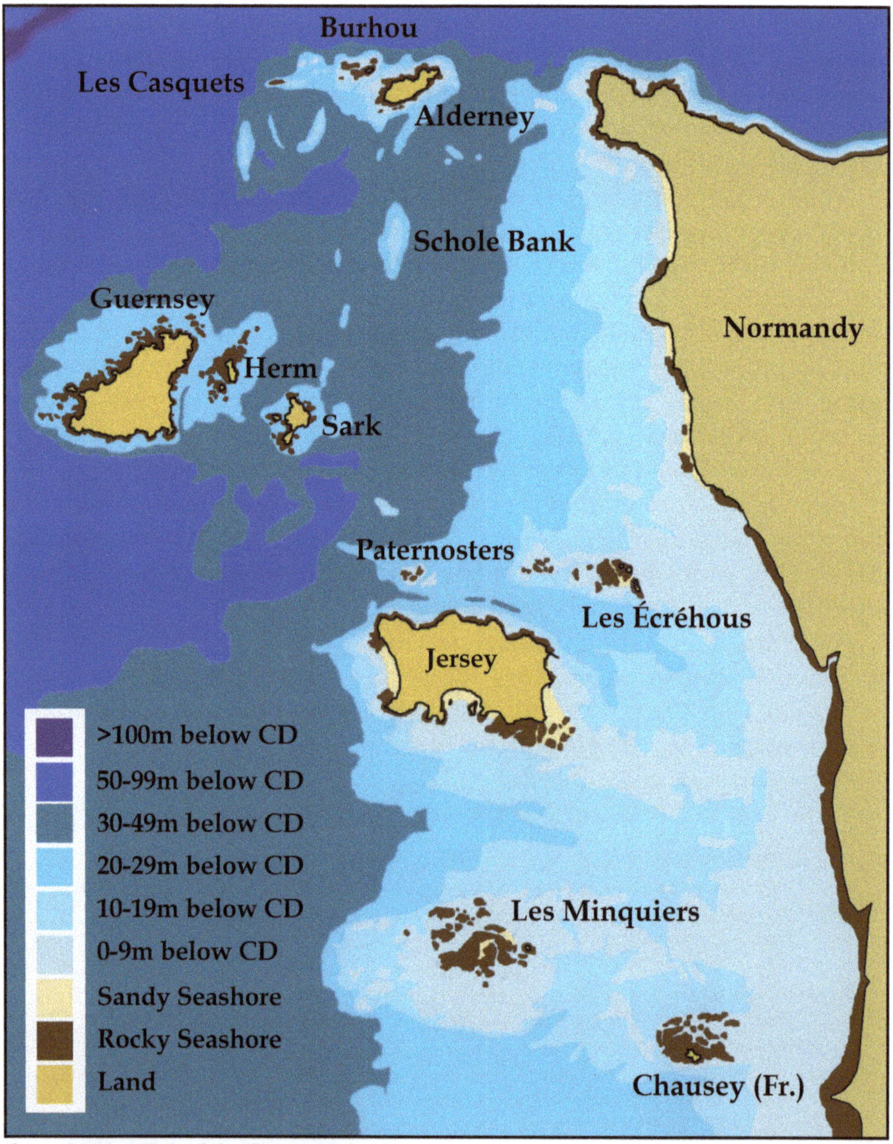

The Channel Islands

With clear, nutrient rich waters and a varied underwater landscape, the Channel Islands are a haven for divers, anglers and beachcombers.

The Channel Islands are located in the Normano-Breton Gulf, an area of shallow sea in the western English Channel that is bounded by the Normandy and Brittany coastlines. There are five larger islands (Jersey, Guernsey, Alderney, Sark and Herm) which are formed into two self-governing Crown Dependencies. The Bailiwick of Jersey contains the island of Jersey and a collection of offshore reefs (most notably Les Écréhous and Les Minquiers); while the Bailiwick of Guernsey is formed of the inhabited islands of Guernsey, Alderney, Sark and Herm plus a collection of islets and reefs.

Both bailiwicks are dependencies of the English Crown but they are not part of the United Kingdom. This is a legacy of the Norman Conquest when the Duchy of Normandy, under William the Conqueror, captured the English throne at the Battle of Hastings in 1066. When Normandy was lost to France in 1204, the Channel Islands elected to remain with England creating a small British archipelago off the northern coast of France.

The seas around the Channel Islands are famous for their large tides (reaching nearly 13 metres at Les Minquiers), lack of pollution and diverse marine life. The islands are home to many southern European marine species, such as the Ormer (*Haliotis tuberculata*), whose northerly range is reached at the English Channel. There are several species of fish found locally (e.g. seabreams and jacks) that are more often associated with the Bay of Biscay although, conversely, there are colder water species that are either rare or absent from the islands (see page 278).

The sea area administered by the Channel Islands is 6,200 km^2 and is split into two distinctive oceanographic regions with a dividing line that almost exactly follows the maritime border between Jersey and Guernsey. To the north of this line the waters are deep and exposed to currents and weather from the English Channel while to the south the seabed around Jersey and Les Minquiers is shallower (mostly <20 metres) and topographically complex. This means that the waters around Guernsey and Alderney tend to be deeper, stratified and open to water movements from the English Channel. The waters around Jersey are influenced by a complex series of gyres that operate around the reefs and islands, trapping seawater and nutrients in the area and creating warmer summer sea temperatures.

Although the islands share a majority of their marine species, the differences in oceanography and seabed topography produce subtle differences. Guernsey tends to receive more deeper water species and oceanic pelagic fish while Jersey's extensive shallow marine areas encourage inshore species and benthic feeders. With such a diversity of ecological niches and with the Bay of Biscay and Atlantic Ocean close by, it is little wonder that the Channel Islands have so many fish species in such a small geographic area.

Unsurprisingly, the Channel Islands have a rich tradition of coastal fishing both from a commercial and recreational perspective. There is also a strong tradition of natural history recording and scientific investigation. These two traits helped provide the wealth of historical and contemporary information that were used to create the species list used for this book. The main information sources are discussed below.

Information Sources

The location of the Channel Islands on the southern fringe of the British Isles has attracted naturalists from both the United Kingdom and France. The subtly different maritime flora and fauna allowed Victorian biologists to extend their specimen collections although it was not until the twentieth century that scientists accepted that Channel Island marine species were part of the list of British flora and fauna. As well as welcoming visiting experts, the Channel Islands developed proficient naturalists of their own, some of whom founded the Société Jersiaise (1873) and the Société Guernesiais (1882), learned organisations that have provided a centrepoint for historical, cultural and biological studies across the two bailiwicks. Recently these institutions were joined by the Alderney Wildlife Trust, the Guernsey Biological records Centre and the Jersey Biodiversity Centre, all of which are devoted to natural history studies and gathering wildlife records.

This long tradition of natural history studies means that the Channel Islands have a remarkable documentary record of their native and (more recently non-native) plant and animal species. This includes most marine groups many of which have been documented since early Victorian times. From the outset particular attention was paid to the islands' fish species some of which were not then known in the UK. It is this mass of fish related biological data that has been gathered together, analysed and sifted to produce the list of species that form the basis of this book.

Over 12,000 fish records were collected by the authors via painstaking searches through libraries, journals, books, newspapers and institutional archives. The authors searched for local references in classic Victorian fish volumes written by the likes of Jonathan Couch, Francis Day and Paul Gervais. They also searched through the annual bulletins produced by the Société Jersiaise and Société Guernesiaise where many unusual fish captures were reported. Additionally, institutional records from the States of Jersey and Guernsey, ICES, FAO, CEFAS, Seasearch and others were requested and studied. All this information was inputted into a database held by the Marine Biology Section of the Société Jersiaise and then updated to reflect changes in species names, taxonomy, etc.

As well as individual records, sightings and reports, this book was able to draw on a number of summary lists of local fish species made at various times over the past two centuries. The oldest such list was compiled by Jonathan Duncan in 1841 and was followed twenty years later by a wider Channel Island list put together by the respected Guernsey naturalist Frederick Lukis. At the turn of the twentieth century a spat with his son-in-law persuaded the Jersey museum curator and taxidermist Joseph Sinel to publish his own Channels Island fish list, complete with comments on their distribution and abundance.

In 1967 a short book on Jersey fish was published in memory of Ronald le Sueur whose knowledge of local marine biology was at the time unrivalled. The most recent list of local fish species was produced in 2009 by the French Ifremer scientist Patrick le Mao who collected hundreds of regional records as part of a broader project to document several key marine groups from the Normano-Breton Gulf. Finally, in 2006 CEFAS started annual scientific beam trawl surveys in the English Channel which have produced a wealth of information about the benthic offshore species in and around the Channel Islands.

These species lists provide snapshots in time concerning the commonality and constitution of the Channel Islands' fish population with the gaps between being infilled with a wealth of casual data. Through the careful study and interpretation of these and other records it has been possible to detect the arrival of new species, such as the Triggerfish, and the disappearance of existing ones, such as the Common Skate. It is also possible to estimate changes in abundance and distribution for some of the more common species.

The end product of this research is a list of over two hundred fish species reported from the islands since the start of the nineteenth century. This is a remarkably diverse list for such a small area and it is probable that some of these reports are erroneous - the reasoning for such doubts is explained in the relevant entries. However, the majority of species documented here are valid, which makes the Channel Islands one of the most diverse fish areas in the British Isles.

The Scope of this Book

This book was written as a comprehensive guide to all the known fish species from the Channel Islands. Each species has its own entry that includes a basic illustration and biological information as well as a brief written summary of cultural, historical, biological and other information relating to the fish. Capture and bait information are provided for species that are commonly targeted by anglers. Conservation information is provided where relevant, as are catch statistics and photographs.

Please note that this book was designed to be a popular guide to the diversity of local fish species. It is not an identification guide nor is it a scholarly study into the science of fish populations or the history of the islands' fisheries. Those requiring an identification guide that covers most Channel Island species could try consulting the *Identification Guide to Inshore Fish of the British Isles* (Henderson, 2014) or *A Field Guide to the Marine Fishes of Wales* (Kay and Dipper, 2009). For a regional perspective on the marine environment and aspects of local fisheries see *Les Minquiers: A Natural History* (Chambers, Binney and Jeffreys, 2016) or *Les Écréhous* (Rodwell, 1996).

The hidden lifestyle of marine fish and their ability to move about makes it difficult for anyone to know precisely where fish are living, how abundant they are and how they may be behaving. The annals of fishing are filled with discussions and arguments between anglers, fishermen, politicians, naturalists and scientists, each of whom may have individual theories about what is happening within a fishery and how it should best be managed. There can be few other areas in science where the gulf between anecdotal and empirical evidence is so wide and where the former may still play a central role in decision-making.

Within this uncertain and conflicted landscape a book such as this will never be able to please all of its readers, all of the time. However, we hope that our careful evidence gathering and assessments (although often based on limited information) means that this book will please most of its readers, most of the time. We would welcome any comments, criticism or corrections and can be contacted via the Marine Biology Section of the Socété Jersiaise.

Fish Species of the Channel Islands

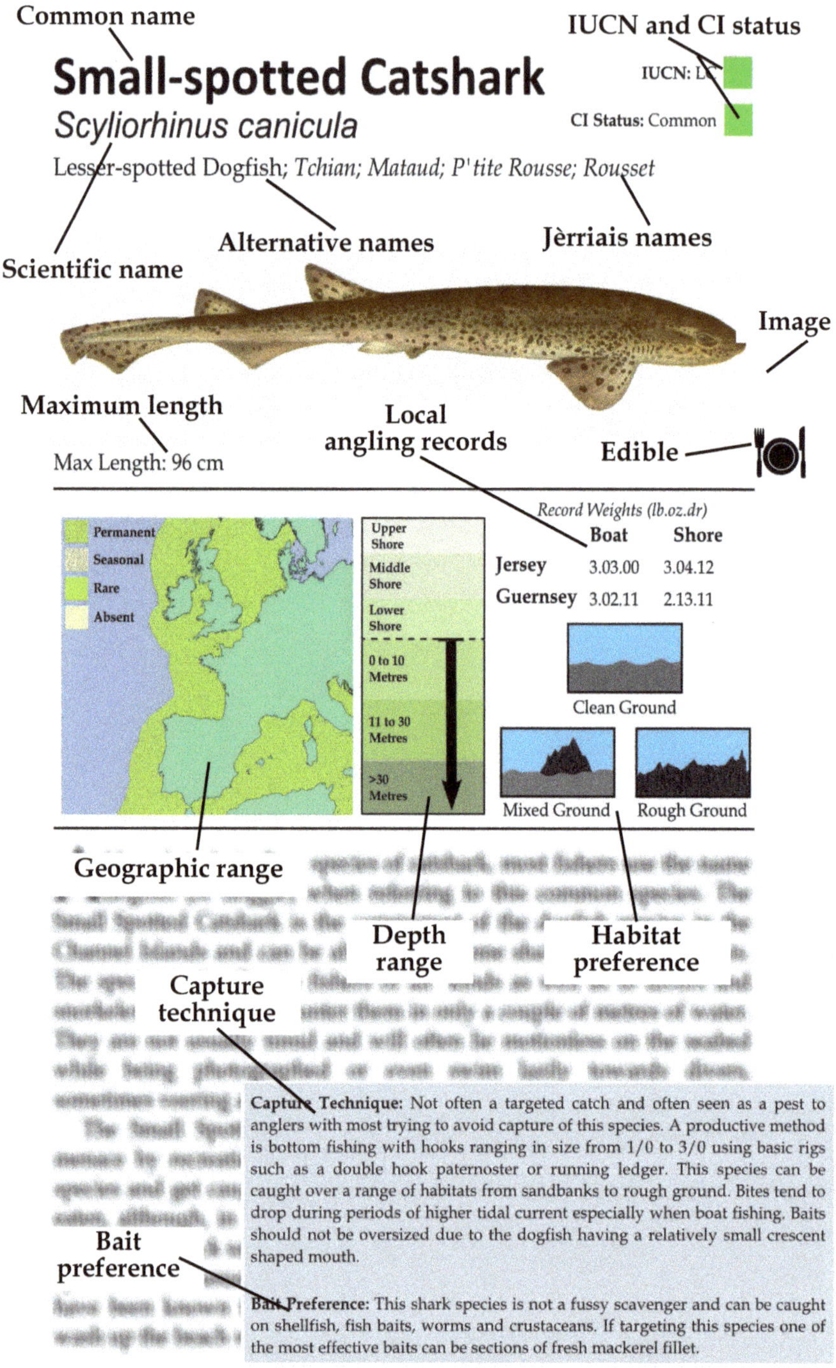

Common name
IUCN and CI status
Small-spotted Catshark
Scyliorhinus canicula
IUCN: LC
CI Status: Common
Lesser-spotted Dogfish; Tchian; Mataud; P'tite Rousse; Rousset
Alternative names
Jèrriais names
Scientific name
Image
Maximum length
Local angling records
Edible
Max Length: 96 cm
Record Weights (lb.oz.dr)
Boat
Shore
Jersey 3.03.00 3.04.12
Guernsey 3.02.11 2.13.11
Permanent
Seasonal
Rare
Absent
Upper Shore
Middle Shore
Lower Shore
0 to 10 Metres
11 to 30 Metres
>30 Metres
Clean Ground
Mixed Ground
Rough Ground
Geographic range
Depth range
Habitat preference
Capture technique
Capture Technique: Not often a targeted catch and often seen as a pest to anglers with most trying to avoid capture of this species. A productive method is bottom fishing with hooks ranging in size from 1/0 to 3/0 using basic rigs such as a double hook paternoster or running ledger. This species can be caught over a range of habitats from sandbanks to rough ground. Bites tend to drop during periods of higher tidal current especially when boat fishing. Baits should not be oversized due to the dogfish having a relatively small crescent shaped mouth.
Bait preference
Bait Preference: This shark species is not a fussy scavenger and can be caught on shellfish, fish baits, worms and crustaceans. If targeting this species one of the most effective baits can be sections of fresh mackerel fillet.

A Guide to the Species Pages

Each fish species in this book has an individual entry which provides summary information about its local occurence, ecology, biology, angling potential and status. Where possible this information is presented visually - a key to the page layout is shown opposite and a written description is provided below.

The fish list is presented in approximate taxonomic order - i.e. those species that possess what might be considered primitive biological characteristics are presented first while the more biologically advanced ones come later. This is standard practice and reflects the rough evolutionary history of marine fish over the past 500 million years.

There are introductory summaries for some of the larger or more complex groups of fish (such as sharks, gobies, etc.) but, for reasons of space, we have not provided a write up for every fish family. Those seeking additional information about any of the fish species or the family they belong to should consult the references given in the **Bibliography** section (page 284).

Common and Scientific Names

Every animal and plant species on Earth that has been formally identified is given a two part **scientific name** (e.g. humans are *Homo sapiens*). This name is unique and is used by scientists to identify the organism and also to locate its evolutionary position in relation to every other species, living and extinct. Scientific names will alter with time as researchers discover new biological and genetic affinities between species. The scientific names in this book are taken from the WORMS website (www.marinespecies.org) as this is widely viewed as an accesible, reliable and up-to-date resource.

The **common names** used for plants and animals are not fixed or unique and will change with time, language, location and fashion. Most fish species will have a common name and some may have several. In this book we have provided the most often used English common names for each fish but also any local names in **Jèrriais** which is the traditional Norman-French language of Jersey. The Jèrriais names are given in italics and were taken from a list compiled by the Société Jersiaise. All the Channel Islands have their own Norman-French derived languages but we were unable to find similar lists for Guernsey, Alderney and Sark. The Channel Island languages are no longer widely spoken and so the local fish names are rarely used today.

Local Angling Records

The Channel Island **rod-caught fish records** were kindly provided by the Bailiwick of Guernsey Rod-Caught Fish Committee and the Jersey Rod-Caught Fish Committee. These were valid at the point of publication but often change as bigger fish are caught. An **asterisk** next to a weight denotes it is a British weight record as well as a local one.

Biological Statistics

Biological data such as **maximum length, depth range, geographical distribution** and **habitat preference** were taken from standard resources including several published works on European fish species as well as the data provided by Fishbase (www.fishbase.org). The length, depth and distribution map are self-explanatory. The habitat symbols can be explained as follows.

Clean ground represents sedimentary seabeds with few rocks or protrusions. **Mixed ground** refers to a mixture of sandy and rocky seabeds. **Rocky ground** is a hard, often complex, rocky seabed of bedrock, cobble or boulders. **Pelagic** refers to fish that live mid-water and **seagrass** refers to offshore seagrass beds (*Zostera marina*) or sometimes also dense seaweeds.

This information was modified where necessary to reflect known local differences in behaviour and habitat preference (e.g. the Channel Islands' large tidal range means some traditionally shallow marine species can be intertidal). Quoted **catch statistics** were taken from data submitted to ICES and the FAO by the Jersey and Guernsey governments. These were analysed both for possible regional trends but also to gauge the geographical distribution of commercial species.

Images and Photographs

This book is not meant to be an identification guide and the **drawings** and **photographs** provided are for illustrative purposes only. Most of the drawings were taken from Jonathan Couch's multivolume Victorian work *A History of the Fishes of the British Islands* which has been out of copyright for many years. An unbound set of hand-coloured plates from this work were provided by Roger Long to whom we are grateful. Each plate was digitally scanned and then cleaned using Photoshop.

Where no plate could be found, other sources were found with drawings being preferred to photographs although, in some instances, this could not be avoided. A list of the illustrations used for this book and their origin is provided on page 285.

Capture Technique and Bait

The angling information included in this book focuses on those fish species that are most popular with recreational rod fishers within the Channel Islands. The principal descriptions are on **capture technique** (such as the hook sizes, line strength, etc.) and the species' **bait preference**. This information comes directly from the authors' knowledge and experience of angling in Channel Island waters. A 'knife and fork' symbol has been used to indicate those **edible fish** that are traditionally considered to be good to eat.

Fishing Rules and Regulations

Like all other European fisheries, the bailiwicks of Jersey and Guernsey have **fishing regulations** that dictate minimum landing sizes, equipment standards, catch and release, protected species, bag limits, etc. These may relate to commercial and recreational fishing. Effective fisheries management is reflexive and rules can change quickly and so this book does not provide information relating to the fishing rules and regulations of Jersey and Guernsey. We strongly recommend that anglers should check websites for the States of Jersey and Guernsey so that they know the latest regulations before they go fishing.

IUCN Status

Overfishing, climate change, habitat destruction, pollution and other issues have caused changes in fish populations across the globe including within the Channel Islands. Changes in local fish stocks are often (but not always) due to factors that operate on a regional or international basis (e.g. overfishing in the English Channel) rather than just within the islands. The desire to have clean seas with sustainable fishing has gained much publicity in recent years and there are a number of organisations which provide independent assessments on the current status of the world's marine fish, usually in relation to the size of their unfished population and the possibility of a species' extinction.

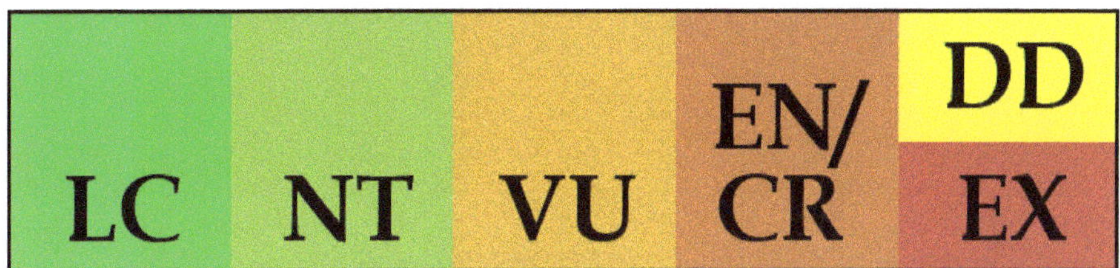

The 'traffic light' colours used to indicate a fish's assessment within the IUCN threatened species index (see www.iucnredlist.org for more details). The abbreviations are as follows:

LC = **least concern**; *NT* = **near threatened**; *VU* = **vulnerable**; *EN* = **endangered**; *CR* = **critically endangered**; *EX* = **extinct**; *DD* = **data deficient**.

In this book we have used two different systems to offer an indication of each fish species' population status. The first is an international assessment from the **IUCN Red List of Threatened Species** which categorises plants and animals in relation to the threat of them becoming extinct. The scale runs from 'least concern' through to 'extinct' and is widely regarded as a reliable indicator of the health of individual species' populations on a global scale. For more information on the assement criteria, see the IUCN website (www.iucnredlist.org).

Channel Islands (CI) Status

A second measure used to assess each species' status is the authors' own creation which we've called CI Status. This offers an indication as to the present abundance of a species within the Channel Islands. This scale is designed to reflect each species' local commonality by indicating how easy it would be for a skilled angler/naturalist to find a particular fish if fishing/searching within its preferred habitat and depth range by using the correct equipment/technique. The CI Status scale has the following categories.

Common (many specimens could be found); **Frequent** (a small number could be found); **Occasional** (one or two might be found); **Rare** (specimens are unlikely to be found easily); **Expirated** (a historically recorded species that is no longer found locally); **Vagrant** (a species that is not resident but may visit the area); **Unconfirmed** (where a historical record seems improbable or needs confirmation).

The assigned CI Status categorisation is based on an analysis of the local records and other information gathered for this book. This includes the views of commercial fishers, recreational anglers and local naturalists. However, many local fish species are data deficient and so the CI Status of a species is often an educated judgement based on a balance of probabilities and should be treated as such.

The 'traffic light' colours used to indicate a fish's assessment within the Channel Islands (CI) Status classification. The abbreviations are as follows:
Co = **common**; *Fr* = **frequent**; *Oc* = **occasional**; *R* = **rare**; ; *Ex* = **expirated**; *Un* = **unconfirmed**.

Jawless Fish and Sharks

The jawless fish, sharks and rays (known as elasmobranchs) are primitive vertebrates whose skeleton is composed principally of cartilage, a rigid but flexible substance which makes up much of the human nose. There are several common species of shark in the Channel Islands but just one species of jawless fish, the Sea Lamprey.

The jawless fish belong to the fish group called 'agnathans' which evolved over 500 million years ago and which, as the name implies, lack jaws but have teeth, often arranged within a circular mouth. Only one species of Channel Island fish-like chordate is more primitive than the Sea Lamprey and that is the Lancelet (*Branchiostoma lanceolatum*) which possesses a notochord (spinal cord) but no backbone. The Lancelet is not uncommon around the islands but being an invertebrate and not a true fish, is not covered in this book.

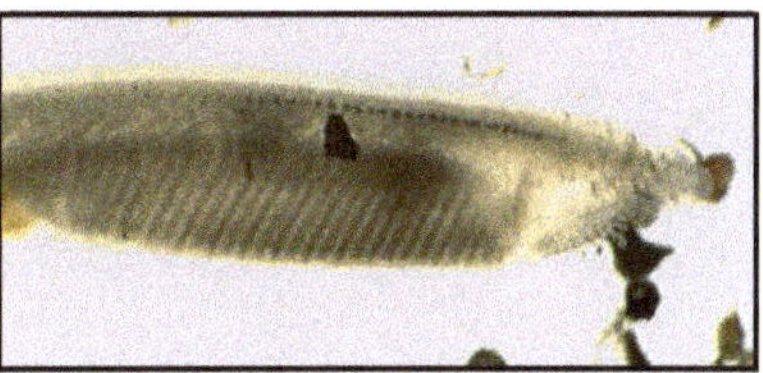

A Lancelet from near La Rocque, Jersey (length = 3 cm).

Sharks evolved later than the jawless fish (circa 420 million years) and possess boney jaws armed with teeth. As a group, sharks have been highly successful with nearly 500 living species and they often occupy the role of top predator within a food chain.

There are around twenty species of shark that can be found in the English Channel, twelve of which are definitely known from the Channel Islands while another two (the Hammerhead and Smoothhound) have unconfirmed records. As local seas warm, it is possible that some southern European shark species may be more regularly seen, such as the Bigeye Thresher (*Alopias vulpinus*) and even the notorious White Shark (*Carcharodon carcharias*). There have already been anecdotal reports of White Sharks locally but these are almost certainly misidentifications of Porbeagle Sharks. The nearest definite reports are from La Rochelle and, as with other Bay of Biscay fish species, vagrant White Sharks reaching the English Channel is not impossible.

Most of the larger, pelagic sharks are late maturing and often have complex reproduction cycles that require lengthy sea migrations. This makes them vulnerable to overfishing and some of the larger Channel Island species, such as Blue and Porbeagle Sharks, are endangered.

Contrary to their Hollywood depiction, most sharks avoid humans and so will often come and go into an area undetected. More information is needed about most Channel Island sharks and we would encourage people to report sightings to one of the local wildlife record centres.

Sea Lamprey
Petromyzon marinus

Max Length: 90 cm

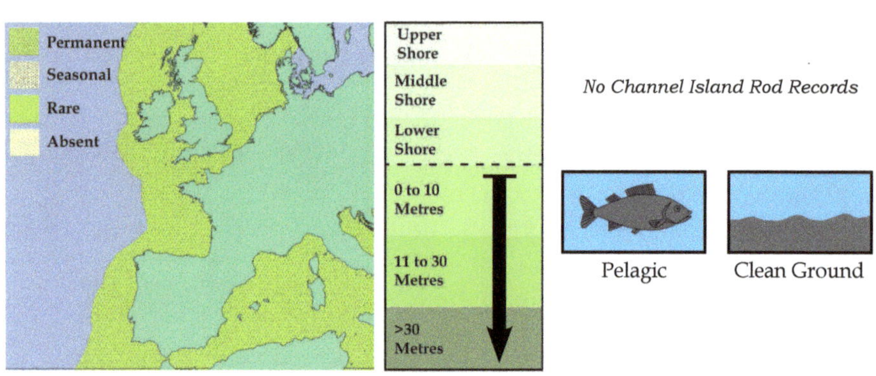

Lampreys are jawless fish which live on soft sediment and attach themselves to other fish. The Sea Lamprey is unlikely to be seen by divers but may occasionally be caught by anglers (usually attached to another fish) or taken in nets and trawls.

The Sea Lamprey is probably an uncommon resident of the Channel Islands with only a handful of known regional records since the 1860s. However, catches are still made with the last known specimen being taken in 2005 by an angler in Guernsey.

The Sea Lamprey population in Europe declined severely after World War II and the species is now protected in several countries. The distinctive circular marks of their jaws may sometimes be seen on corpses, such as the example (shown right) which was on a Common Dolphin washed up in 2018 on Jersey.

Lamprey bite mark on a dead dolphin

Shorkfin Mako Shark

Isurus oxyrinchus

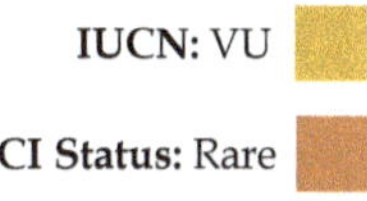

Max Length: 350 cm

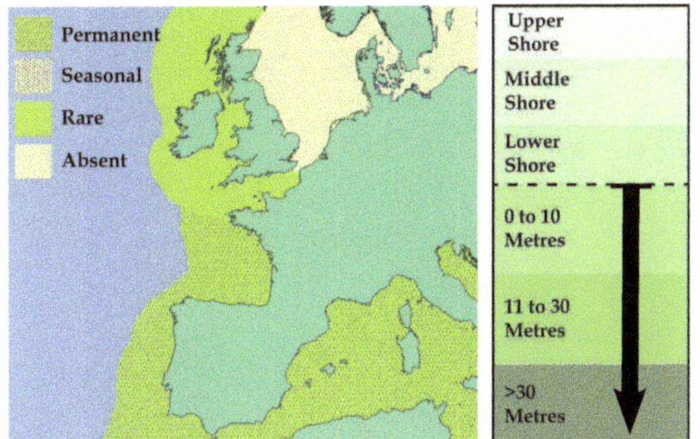

No Channel Island Rod Records

Pelagic

This large shark is a rare visitor to the English Channel but is relatively common in the Bay of Biscay. Records are sporadic and there is just one confirmed Channel Island's record when a specimen was captured and killed just off the Guernsey coast in 1931 (see photograph below). Other reports of this shark in the region are unconfirmed.

The Shortfin Mako is potentially dangerous but most injuries have been due to the animal being caught and not handled correctly.

Overfishing has depleted the global Shortfin Mako population and it is regarded by the IUCN as vulnerable. This is the fastest swimming shark and can reach speeds of up to 42 mph (67 kph).

A Shortfin Mako caught off Guernsey in 1931.

Porbeagle Shark

Lamna nasus

IUCN: VU

CI Status: Occasional

Beaumaris Shark; *Rétchin; Cheurque*

Max Length: 350 cm

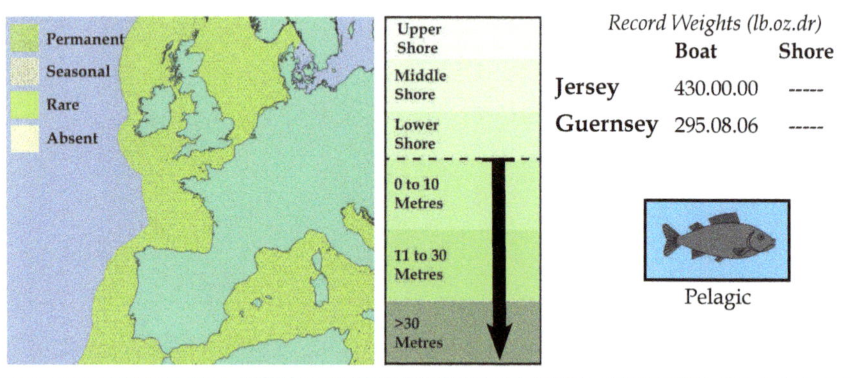

Record Weights (lb.oz.dr)

	Boat	Shore
Jersey	430.00.00	-----
Guernsey	295.08.06	-----

The Porbeagle is the commonest of the large pelagic sharks found around the Channel Islands. It is a shy, predominantly offshore species that is most often seen from boats, usually by anglers. Encounters are typically brief and may just involve the sight of its dorsal fin for a few seconds before it dives to deeper water. However, there are reliable reports of Porbeagle Sharks having swum around surfers in St Ouen's Bay, Jersey, and even of entering harbours at high tide.

Most historical shark reports from the Channel Islands are of Porbeagles which have been caught by people fishing for Conger Eels or, more commonly, netting offshore for Mackerel. One nineteenth century report describes the Porbeagle Shark as being a menace during the 'breaming season' when the sharks would follow fishing lines to the surface, snatching the bream before they could be landed. In 1889 a large Porbeagle was killed in a net set off Rocquaine, Guernsey, and for several days afterwards the body was displayed in St Peter Port.

The Porbeagle is large and is in the same family as the much feared White Shark. Although it looks aggressive, this shark is actually harmless to humans unless severely provoked. It is almost never seen by divers and will generally steer clear of boats unless there is potential food in the water. It will occasionally follow caught fish or bait to the surface giving anglers a good view but otherwise its dorsal fin will sometimes be seen briefly at the surface before the animal dives rapidly to the depths.

The Porbeagle Shark has a commercial value, primarily for its dorsal fin, and until recently there were infrequent landings recorded against the Channel Islands. Their commercial sale is now prohibited locally but this shark is still pursued by anglers as a sport fish, usually on a catch and release basis. As a slow growing and maturing species, the global population of Porbeagles has been severely depleted by commercial fishing and it is expected to join the list of legally protected EU marine species imminently.

Amateur studies in the 1950s and 60s by the Jersey naturalist Ronald le Sueur suggested that the islands might be a nursery area for Porbeagle Sharks. He studied specimens taken by sport anglers and found that a higher than expected number were female and carrying embryos. A satellite tagging project off Portugal tracked a Porbeagle to the Channel Islands suggesting that they may migrate here from the open ocean.

The fragility of the world's pelagic shark population (including the Porbeagle) makes angling for them innapropriate, even on a catch and release basis. At least ten percent of Porbeagles are known to die within two days of being released from commerical fisheries and the prolonged fight of a shark caught on incorrect tackle will exhaust many animals beyond the point of recovery. The IUCN lists the Porbeagle as vulnerable and any sightings should be made to a local records centre.

*The White Shark (*Carcharodon carcharias*) has no confirmed records from the English Channel but it is closely related to the Porbeagle and looks similar. It is probable that anecdotal reports of White Sharks in the Channel Island waters are misidentifications of Porbeagle Sharks.*

Basking Shark

Cetorhinus maximus

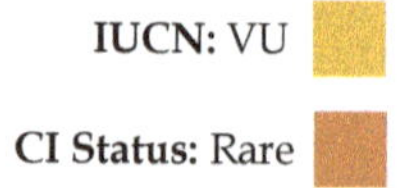

Max Length: 1100 cm

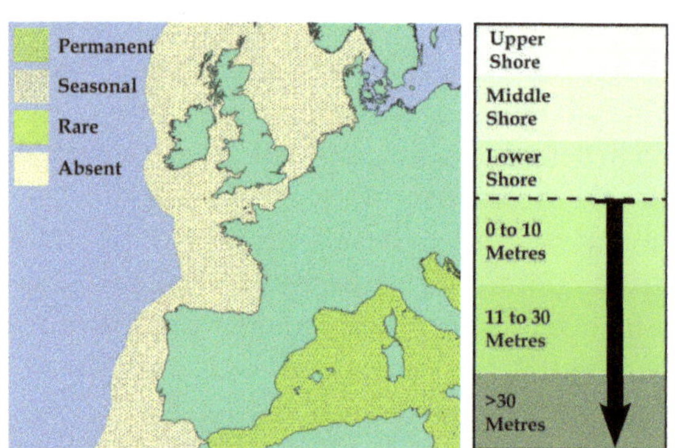

No Channel Island Rod Records

Pelagic

The Basking Shark is the second largest fish in the sea (the largest being the Whale Shark) with large individuals reaching lengths of more than ten metres and weighing over four tonnes. It is an open ocean fish that feeds on plankton and, despite its impressive size and shark shape, is harmless to humans. The behaviour of Basking Sharks remains little understood although satellite tracking has revealed that they can migrate for hundreds or even thousands of kilometres and will generally be found in the English Channel during the summer months.

These sharks are generally observed as lone individuals and are more common to the north of the islands. They are regularly seen off the Cornish and Welsh coasts but sightings in Channel Island waters are rare and generally occur in deeper waters to the west of Guernsey and south of Sark. They can often be spotted some distance away because of their large, dark dorsal fin but, if seen, should not be approached too closely in a boat as they can swim erratically. Diving or snorkelling with Basking Sharks is possible but they are powerful animals with rough skin and so, to avoid injury and to respect the animal, keep a distance of five metres or more. There used to be an important fishery for Basking Sharks in Europe but this has led to their numbers declining dramatically and they are now legally protected in many countries.

For such a large and obvious fish, the number of Channel Island records is remarkably small. It appears on some nineteenth century fish lists but reports are sporadic thereafter. Currently there are usually no more than one or two reports a year, mostly by leisure boaters during the summer. More information is urgently needed on this species' presence in the Channel Islands so any sightings should be passed on to a local records centre.

The most unusual (and tragic) local event concerning a Basking Shark occurred in July 1951 when a juvenile (3.5 metres long) became stranded at low tide in the seawater swimming pool at Havre des Pas, Jersey.

The shark became distressed and started to thrash wildly sending bathers scrambling out of the pool. A large crowd gathered to watch the trapped animal but before long members of the Jersey Rifle Association arrived and proceeded to shoot at the animal until it died. After lots of pictures for the local newspaper, the body was carted off to the abattoir.

SHOOTING THE SHARK

Our pictures show Mr. G. H. Brée shooting the shark, the carcase brought ashore, and the two lads who first saw the unusual visitor, each holding one end of the rope round the carcase

'Shooting the shark' - the stranding of a Basking Shark at Havre des Pas, Jersey, made headline news in 1951.

Thresher Shark

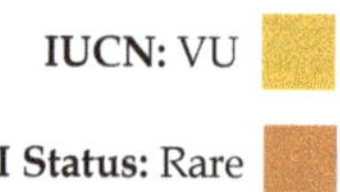

Alopias vulpinus

Fox Shark; *Érnard; Érnaûd; R'nard; R'naûd*

Max Length: 600 cm

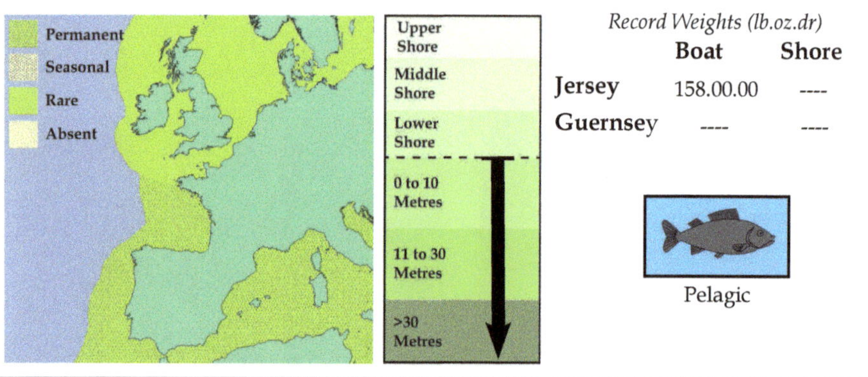

Record Weights (lb.oz.dr)

	Boat	Shore
Jersey	158.00.00	----
Guernsey	----	----

The Thresher Shark is generally an open water and solitary fish which is only rarely encountered in the English Channel. Reports from the Channel Islands are sporadic and several years may pass between confirmed sightings. The oldest known encounter was in July 1860 from a mackerel angler working nine miles south-west of Jersey who had a four metre long Thresher Shark tangled in his net. After a prolonged struggle he landed the shark and the body was put on display in St Helier for ten days. Afterwards it was stuffed and displayed at local horse racing events.

Other reports come from 1920 (St Brelade's Bay); 1961 (Les Écréhous); 1999 (Guernsey) and 2004 (Alderney). The global Thresher Shark population has been severely depleted by commercial fishing and, like most pelagic sharks, the species is considered to be vulnerable. Caught specimens should be handled and released in the water and a report made to one of the local records centres.

Blackmouth Catshark

IUCN: LC

CI Status: Unconfirmed

Galeus melastomus

Blackmouth Dogfish

Max Length: 80 cm

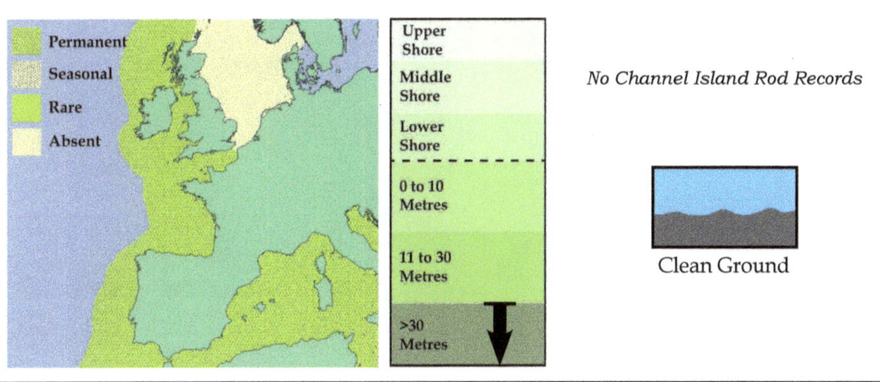

No Channel Island Rod Records

Clean Ground

The only record for the Blackmouth Catshark in this region comes from an 1862 list of Channel Island fish provided by local naturalists for a comprehensive tourist guide to the islands and their wildlife. The Blackmouth Catshark is generally a deeper water shark that lives below 150 metres and so is unlikely to have been found locally. It is therefore possible that the lone out of context historical record from 1862 is based on a misidentification or other error. However, Blackmouth Catsharks have been caught in shallower waters but without further proof, this species should be considered as doubtful for the Channel Islands.

Small-spotted Catshark

Scyliorhinus canicula

Lesser-spotted Dogfish; *Tchian; Mataud; P'tite Rousse; Rousset*

Max Length: 95 cm

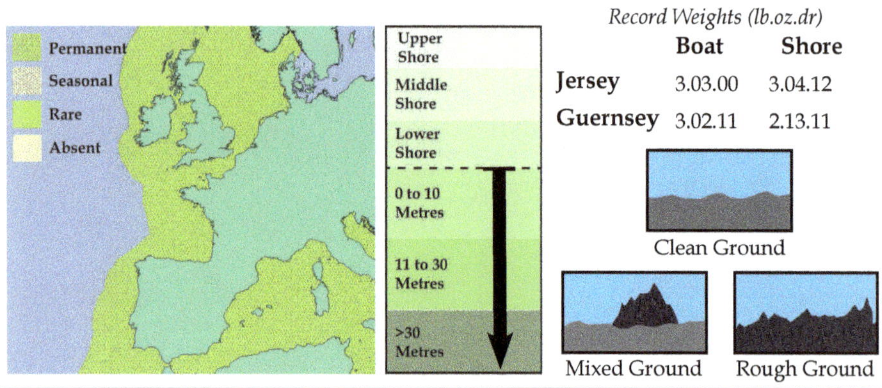

Record Weights (lb.oz.dr)

	Boat	Shore
Jersey	3.03.00	3.04.12
Guernsey	3.02.11	2.13.11

Although technically a species of catshark, most fishers use the name dogfish (or doggie) when referring to this common species. The Small-spotted Catshark is the commonest of the dogfish species in the Channel Islands and can be abundant in some shallow marine habitats. It is familiar to fishers of all kinds as well as to divers and snorkelers who may encounter them in only a couple of metres of water. They are not usually timid and will often lie motionless on the seabed while being photographed or even swim lazily towards divers, sometimes veering away at the last second.

The Small-spotted Catshark is considered to be something of a menace by recreational anglers as it will take bait intended for other species and regularly gets caught across a variety of habitats. It is a rarely eaten fish although, in an attempt to give them market value, it has been marketed as 'rock salmon' in some parts of the UK. Recreationally caught specimens are usually returned alive although shore netters in Jersey have been known to kill catsharks deliberately, leaving the bodies to wash up the beach with the tide.

Commercial fishing boats will usually land catsharks as bycatch from trawling, angling and potting, generally to be sold for pot bait (especially for whelks). As such, the Small-spotted Catshark is one of those low value species that can be taken in a large enough quantity to make it economically valuable. Annual catches in the Channel Islands peaked at 80 tonnes in 2005 and are currently around 20 tonnes. Landings in France have run into 1000s of tonnes in some years.

The Small-spotted Catshark has a historical record going back at least two hundred years and is common around all the Channel Islands. Despite being heavily commercially fished in some parts of Europe, the population is believed to be healthy. This may be because it is a generalist species that can live in a variety of habitats and eats a wide range of food from live worms and shellfish to dead fish. Its goblet-shaped eggcases frequently wash up on the shore, sometimes in tangled clumps of a dozen or more (see page 63). These are normally laid in the spring months and attached to seaweed or other subtidal features via long stringy threads.

A Small-spotted Catshark resting on the seabed at Les Dirouilles. This pose is typical of catsharks and is how divers will often encounter them.

Capture Technique: Not often a targeted catch and sometimes seen as a pest to anglers, most try to avoid the capture of this species. A productive method is bottom fishing with hooks ranging in size from 1/0 to 3/0 using basic rigs such as a double hook paternoster or running ledger. This species can be caught over a range of habitats from sandbanks to rough ground. Bites tend to drop during periods of higher tidal current especially when boat fishing. Baits should not be oversized due to the catshark having a relatively small crescent shaped mouth although they have been known to engulf incredibly large baits for their size.

Bait Preference: This shark species is not a fussy scavenger and can be caught on shellfish, fish baits, worms and crustaceans. If targeting Small-spotted Catsharks then one of the most effective baits can be sections of fresh mackerel fillet.

Bull Huss

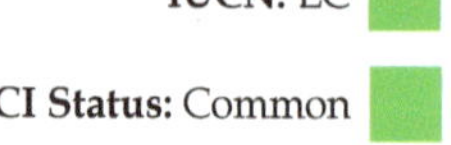

Scyliorhinus stellaris

Nursehound; Greater Spotted Catshark; *Tchian d'mé; Rousse*

Max Length: 160 cm

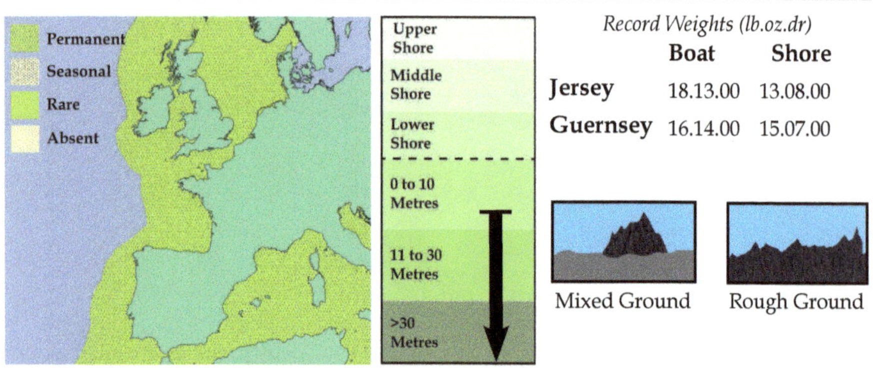

Record Weights (lb.oz.dr)

	Boat	Shore
Jersey	18.13.00	13.08.00
Guernsey	16.14.00	15.07.00

The Bull Huss looks similar to the Small Spotted Catshark but may usually be distinguished by its larger size and bulk. Although not rare, the Bull Huss is less often encountered by recreational anglers and divers, it being more selective in its habitat with a preference for rocky ground in deeper water. They are more commonly seen by commercial fishing boats who will capture them in lobster pots, nets and trawls. Like the Small-spotted Catshark, the Bull Huss will be retained as a bait species with the landing figures being generally recorded as 'dogfish'.

The natural history of the Bull Huss is similar to that of the Small Spotted Catshark with reproduction being via a large and distinctive eggcase (see page 63). These eggcases are rarely washed onto the shore and yet the adult animal is very common locally and their eggcases are common in the UK. This was something of a puzzle and it was wondered whether the species did not breed in local waters. Then a few years ago divers started reporting dozens of Bull Huss eggcases wrapped around Pink Sea Fans (*Eunicella verrucosa*) on offshore reefs such as Les Minquiers. Some of these eggcases appeared to be quite old but they had been so firmly entangled with the sea fans that they could not wash free.

It is now thought that they do breed in local waters although for unknown reasons the eggcases rarely make it to shore.

Unlike its smaller relative, the Bull Huss is sometimes targeted by recreational anglers, it being powerful enough to give a good fight. Anecdotal reports have suggested that the species has increased in abundance over the past few decades although there is no independent evidence for this with the species having been described as being abundant in the nineteenth century. It is common around all the Channel Islands and the population is believed to be stable.

Bull Huss often get trapped inside lobster pots and in the Channel Islands they may be retained as bait for the whelk potting industry.

Capture Technique: A species mostly found over rough ground habitat or near submerged reefs. Due to this species having teeth, hook lengths should be over 60 lb breaking strain. Simple rough ground rigs such as pulley rigs and running ledgers will be most effective paired with a weak link attached to the sinker. Hook sizes should be relative to the size of the bait and be in the region of 4/0 - 6/0.

The Bull Huss has a tendency to cling onto baits until hitting the surface when it will let go. Night fishing tends to be more productive when fishing for Bull Huss especially from the shore but they can be caught in deeper water during daylight hours. Bull Huss should be handled with care due to their abrasive dermal denticles. For best handling practices, hold them by their tail and behind the head.

Bait Preferences: Baits that are most popular tend to be mackerel, sandeel and squid but this is a scavenger that is not fussy.

Tope

Galeorhinus galeus

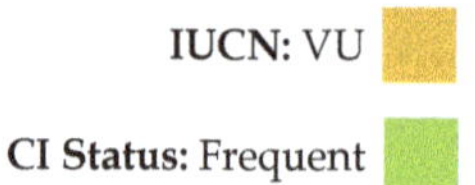

Penny Dog; White Hound; *Haû*

Max Length: 200 cm

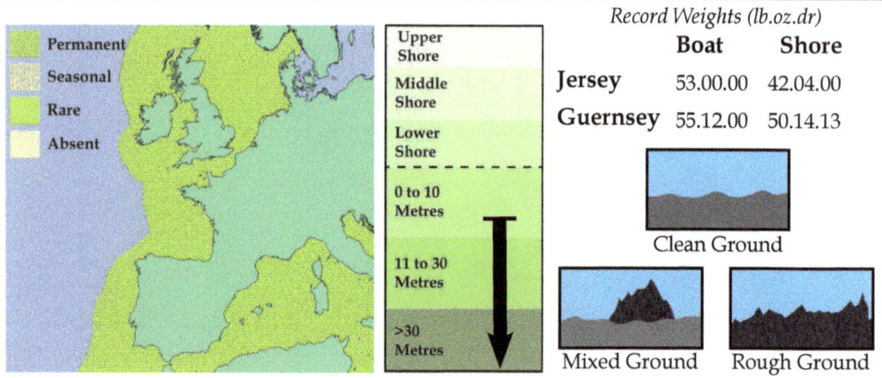

Record Weights (lb.oz.dr)

	Boat	Shore
Jersey	53.00.00	42.04.00
Guernsey	55.12.00	50.14.13

The Tope is an elegant, medium-sized shark that usually lives close to the seabed from just offshore to quite deep waters. Local records normally come from boat anglers with the exception of Alderney where there is a noticeable number of shore caught reports. The animal seems to favour the large sand and gravel banks that are found in Channel Island waters, especially where there are strong currents. Divers and snorkelers may occasionally encounter this species, especially in summer when the females move closer inshore to breed.

Historically the Tope has been described as being 'very common' but the species has been heavily overfished in Europe leading to a population decline. It has been commercially fished in Channel Island waters with recent landings of up to 40 tonnes in Guernsey and three tonnes in Jersey. At the time of writing the Tope is a zero quota species for EU fishing boats meaning that it cannot be landed.

As a powerful shark, the Tope is most commonly fished for sport around the islands with specimens usually being returned alive. Unlike some of the larger pelagic sharks, it is believed to have a good survival rate after being released. The Tope is long-lived (up to 60 years) and slow-growing with sexual maturity not being reached until the animal is around nine or ten years old. This makes it vulnerable to overexploitation and so any specimens that are caught angling should be returned alive, especially the females. A tagging project for Tope has operated off Jersey for several years with the help of charter anglers but the results for this are not yet available.

The Tope is listed as 'vulnerable' on the IUCN Red List and the true status of its local population is not known. Anecdotal reports suggest that it is probably tolerably common off all the Channel Islands but possibly not as common as it was prior to World War II.

A Tope investigates a camera off Corbiére, Jersey, during a 2016 scientific study of fish behaviour using baited remote underwater video units (BRUVs).

Capture Technique: One of the hardest fighters in CI waters, Tope need heavy gear compared to most other targeted species. For lowest mortality, rigs should consist of heavy monofilament hook lengths and large circle hooks to increase the chances of lip hooking the fish. Wire leader tends to cut the hooked area of the animal during the fight. Traditional J hooks should be avoided. This species is mostly targeted from boats where fishing is best in areas of mixed ground with high tidal run. If at anchor, a chum sack can be lowered to provide a stronger scent trail. Once at the surface, it is best practice to release the shark at the side of the boat with the use of a T bar.

Bait Preference: Tope are demersal scavengers that feed on a variety of fish. Some of the most productive baits tend to be Mackerel, flatfish and Black Bream.

Starry Smoothhound

Mustelus asterias

Sweet William; *Demoiselle*

Max Length: 140 cm

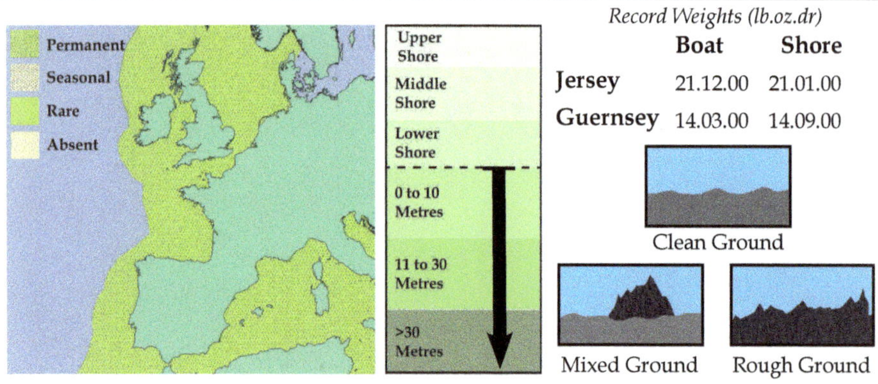

Record Weights (lb.oz.dr)

	Boat	Shore
Jersey	21.12.00	21.01.00
Guernsey	14.03.00	14.09.00

There are very few Starry Smoothhound records from Channel Island waters with the oldest being from the 1870s when several specimens were sent to the Natural History Museum (London) for preservation. Based on this it might be assumed that the Starry Smoothhound is rare locally but a series of scientific beam trawl surveys made annually by CEFAS from 2006 onwards produced specimens with virtually every haul from locations across all the Channel Islands. This is therefore probably one of those species whose formal recording does not reflect the frequency with which it is caught in the Channel Islands by both recreational and commercial anglers.

One possible explanation for this is that Starry Smoothhound specimens have been misidentified as Common Smoothhounds, a species whose presence in the English Channel has been recently questioned (see entry for Common Smoothhound).

The Starry Smoothhound is a shallow water shark that lives on a variety of habitats and has a wide diet. It is more common in the spring and summer months when individuals may be found close to shore. They are infrequently seen by divers and will sometimes lie perfectly still on the seabed and can be approached quite closely. A combination of probable under-reporting and taxonomic confusion means the status of the local population is unknown but anecdotal reports suggest it is not uncommon locally and that the population is probably not under pressure.

Angler Paul Wheaton in 2006 with a Jersey boat caught record Starry Smoothhound (21 lb 12 oz).

Capture Technique: A seasonal visitor to CI waters. Smoothhounds are best targeted using heavy bottom fishing gear consisting of 40 to 60 lb hook lengths and hooks ranging in the size of 2/0 to 5/0. Simple rigs such as single hook clipped down rigs and running ledgers will all catch. This species of shark does not have sharp teeth, therefore eliminating the need for heavy hook lengths. The best time to target this species is from May to August. Their main diet consists of crustaceans and can be found inshore over mixed and clean ground, similar places to where spider crabs are moulting.

Bait Preference: Top baits include peeler and green crab with squid also being a top choice. Bait elastic can be useful to keep the more delicate baits in place with the hook point staying prominent.

Common Smoothhound

Mustelus mustelus

Max Length: 200 cm

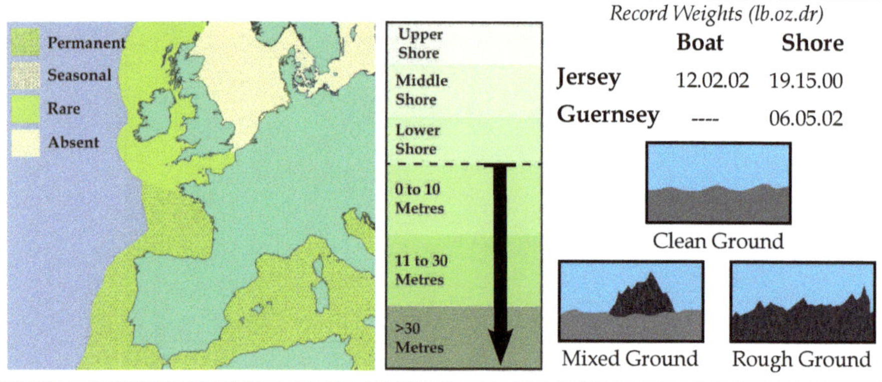

Record Weights (lb.oz.dr)

	Boat	Shore
Jersey	12.02.02	19.15.00
Guernsey	----	06.05.02

Although historically recorded from many parts of the UK, some modern studies cast doubt on all British Common Smoothhound records, it being claimed that they are misidentifications of the Starry Smoothhound (*M. asterias*). The debate over the validity of this is ongoing although current weight of opinion seems to be in favour of there being just one British Smoothhound species.

There are quite a few Channel Island records of the Common Smoothhound going back as far as the 1840s including several regional ones which were gathered as part of scientific surveys. This includes records from 2006 and 2008 in Guernsey waters made as part of the CEFAS beam trawl work. Such scientific reports ought to be accurate and it seems unlikely that all these identifications will be erroneous. If taken at face value, then the Common Smoothhound is present in Channel Island waters which goes against the lumping together of Common and Starry Smoothhound records that has occurred elsewhere in Britain.

Smooth Hammerhead

Sphyrna zygaena

IUCN: VU

Max Length: 400 cm

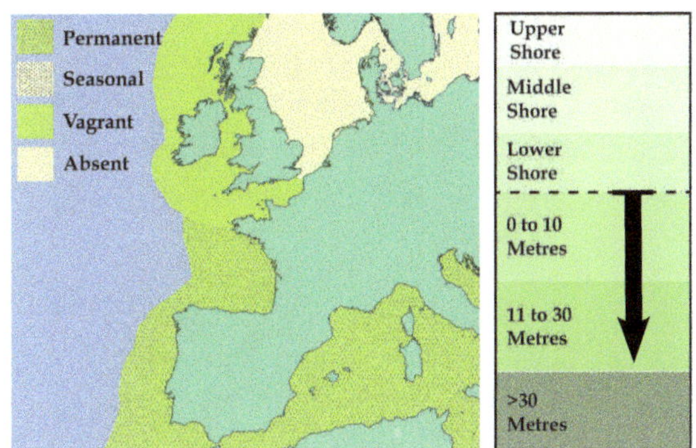

No Channel Island Rod Records

Pelagic

The Hammerhead Shark is instantly recognisable because of its size and wide, flattened head. There are no verified records of the Smooth Hammerhead in local waters but there are two recent unconfirmed encounters by divers from south of Les Minquiers and off the Paternosters reef. The location of the Channel Islands is within the Smooth Hammerhead's summer range and its preference for the sort of productive shallow coastal waters that are found in the islands, makes it probable that this shark does migrate into local waters, albeit rarely.

There are sporadic reports of this shark from the English Channel and Irish Sea including reports from the early nineteenth century as well as more recently. Most reports are from south-west England, Wales and Ireland which ties in with its summer migration from southern Europe into cooler waters. The species is not uncommon to the south of the English Channel and it is a shark that is predicted to become regionally more common with rising sea temperatures. Any sightings or captures should be reported to a local biological records centre.

Blue Shark

Prionace glauca

Max Length: 400 cm

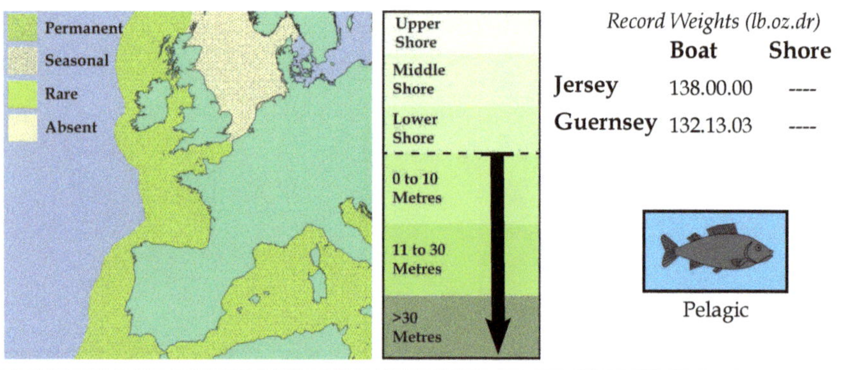

Record Weights (lb.oz.dr)

	Boat	Shore
Jersey	138.00.00	----
Guernsey	132.13.03	----

Although a frequent summer visitor to Channel Island waters, the Blue Shark is a large pelagic predator which prefers deep, open waters and so is not usually seen close to the coast. However, there are records of Blue Sharks coming close inshore including a large specimen that was caught in Grouville Bay, Jersey, at the end of the nineteenth century and a juvenile that entered St Helier Harbour, Jersey, in February 2011.

The Blue Shark is inquisitive and has been known to approach divers which has led to them being the subject of cage diving tourism in south-west England. The only known Channel Island unpleasant shark incident probably involved a Blue Shark that approached a swimmer in St Aubin's Bay in 1879. The bather was in shallow water and spotted the shark coming. He had the time to find and pick up a rock which he then used to stun and then kill the shark before dragging it onshore. This may also be the species of shark that was responsible for aggressively interacting with local boats off Jersey on two separate occasions. Once in 1876 off the north coast when 4.8 metre shark harassed a boat for several minutes and on the second occasion in 1929 when a 3.5 metre shark nearly capsized a boat off Corbiére Point.

Blue Sharks are a popular sport fish around the world and, like the Porbeagle Shark, have historically been targeted by recreational fishers in the Channel Islands, sometimes through deep sea fishing clubs. The probable commonality of Blue Sharks was illustrated in the autumn of 2018 when Jersey anglers targeting Bluefin Tuna unintentionally hooked sharks as well.

Only the Blue Shark's dorsal fin has a commercial value and the Blue Shark was at the centre of a European 'finning' industry which would involve cutting the fins from living sharks and then discarding the body at sea. This practice led to the Blue Shark being the most heavily fished shark species in the world but, as a slow growing species with a nine month gestation time, populations have declined sharply. Finning was recently banned by the EU and there is the prospect of further protection on the horizon both internationally and in the Channel Islands. Local commercial landings have always been very low and generally from bycatch.

The Blue Shark is an offshore species that is unlikely to be seen by anyone other than those deliberately fishing for it, a practice that is not recommended, even on a catch and release basis, as post-release mortality rates may be as high as 22 percent. As a migratory species to the islands, the local Blue Shark population status will reflect the 'near threatened' assessment afforded to it by the IUCN.

Distinguishable by its size, sleek shape and long pectoral fins, the Blue Shark can be curious and is the shark most likely to be seen by divers.

Spurdog

Squalus acanthias

Piked Dogfish; *Brotchet*

IUCN: VU

CI Status: Expirated

Max Length: 125 cm

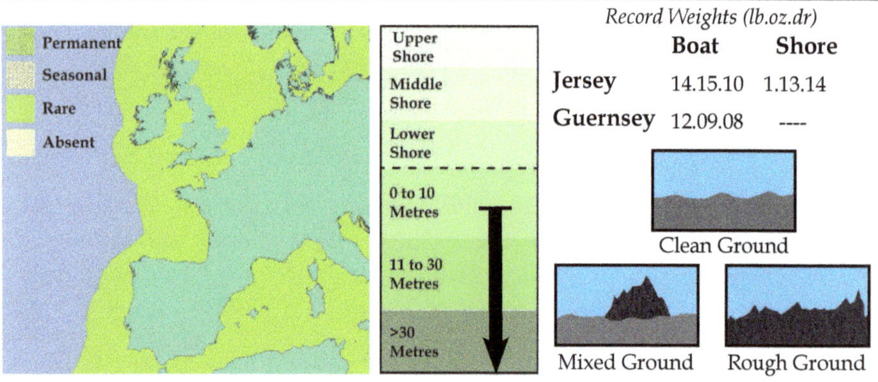

Record Weights (lb.oz.dr)

	Boat	Shore
Jersey	14.15.10	1.13.14
Guernsey	12.09.08	----

The Spurdog was regarded as abundant in the Channel Islands during the nineteenth century but it is a slow-growing and late maturing species, which renders it vulnerable to overfishing. By the 1960s the Spurdog was listed as being scarce in the islands and by 2000 this species was regarded as functionally extinct within the Normano-Breton Gulf. This local population collapse follows an international trend which has seen Spurdog populations decline steeply to a point where the species is listed as threatened by several international conventions and organisations.

The last definite Channel Island records are two rod caught specimens taken off Jersey in 1980 and 1994 but, while the Spurdog is probably locally extinct, it is possible that future specimens will be caught as catches are still being made in neighbouring regions. Since 2010 there has been a European Union ban on commercial fishing for Spurdogs and any caught specimens should be immediately released and the details reported to a local biological records centre.

Bramble Shark

Echinorhinus brucus

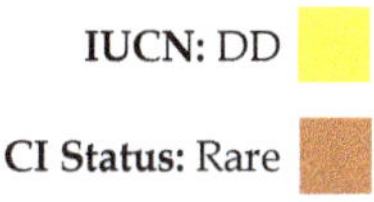

Max Length: 310 cm

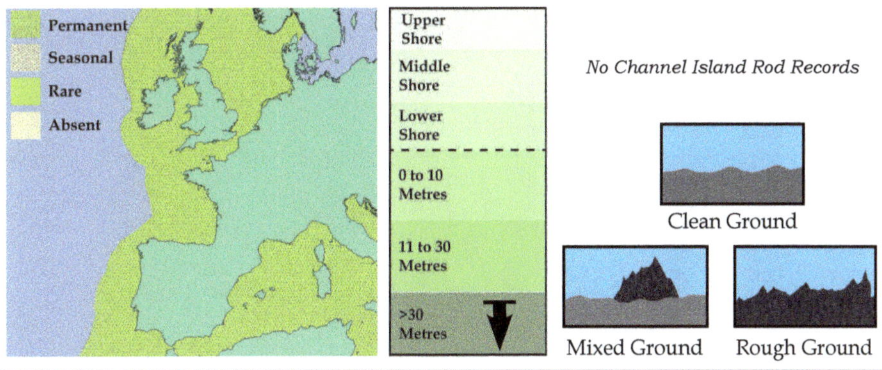

The Bramble Shark is a deep water species that would not ordinarily be expected to be found in shallow coastal regions such as the Channel Islands. Nonetheless, in 1902 a specimen was caught by an angler at Bonne Nuit Harbour, Jersey, and passed to the local naturalist Joseph Sinel. The fish was preserved and presented to the Natural History Museum (London) where it still resides. This represents the only known regional record for this species.

Not much is known about the biology and behaviour of the Bramble Shark although historically specimens were infrequently caught off south-west England and Scotland. The Bramble Shark is considered to be critically endangered in European waters and is highly unlikely to be encountered in the Channel Islands.

Angelshark

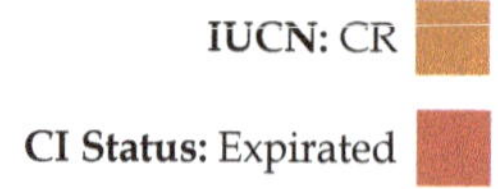

Squatina squatina

Monkfish; *Ange dé Mé; Mouaingne; Violon*

Max Length: 240 cm

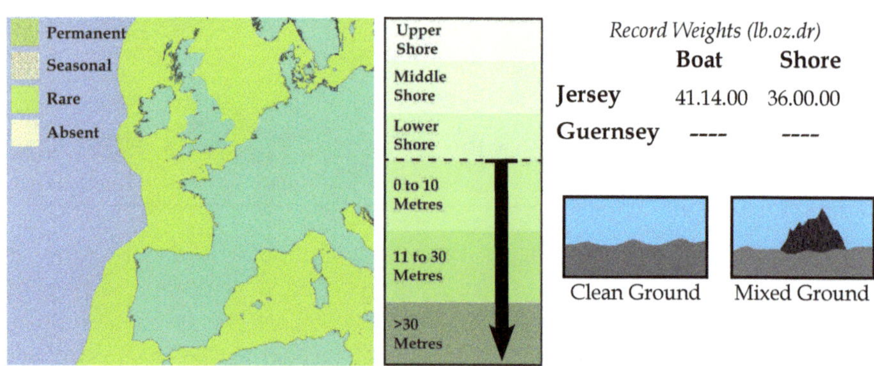

Record Weights (lb.oz.dr)

	Boat	Shore
Jersey	41.14.00	36.00.00
Guernsey	----	----

The Angelshark was common in Channel Island waters during the nineteenth century and was said to be 'very frequently taken' in 1904. By the Second World War it had become scarce and there is just one Angelshark record during the entire 1950s. The last traceable local (and indeed regional) report was in 1971 when an 18 kg specimen was caught by an angler off Jersey. With no records anywhere in the Channel Islands or adjacent coast since then, the species is either exceptionally rare or, more probably, locally extinct.

Collapses in the Angelshark population have been seen right across Europe and it has been declared extinct in several marine areas. Overfishing is the probable cause and there is currently a European Union ban on commercial fishing for Angelshark.

Skates and Rays

Skates and rays are immediately recognisable by their broad, flattened and muscular bodies often with a thin, stick-like tail. They are close relatives to the shark and have the same cartilaginous skeleton and ancient ancestry. The body shape and large size means that most skates and rays live close to the seabed although they are powerful swimmers and can use their wings to push themselves through the water at speed. Some species, such as the Eagle Ray, are more agile and will swim in the water column or even near to the surface. Most species will eat a variety of fish, crustaceans and other smaller species. Some will lay durable eggcases (see page 63) while others give birth to live young.

When looked at historically, the Channel Islands had a remarkably diverse range of ray and skate species. This may be because the islands are at the crossroads between the northern and southern European marine fauna but also because the shallow, invertebrate rich coarse sedimentary habitats favour ray and skate. However, of the fifteen species reported from local waters, only six currently occur with any regularity and of these just four are common. This is due to some species having probably been misidentified but, like many parts of Europe, there are also skate species that were once common but which have since become locally extinct. As with sharks, longevity and late sexual maturity makes many ray and skate vulnerable to overfishing and it is only in the last decade that European fisheries have begun to recognise that there is a potential sustainability issue with some species. There is much still to learn about these remarkable animals including in local waters where their distribution and behaviour is not fully understood.

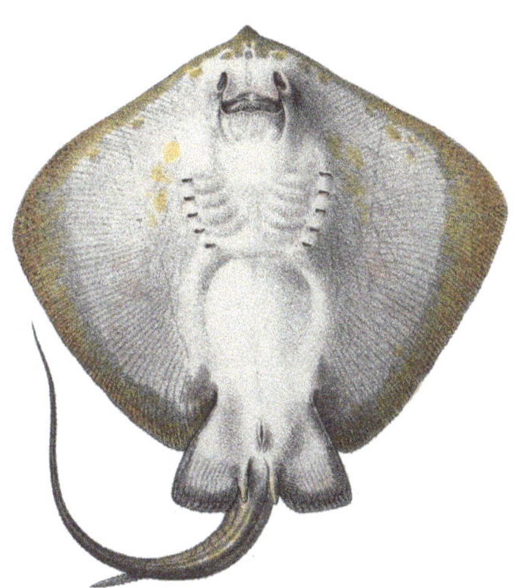

The underside of a Common Stingray showing the position of the mouth, nostrils (nares) and gill slits. Skates and rays will often lie partially buried in sediment but can still breathe by drawing in water from slits (called spiracles) located behind their eyes.

Marbled Electric Ray

Torpedo marmorata

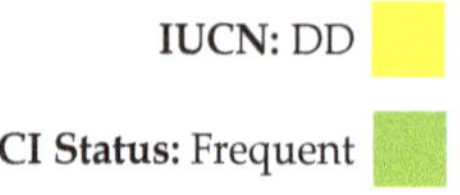

Max Length: 100 cm

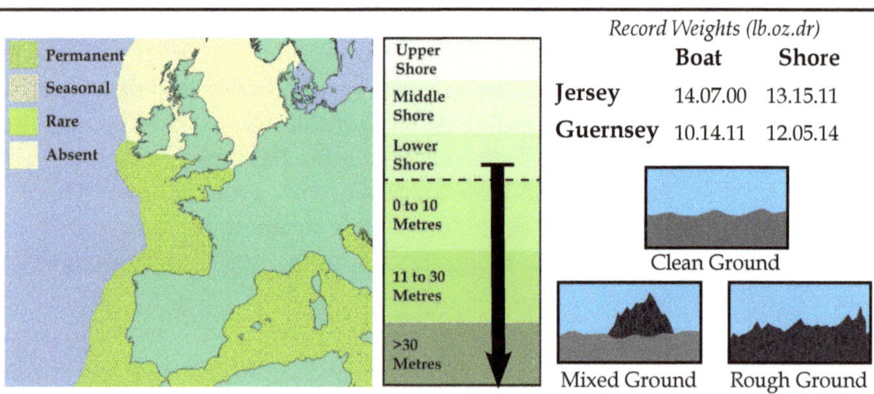

Record Weights (lb.oz.dr)

	Boat	Shore
Jersey	14.07.00	13.15.11
Guernsey	10.14.11	12.05.14

The Marbled Electric Ray is common across the Channel Islands but is rarely encountered further north in the English Channel. This is a shallow water, nocturnal species that is often seen by divers and which may sometimes be encountered in deep rock pools on the lower shore. The Marbled Electric Ray can survive in low oxygen environments such as rock pools and can even stop breathing when oxygen levels are extremely low, sometimes for up to five hours. There are stories of people low water fishing for sandeels having received an electric shock after having spiked a torpedo ray with a metal rake. They prefer sedimentary environments and can reach a considerable size.

When disturbed by divers, electric rays will sometimes perform backward rolls on the seabed. The reason for this behaviour is unknown but it is probably a defence tactic or a means of readying the animal to deliver an electric shock.

A Marbled Electric Ray caught inside a lobster pot.

Prior to the 1950s there was a lone Channel Island record for the Marbled Torpedo Ray which came from 1904, when the fish was said to be rare. By 1963 the naturalist (and accomplished fish expert) Ronald le Sueur noted that he had encountered five specimens, one of which had delivered a shock to an angler when being removed from a trot line. The population seems to have increased markedly during the 1970s and it is now regularly seen by divers and even turns up in lobster pots on occasion. The local history of the Marbled Torpedo Ray suggests that it is one of those southern European species whose range has expanded northwards in recent decades. As with all electric rays, it should not be handled or touched as the resultant shock, while unlikely to be fatal, will hurt.

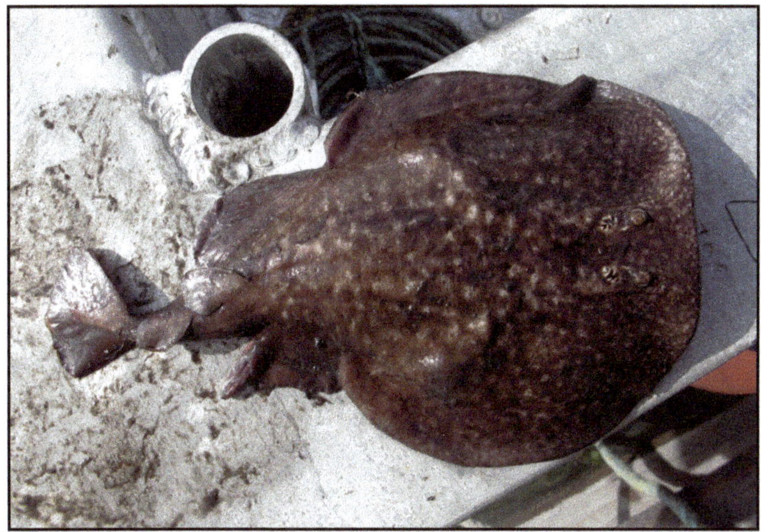

A Marbled Electric Ray on the deck of a Jersey fishing boat off Gorey Harbour, Jersey. They must be handled with care.

Atlantic Torpedo Ray

Tetronarce nobiliana

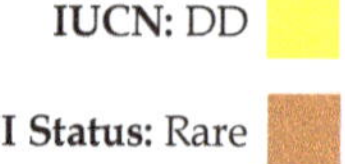

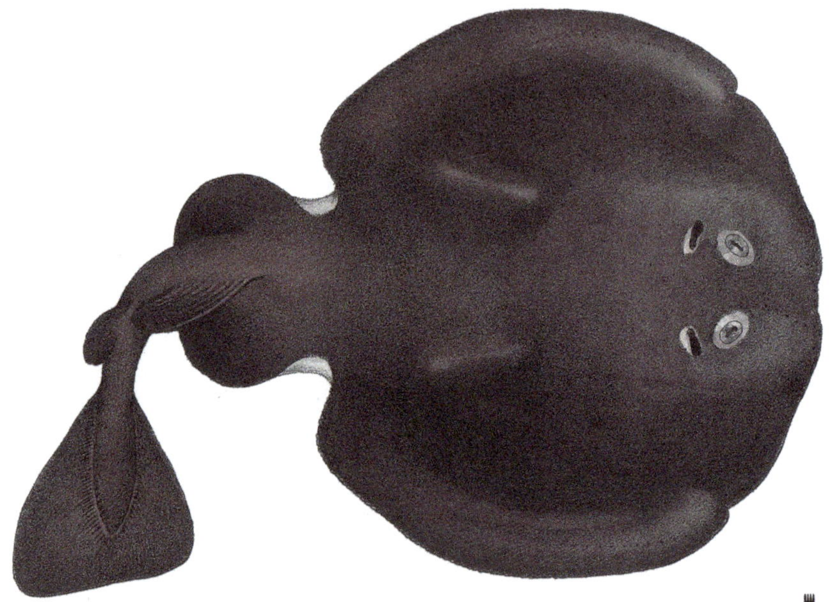

Max Length: 180 cm

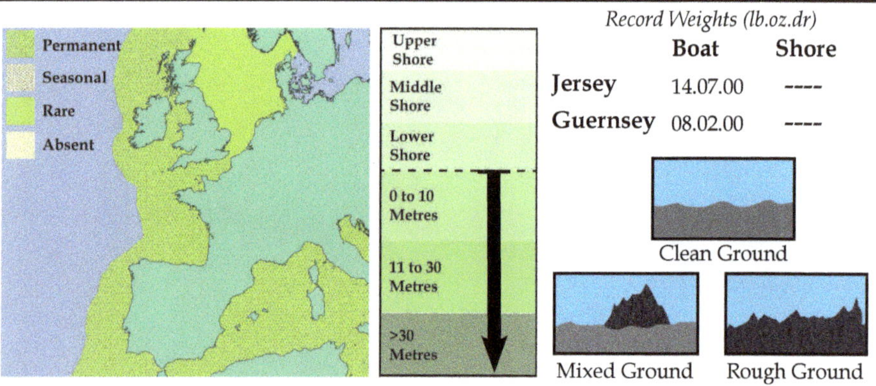

Record Weights (lb.oz.dr)

	Boat	Shore
Jersey	14.07.00	----
Guernsey	08.02.00	----

There are many local reports of the Atlantic Torpedo Ray from the nineteenth and early twentieth centuries but only a handful since. It resembles the Marbled Electric Ray (but can be much larger) and early naturalists may have confused the two species. However, with modern day reports being so much rarer than historical ones, it is possible that the southern European Marbled Torpedo Ray, which has few historical records, has expanded its range displacing the colder water Atlantic Torpedo Ray. If caught this animal can deliver a strong electric shock and should be handled with extreme caution.

White Skate

Rostroraja alba

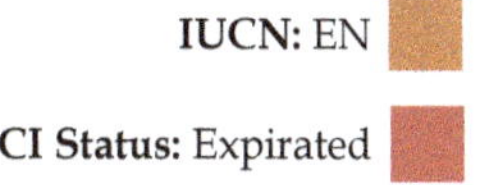

Max Length: 200 cm

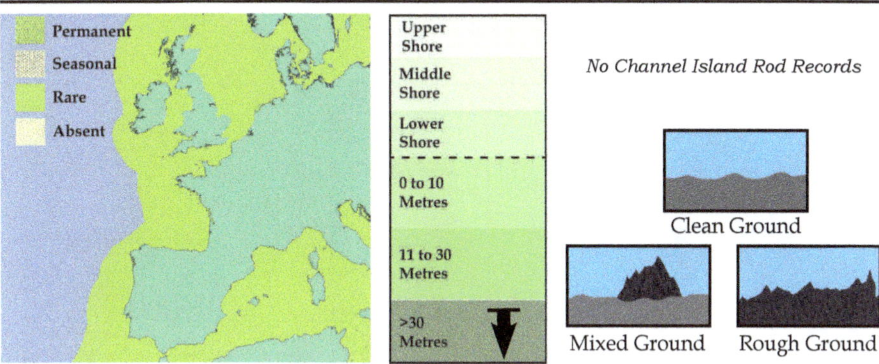

The White Skate was known from Channel Island waters during the nineteenth century but there have been no local captures (or eggcases) reported since at least 1900. A recent review of fish species in the Normano-Breton Gulf by Patrick Le Mao concluded that this species had become locally extinct by 1980 although it had probably been absent from the Channel Islands some considerable time before this.

The White Skate is not common across any part of its range and the species is listed as endangered by the IUCN. ICES research suggests that the European White Skate population has been severely depleted by overfishing and it is currently a protected species under the Bern Convention.

Common Skate

Dipturus batis

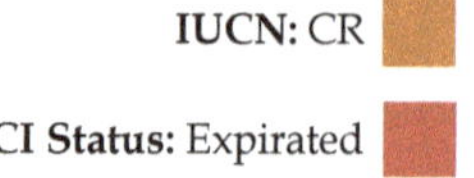

Blue Skate; *Dravan; Fliaue; Fliée*

Max Length: 285 cm

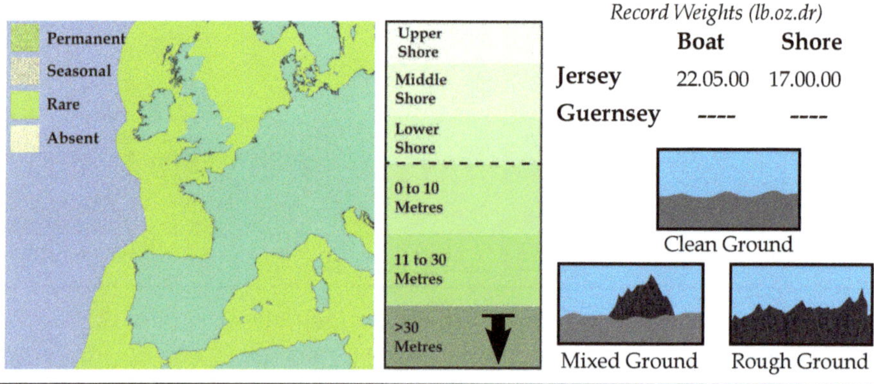

Record Weights (lb.oz.dr)

	Boat	Shore
Jersey	22.05.00	17.00.00
Guernsey	----	----

The Common Skate was said to be infrequently caught in Channel Island waters during the nineteenth century. However, there have been no records in over fifty years and it seems probable that the species is locally extinct. This follows a pattern seen in many European areas where overfishing has led to a severe decline in skate populations. Their slow growth and late sexual maturation does not favour modern mass fishery techniques. The Common Skate is protected by the European Union and the species is listed as critically endangered by the IUCN.

Long-nosed Skate

Dipturus oxyrinchus

IUCN: NT

CI Status: Unconfirmed

Max Length: 150 cm

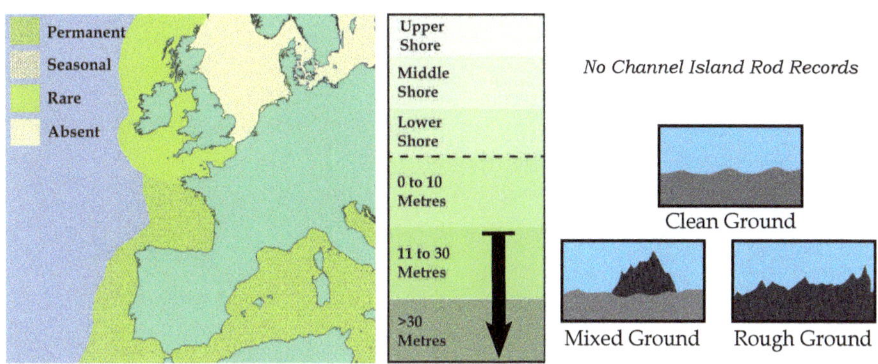

Although reported to be occasionally captured by fishing boats during the nineteenth century (and more rarely in the early twentieth century) the Long-nosed Skate is a deeper water species whose geographic range does not traditionally include the English Channel.

The Long-nosed Skate features in the fish lists of Joseph Sinel and Ronald le Sueur both of whom were proficient at identification, but the lack of any other English Channel records is perplexing. Fishing and scientific trawl records suggest it is not currently present in the Normano-Breton Gulf and until further evidence is forthcoming local historical reports should be treated with caution.

Shagreen Ray

IUCN: VU

Leucoraja fullonica

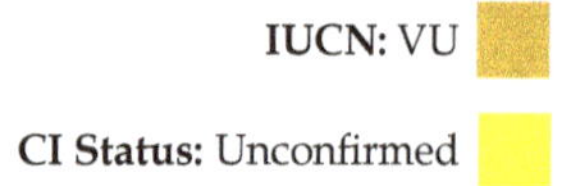

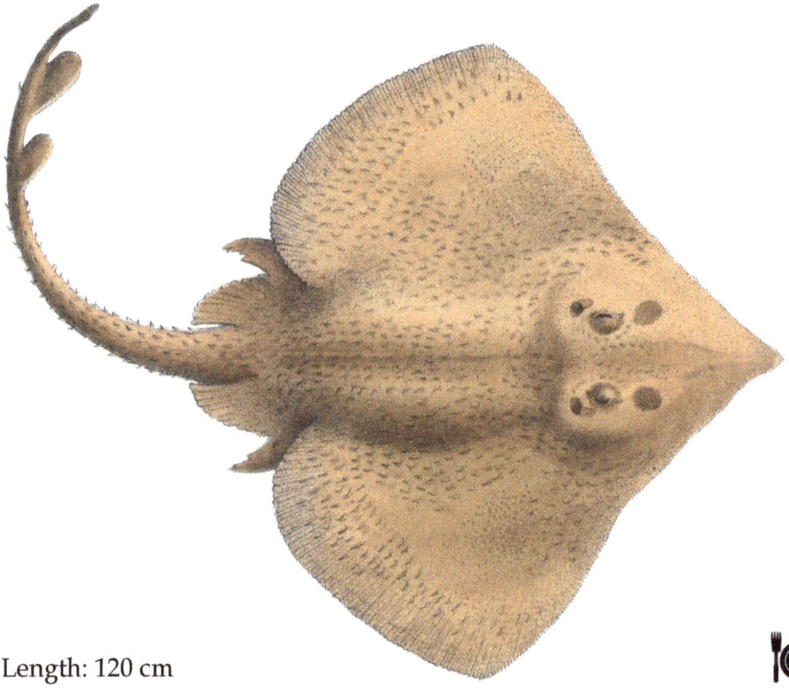

CI Status: Unconfirmed

Max Length: 120 cm

No Channel Island Rod Records

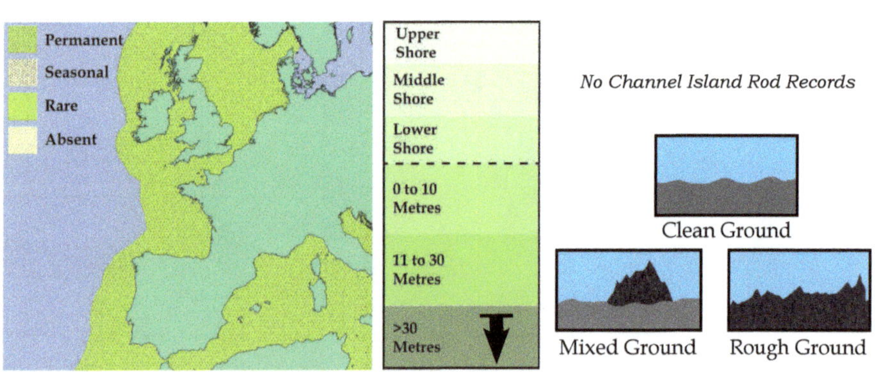

The only local record for the Shagreen Ray is in a list of local fish species provided by local naturalists for an 1862 guide to the Channel Islands. This is a shallow water species which is known from the English Channel and so could have been caught in Channel Island waters. A lack of any other records suggests that it was either exceptionally rare or that its inclusion on the 1862 list was an error. It is not currently present in the region and its inclusion in the Channel Islands' list of fish species should be treated with caution.

Cuckoo Ray
Leucoraja naevus

IUCN: LC

CI Status: Unconfirmed

Max Length: 75 cm

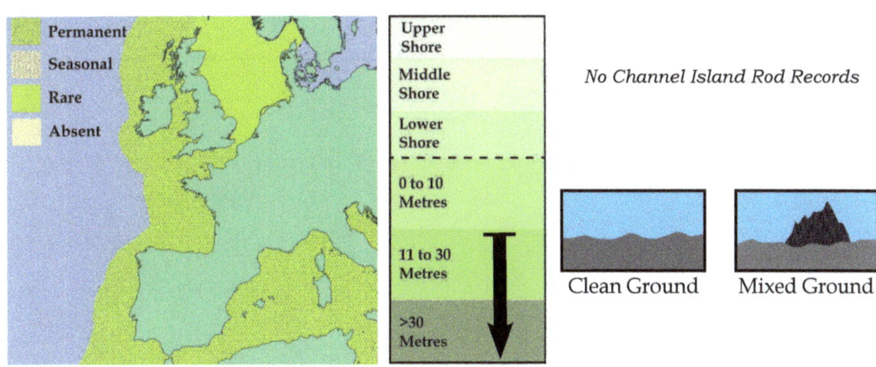

The Cuckoo Ray has not been formally recorded from either the Channel Islands or the wider Normano-Breton Gulf. It is included in this book because specimens of its distinctive eggcase have been collected from beaches around Jersey (see page 63). Since 2013 a handful of Cuckoo Ray eggcases has been found each year, usually in January or February. They are often in good condition which makes it possible that they originated from within the general region. However, a 2017 appeal for information about Cuckoo Rays from local anglers produced no records. The Cuckoo Ray is a shallow water species that occurs elsewhere in the English Channel. It is conceivable that Cuckoo Rays are found in the Normano-Breton Gulf but perhaps only very rarely.

Blonde Ray

Raja brachyura

Max Length: 120 cm

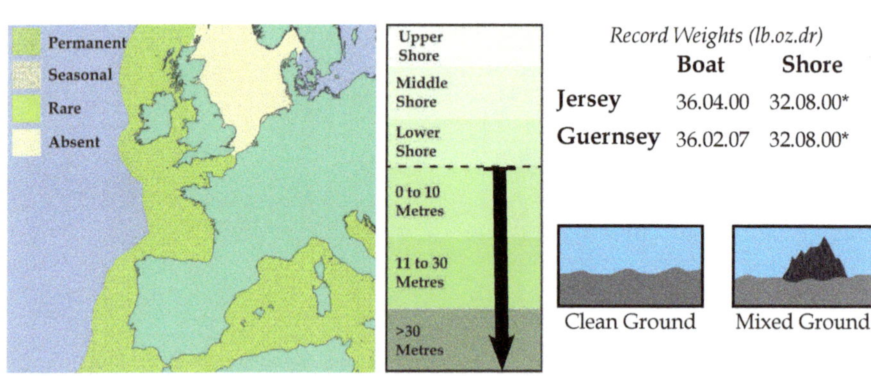

Record Weights (lb.oz.dr)

	Boat	Shore
Jersey	36.04.00	32.08.00*
Guernsey	36.02.07	32.08.00*

Although currently not uncommon in Channel Island waters, the recorded history for Blonde Rays only starts in the 1970s. This has led to suggestions that it has been historically confused with the Spotted Ray (*q.v.*) which it closely resembles. However, Blonde Rays are larger and heavier than Spotted Rays so such confusion would probably only occur in juvenile specimens. The balance of probabilities suggests that the Blonde Ray is either a recent arrival to the Channel Islands or has become more common in recent decades.

The Blonde Ray is a minor commercial species in Europe but it has assumed more importance in Guernsey and Jersey where, following fishing bans on Undulate and Small-eye Ray, it is one of the few locally occurring ray species that can be legally landed. A survey off Jersey in 2006 found that Blonde Rays constituted 22 percent of the rays caught by trawlers while their eggcases make up 40 percent of those washed up around the island.

A Blonde ray caught off Jersey.

The Blonde Ray is an offshore species which prefers a sandy or gravelly seabed. Specimens (especially juveniles) will often stray closer inshore than the adults where they may be encountered by divers, generally below 20 metres. Most recreational angling catches are from boats while commercial catches are made using benthic trawls or nets.

The Blonde Ray is slow-growing and does not breed until it reaches at least eight years (often older) and, in natural settings, is reckoned to live up to around 15-years. The late maturation age makes the Blonde Ray susceptible to overfishing and some European populations are reported to be declining rapidly. The IUCN lists the Blonde Ray as near threatened and it is recommended that specimens under 92 cm in total length (the minimum breeding size) should be released alive.

Capture Technique: A species caught regularly from the shore and from vessels around the Channel Islands. The Blonde Ray is caught using bottom-fishing techniques. Sandbanks can be productive fishing grounds offshore at anchor whilst clean, sand dominated areas and mixed ground being best from shore. Tackle should consist of hook lengths of 40 to 80 lb test tied onto rigs such as a running ledger or pulley rig. Pennel rigs are also popular for ray species. Whilst boat fishing, the most productive time is normally when the current picks up. Initial bites from all ray species should be left for the bite to progress due to the fish often landing on the bait and smothering it, causing small knocks on the rod tip whilst the animal is still homing in on the scent. Strong 4 to 8 oz rods should be used from the shore and 20+ lb tackle from a boat.

Bait Preference: Blonde Rays do not have sharp teeth but instead have powerful jaws armed with crushing plates. Popular baits include mackerel fillets, squid and sandeel with many anglers having success using 'cocktails' made of these popular baits.

Thornback Ray

Raja clavata

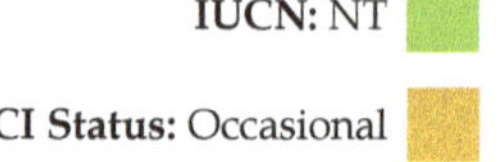

Max Length: 130 cm

Permanent
Seasonal
Rare
Absent

Upper Shore
Middle Shore
Lower Shore
0 to 10 Metres
11 to 30 Metres
>30 Metres

Record Weights (lb.oz.dr)

	Boat	Shore
Jersey	22.09.00	18.00.00
Guernsey	18.04.00	----

Clean Ground
Mixed Ground

The Thornback Ray was consistently reportedly as being common across the Channel Islands prior to the 1970s and CEFAS beam trawl surveys in 1991 and 1992 produced specimens with almost every haul. However, a 2006 scientific study around Jersey produced just seven out of 814 ray specimens caught and the annual beam trawl surveys made by CEFAS since 2006 have produced no specimens at all. Whether this represents a local decline in the Thornback Ray population is uncertain as prior to 2010 commercial catches of rays were not recorded to species level. Since 2009, recorded commercial landings of Thornback Ray have been under 200 kg annually.

The Thornback Ray can be highly variable in its patterning and is easily confused with other local species, such as the Undulate Ray. It lives at a wide range of depths down to about 300 metres but is most common in waters shallower than 30 metres, especially in the early part of its life, and can be caught from the shore. Biological studies into its growth rate and maturity age have produced differing figures but it probably becomes sexually mature at around eight years. The eggcases collected since 2013 constitute around five percent of those washed up around Jersey which is consistent with its low abundance in recent trawl surveys.

Outside of the Channel Islands there is a strong commercial fishery for Thornback Rays and in the UK it is one of the most commonly caught rays from the shore. As with other skate and ray species, a late maturation age makes the Thornback Ray susceptible to overexploitation and it is subject to various management measures at EU and regional levels. The IUCN lists it as near threatened and specimens below 80 cm total length (the probable minimum breeding size) should be released alive.

Small-eyed Ray

IUCN: NT

CI Status: Frequent

Raja microocellata

Raietelle; Rêtelle

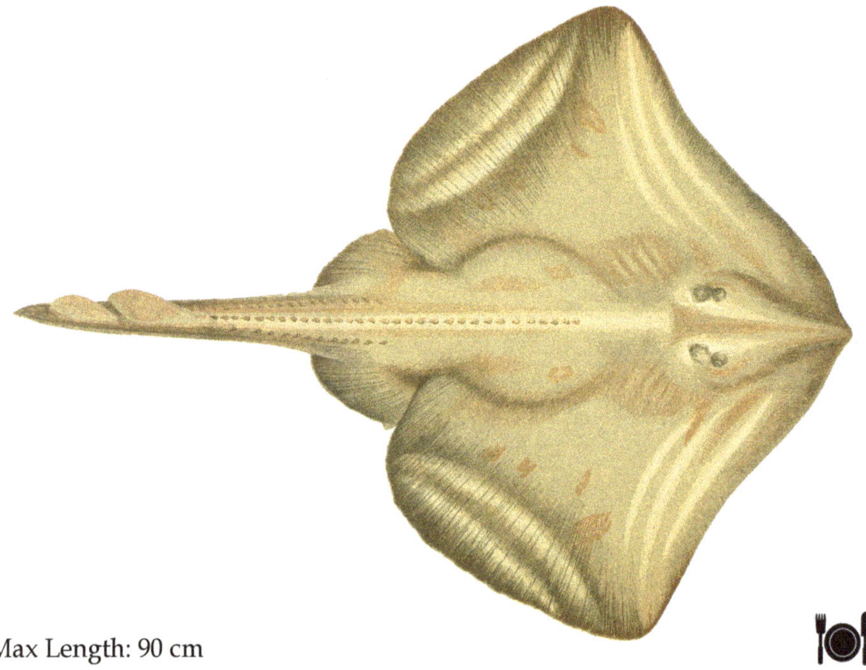

Max Length: 90 cm

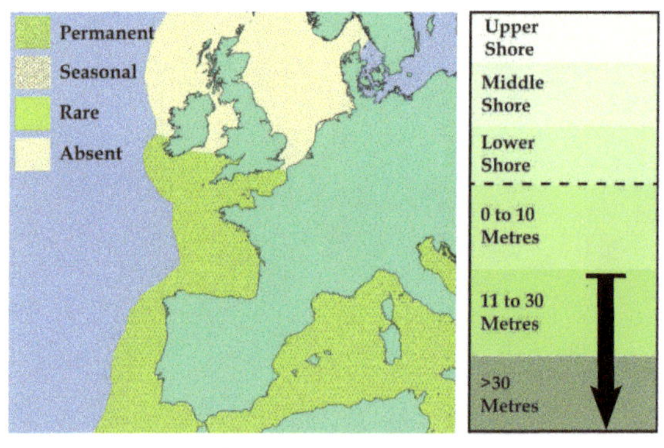

Record Weights (lb.oz.dr)

	Boat	Shore
Jersey	15.04.00	13.00.00
Guernsey	12.13.12	14.07.10

The Small-eyed Ray is a common ray species caught on rod and line in the Channel Islands and was the most frequently caught ray in a 2006 trawl survey around Jersey, making up 64 percent of 814 specimens. A similar trawl survey in the Bay of Mont St Michel in 1978 produced just one specimen while CEFAS trawl surveys in 1991 and 1992 produced none at all. This paucity of regional records from outside the Channel Islands seems unusual for a species that has an essentially southern European distribution.

Historical Channel Island records go back to the 1840s and anecdotal descriptions suggest that the local population may have remained steady although the species as a whole is declining across Europe leading to increasingly severe management measures being imposed by EU and national fisheries administrators. Since 2010 local commercial landings have varied between three tonnes and one tonne annually.

Little is known about the Small-eyed Ray's biology and behaviour although it is known to have a wide depth range and a preference for sandy seabeds. Only two percent of stranded eggcases come from this species which, given its apparent commonality in the 2006 trawl survey, suggests that it may not be breeding locally. Like most skate and ray species, the Small-eyed Ray is probably slow-growing and late to mature leading to concerns about potential overexploitation by commercial fisheries. The IUCN lists the Small-eyed Ray as near-threatened and it is suggested by some authorities that fish with a disc width of less than 45 cm should be returned alive.

Capture Technique: This is one of the main ray species caught from the Channel Islands' shoreline as well as on offshore sandbanks. This animal sticks to clean sandy patches and can both be caught during the day and at night. A smaller ray species compared to most, with a double figure fish (lbs) being a great catch. Due to being targeted mostly over clean ground, lighter gear could potentially be used but this is still a strong fighting fish with 4 to 8 oz rods still being preferred while shore fishing. Clip down, pulley and running ledger rigs will all produce with hooks ranging between 2/0 and 4/0.

Bait Preference: A number one bait for Small-eyed Ray fishing is a single large sandeel (or Launce) attached to the hook with the use of bait elastic. The sandeel can be topped and tailed to produce a bait which has a more extensive scent trail.

Undulate Ray

Raja undulata

Painted Ray

Max Length: 120 cm

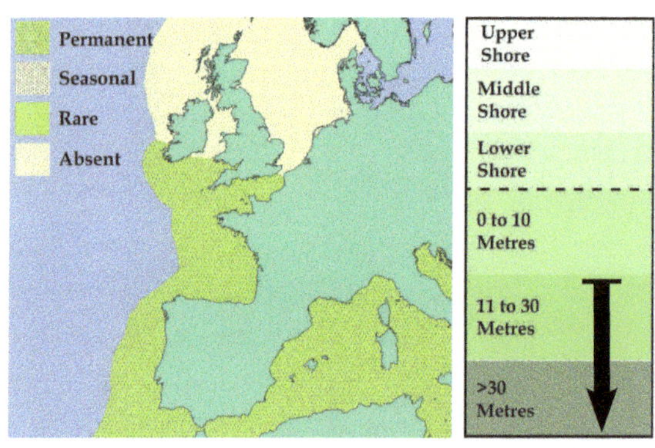

Record Weights (lb.oz.dr)

	Boat	Shore
Jersey	21.08.00	21.04.00
Guernsey	19.06.13	19.00.12

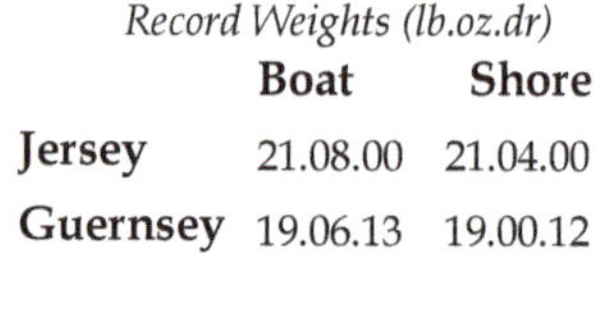

Clean Ground

Mixed Ground

The Undulate Ray is large, distinctive and frequently reported by anglers, commercial fishers and divers. A 2006 trawl survey found that 12 percent of 814 ray caught were Undulates while stranded eggcases make up 40 percent of those stranded on Jersey. Given this, it is remarkable that the oldest Channel Island record for an Undulate Ray only dates to 1952 when a lone specimen was caught off Jersey. In fact, local reports do not become common until the 1970s while in the UK the species was unknown until 1913 which lead one ichthyologist to remark that 'it is difficult to believe that the Undulate Ray has been previously overlooked'.

An Undulate Ray caught off Jersey.

This suggests that the Undulate Ray may be a relatively recent arrival in the English Channel, its range perhaps having expanded north from the Bay of Biscay. However, in 1897 the Undulate Ray was described as being 'not uncommon' off the coast of Granville, Normandy, and an alternative explanation for the lack of local records is that the Undulate was being confused with the Small-eyed Ray. Additionally, both species were commonly called the 'Painted Ray' in textbooks which may have caused further confusion to local naturalists.

While the Undulate Ray is apparently common in the Normano-Breton Gulf, there are concerns at a European level that stocks have been overfished. In 2009 a ban on retaining Undulate Rays was imposed in several EU areas including the English Channel. The Undulate Ray is financially important to the Channel Island fishing fleet and the ban has not been popular. Although listed as endangered by the IUCN, the Undulate Ray remains common locally and it has been suggested that the Channel Islands may be an important breeding area for the species. Specimens smaller that 73 cm total length (the probable minimum breeding size) should be returned alive.

Capture Technique: A relatively rare species in the UK but a frequent capture from the Channel Islands, especially Jersey's shoreline. Caught on clean and mixed ground using 40 to 50 lb hook lengths paired with 2/0 to 4/0 hook sizes. Spring and summer is often the best time for the largest specimens to be caught with captures exceeding 20 lbs from Jersey coastal waters and shoreline. Plain leads can be used to ensure the ray does not feel the spikes of a grip lead when settling over the bait. Another way to ensure this is to use longer trace lengths. This ray has shown a large population boost around the English shoreline, this is most likely due to a commercial ban and most shore and boat anglers returning this species.

Bait Preference: Baits that are productive consist of mackerel, squid and sandeel but one of the top baits being fresh pouting either whole or filleted. When using fresh bait it is vital that the fish are over the minimum landing size for that species.

Spotted Ray

Raja montagui

Max Length: 80 cm

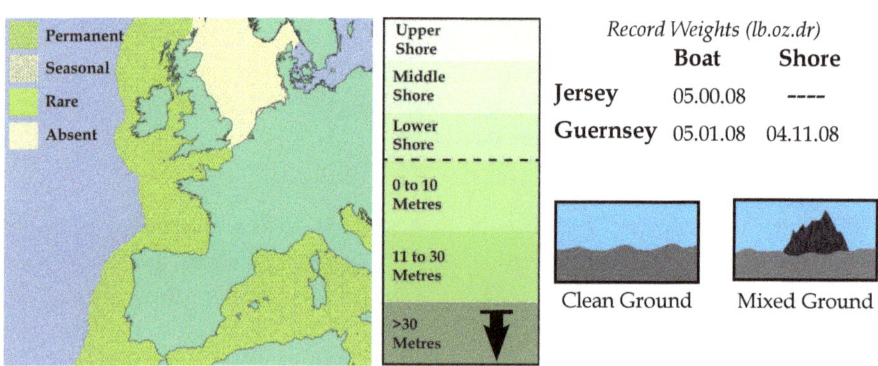

Record Weights (lb.oz.dr)

	Boat	Shore
Jersey	05.00.08	----
Guernsey	05.01.08	04.11.08

In 1904 the Spotted Ray was said to be 'tolerably common on all Channel Island coasts' but by the 1970s records from the Normano-Breton Gulf were scarce. The last confirmed angling records were in Guernsey and Herm, both in 1982, but CEFAS trawl surveys from 2006 have infrequently produced specimens from across the islands.

These records suggest that the Spotted Ray may have declined locally although a similar species, the Blonde Ray (*q.v.*), was rarely reported prior to the 1960s and so perhaps the two animals were confused by anglers. The paucity of records suggests it is a rare species. Eggcases have been found on Jersey but they are also rare, forming under one percent of all eggcases washed up.

Sandy Ray
Leucoraja circularis

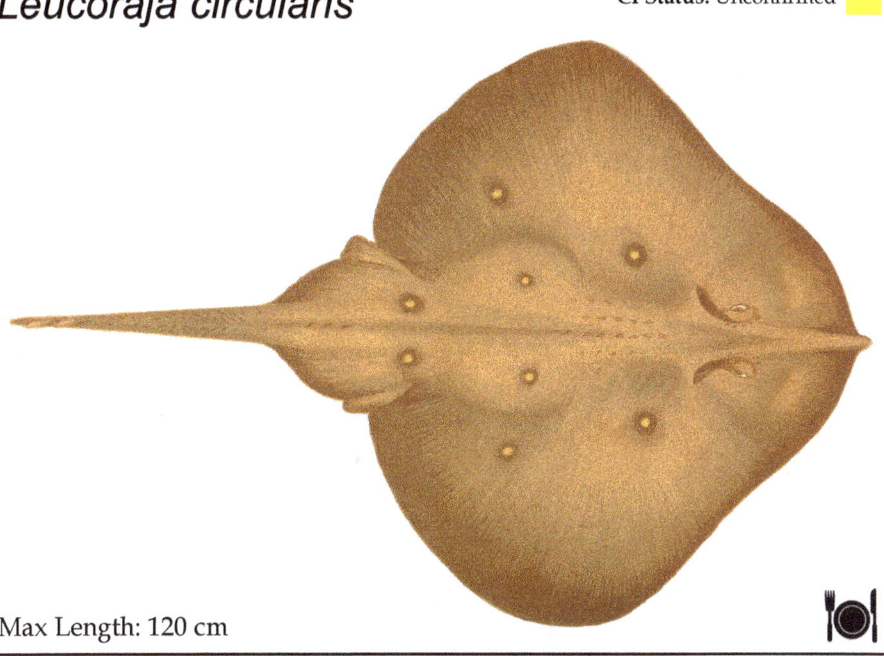

Max Length: 120 cm

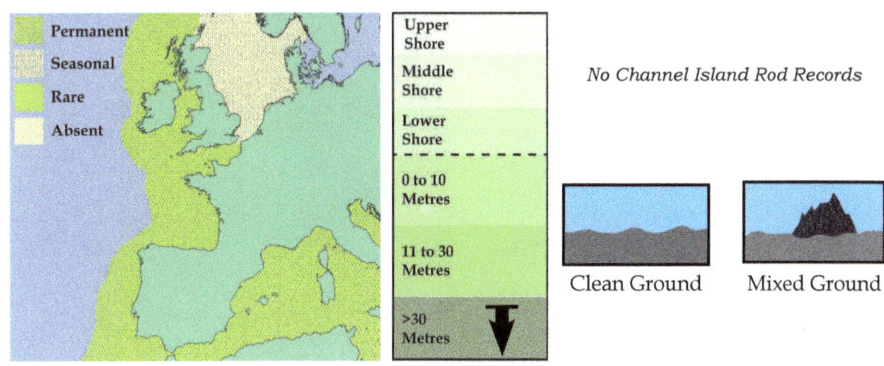

The Sandy Ray is a large deep water fish that rarely comes into areas shallower than 70 metres. It is an unlikely ray species for the Channel Islands and has just a single FAO commercial landing record of five tonnes in 2009. However, the Small-eyed Ray (*q.v.*) was historically known as the Sandy Ray and it seems probable that the FAO represents confusion between the two species, especially as 2009 was the first year that ray catches had to be reported as individual species rather than as a general group. It is possible that Sandy Rays could be found in Channel Island waters but further evidence is needed to confirm it as a local species.

Common Stingray

IUCN: DD

CI Status: Frequent

Dasyatis pastinaca

Raie à Didget; Têgrêsse; Tigre-raie; Tîngrelle

Max Length: 140 cm

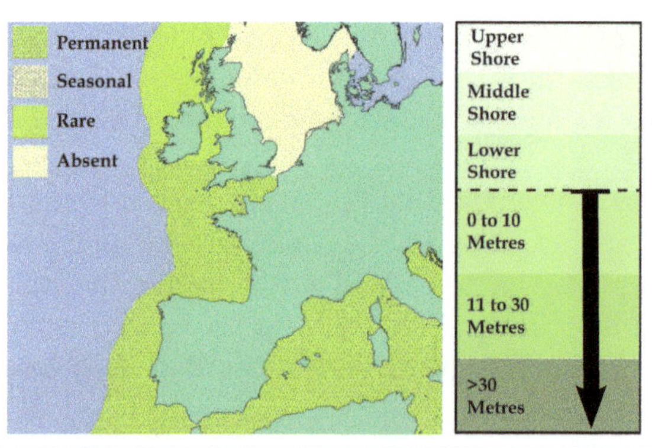

Record Weights (lb.oz.dr)

	Boat	Shore
Jersey	57.02.00	41.00.00
Guernsey	40.12.00	59.00.00

Clean Ground

Regarded as an irregular visitor in the nineteenth century, the Common Stingray is now locally common across the Channel Islands. In Jersey, Stingrays have been observed to move into shallow waters during the spring and summer months, especially in shallow sandy bays where they follow the rising tide, sometimes into water less than a metre deep. Juveniles (and less often adults) are particularly common along Jersey's east coast and it is speculated that this could be a nursery area. They are also common along some of the sandy channels within Les Minquiers. The Stingray gives birth to live young and is close to the northern limit of its breeding range within the Channel Islands.

The Common Stingray is a large fish with a poisonous spine at the base of its tail. They are sometimes seen by bathers, divers and anglers but they are wary of humans and there are no known accidental injuries from Stingrays in Channel Island waters.

This is a predominantly southern species in the British Isles but one whose range could extend further north as the seas become warmer. Studies from the 1970s suggest that there may be two species of very similar looking stingray in the English Channel. The second of these is *D. tortonesei* (Tortonese's Stingray) which is only distinguishable from *D. pastinaca* by a wider distance between the eyes and a membraneous fold below the tail. It may also have a more yellowish tinge to its colour and be slightly larger across the disc. *D. tortonesei* has not been reported from the Channel Islands but a taxonomic study of local stingrays may produce specimens as they share the same range and habitat preference.

Another species to be aware of is the Roughtail Stingray (*D. centroura*), a southern European species whose range currently terminates in the Bay of Biscay but which is possibly moving northwards towards the English Channel.

A Common Stingray swimming in shallow water at Grouville Bay, Jersey. The summer of 2018 saw an influx of stingrays in Jersey's sandy bays.

Eagle Ray

Myliobatis aquila

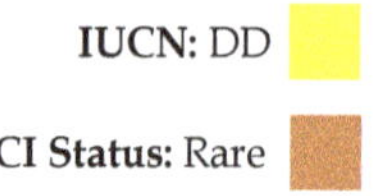

Max Length: 183 cm

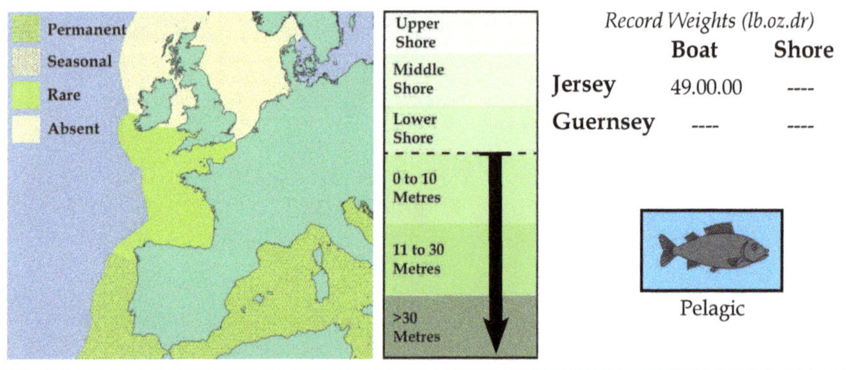

Record Weights (lb.oz.dr)

	Boat	Shore
Jersey	49.00.00	----
Guernsey	----	----

The Eagle Ray is a southern European species that occasionally strays into the English Channel and will sometimes reach the Irish Sea. The first Channel Island report for this species was in May 1999 when an individual was caught off the Schole Bank, Guernsey, and handed to a local fish expert. A second specimen was recently caught off Jersey.

The Eagle Ray tends to forage near the seabed in sandy areas and may be found in quite shallow water. It is of much local scientific interest and any caught specimens should be released and a report sent to one of the islands' record centres. The Eagle Ray is regarded as a temperate water fish but it has the potential to become more common in the English Channel as the sea temperature increases. This fish should be handled with care as there is a venomous spine located at the base of the tail.

Mermaids' Purses (eggcases)

Some species of ray and shark reproduce by laying leathery eggcases which are attached to hard objects or seaweed. The eggcases can become detached and washed up on the shore as 'mermaids' purses' (see www.sharktrust.org). Between 2013 and 2018 the Société Jersiaise collected over 15,000 eggcases from Jersey. Eight species were found. These are illustrated below along with their percentage within the total collection.

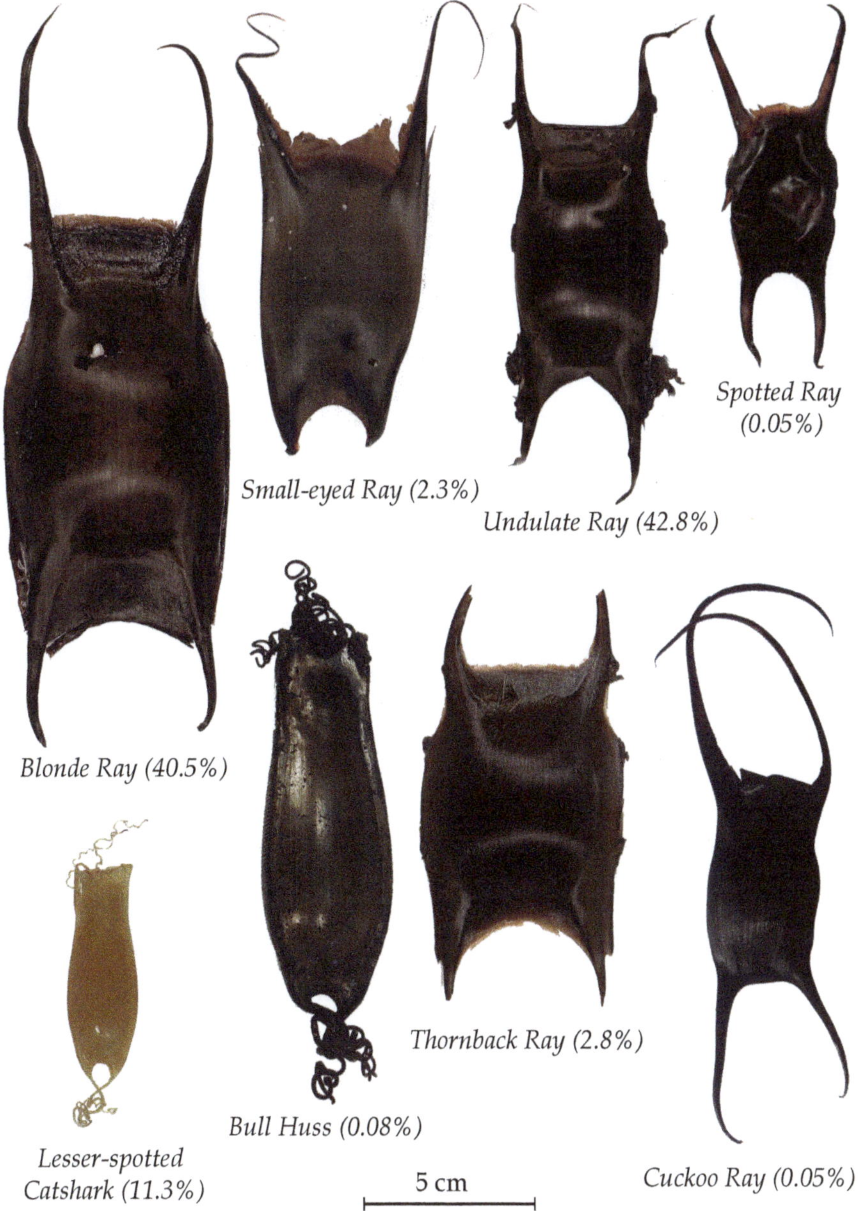

Blonde Ray (40.5%)

Small-eyed Ray (2.3%)

Undulate Ray (42.8%)

Spotted Ray (0.05%)

Lesser-spotted Catshark (11.3%)

Bull Huss (0.08%)

Thornback Ray (2.8%)

Cuckoo Ray (0.05%)

Bony Fishes

A majority of the fish species recorded from the Channel Islands belong to the 'osteichthyes' or bony fishes. Their skeletons are made from hard, inflexible bone that has evolved into a wide array of body shapes, features and sizes. This contrasts with the sharks, skate and rays whose body shape is more consistent and conservative. Other evolutionary innovations, such as scales, a swim bladder and a mouth positioned at the end of the head (rather than underneath it), separate the bony fish from other fish classes. Reproduction usually takes place outside the body but some species have complex reproductive strategies that involve changing sex (e.g. seabreams) or live birth by the males (e.g. seahorses).

There are 184 species of bony fish covered in this book belonging to over 65 different families which include everything from tiny species, such as the gobies, through to massive ones like the Sunfish (see below photograph). This represents an extraordinary diversity of body types, behaviours, habitat preferences and diets which helps explain why the bony fishes are dominant in every sea, including the waters around the Channel Islands.

The identification of individual bony fish species to their family is usually not problematic as the body shape and fin arrangement are often distinctive. Getting to species level should be possible in most cases but requires care and, in the case of small and closely related species, careful examination of a specimen or a clear photograph. This book is not an identification guide and for this we recommend the works of Louisy (2015), Henderson (2014) or Kay and Dipper (2009) - see the Bibliography section (page 284) for more details.

The Sunfish is the world's heaviest bony fish.

Sturgeon

Acipenser sturio

Esturgeon

IUCN: CR

CI Status: Rare

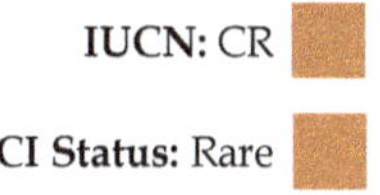

Max Length: 350 cm

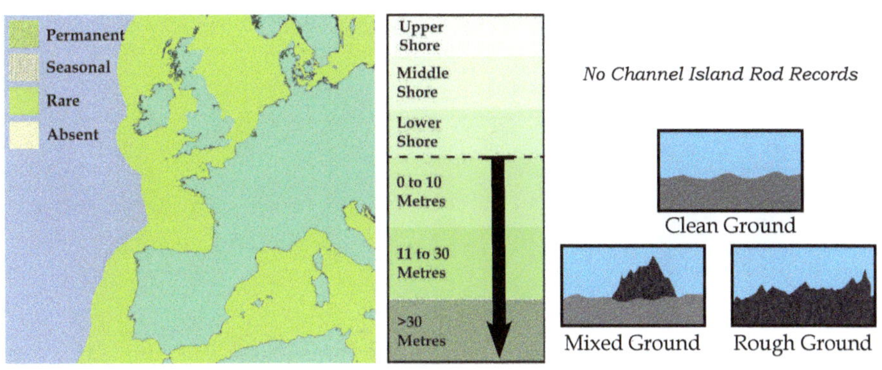

No Channel Island Rod Records

The Sturgeon is famous for producing caviar (roe) and for being a fish that, if caught in British waters, should be offered to the Queen. It is a rare visitor to the Channel Islands with just a handful of records from Guernsey and Jersey. The most unusual of these was of a dead individual found floating off Gorey Pier, Jersey, in 1954. The last known regional record was in 2004 when a Sturgeon was caught off Brittany, tagged and then released near to Les Minquiers.

Sturgeon only begin to breed at 25 years of age by returning from the sea to freshwater. Allegedly abundant in Medieval times, overfishing and dam construction collapsed Sturgeon populations across Europe and it is now listed under several international conventions as being critically endangered.

If caught by anglers, this fish should be released alive and a report sent to one of the Channel Islands' biological records centres.

A Sturgeon on Gorey Pier, Jersey, in 1954.

European Eel

Anguilla anguilla

Common Eel; *Andgulle d'ieau douoche*

Max Length: 120 cm

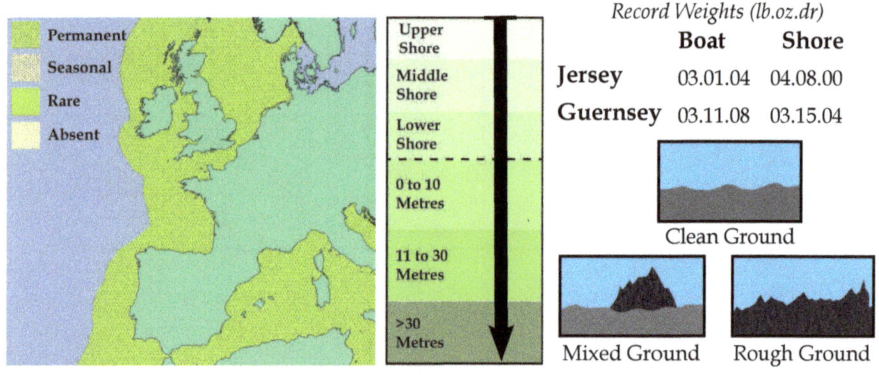

Record Weights (lb.oz.dr)

	Boat	Shore
Jersey	03.01.04	04.08.00
Guernsey	03.11.08	03.15.04

Once abundant throughout Europe, since the 1970s overfishing and mismanagement has led to a collapse in the European Eel population. The complicated reproductive history of this animal is not well understood but it does require a long migration from Europe's rivers and estuaries to the depths of the Sargasso Sea during the autumn, where it spawns and dies. The eel larvae will then ride the Gulf Stream across the Atlantic Ocean back to the shores and rivers of its ancestors.

The European Eel used to be common on Jersey and Guernsey where it would be seen in streams and ponds or, more rarely, in coastal waters. It is still present in freshwater and marine environments but is a rarer sight now than in the past although specimens do still turn up. For example, in 2017 two large eels were washed from a stream onto the shore in St Aubin's Bay, Jersey, following a heavy rainstorm. Such is the concern about the European Eel that it is listed as critically endangered in the IUCN Red Book and, if caught by anglers, should be released.

Moray Eel

Muraena helena

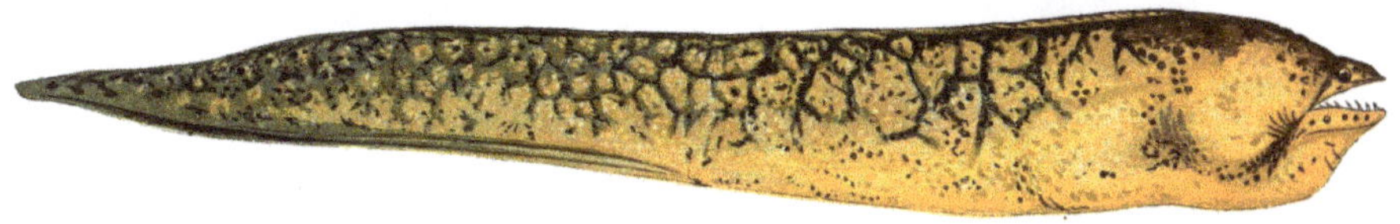

Max Length: 150 cm

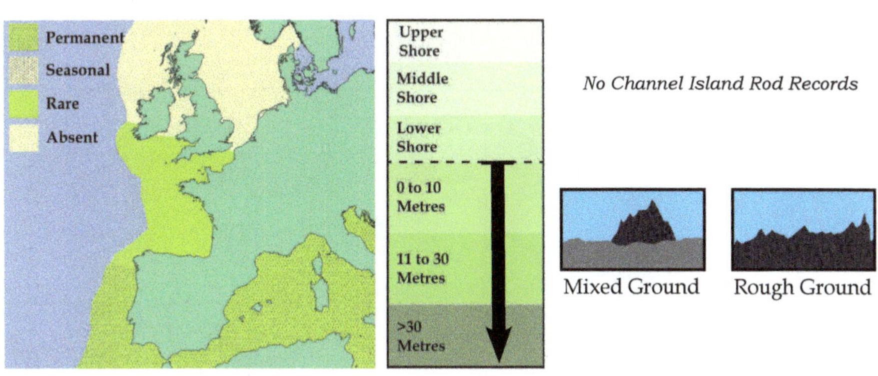

The Moray Eel is familiar to divers in tropical and subtropical seas and, very rarely, individuals will take up residence in the cooler waters of northern Europe. The single Channel Island record was caught off Guernsey in October 1996 and then taken to the Guernsey Aquarium where it lived for many years. In June 2011 the eel was discovered to have choked to death while trying to eat a Grey Mullet. It was apparently the first time it had attempted to eat another inhabitant in its tank. The Moray Eel's body was returned to the sea but later washed up on a Guernsey beach sparking a wave of media interest.

Other Moray Eels have been caught in the English Channel and, with increasing water temperature and a decline in the Conger Eel population, it could be a species that will be reported more frequently from local waters. This is a large, powerful fish with sharp teeth and, as with the Conger Eel, needs to be handled with care if caught.

Conger Eel

IUCN: LC

CI Status: Frequent

Conger conger

Congre; Andgulle; Fîlerêsse [small]; *Filot* [small]; *Fouet* [small]

Max Length: 300 cm

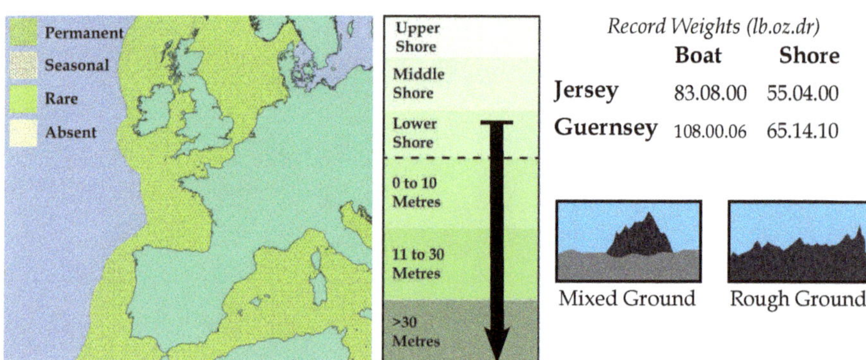

Record Weights (lb.oz.dr)

	Boat	Shore
Jersey	83.08.00	55.04.00
Guernsey	108.00.06	65.14.10

The Conger Eel is a large, powerful fish that is popular with anglers and divers. Some of the earliest references to fishing in the islands come from medieval taxes that were imposed on Conger Eels and on *êpèrquéthie*s which were areas reserved for drying the fish before export. In the nineteenth century Jersey was known as the 'Kingdom of the Conger' with particularly large specimens being caught around Les Minquiers. For centuries the Conger Eel was the mainstay of the Channel Islands' fishing industry and during the 1830s between 100,000 and a million fish were exported annually from the Chausey Islands. In the first two weeks of July 1880 over 14,000 kg of Conger was sold through Jersey's fish market but by the 1890s biologist James Hornell believed that the local population had decreased by 40 percent due to overfishing.

The Conger is a particularly bony fish that has become unpopular with diners in recent decades but it still retains a commercial value for use in soups and stocks. During the late 1980s and early 90s annual landings in the islands were up to 240 tonnes before rapidly declining.

Catches in Guernsey (but not Jersey) rose again at the turn of the twenty-first century before declining steeply from 2007. Only a few tonnes a year are landed currently.

Like the European Eel, the Conger migrates a long distance offshore to spawn in deep water before dying. Juvenile Congers migrate back to coastal waters but there are concerns that this complex reproductive cycle has made the animal susceptible to overfishing as any Conger caught and killed in coastal waters will not yet have spawned.

Peter Gay with the Jersey boat caught record (83 lb 08 oz).

Anecdotal and statistical evidence suggest that the Channel Island Conger population is a fraction of what it was historically and that much of this decline has occured in recent decades. The phenomenon of shifting baselines (where gradual changes go unnoticed between generations) may have masked the decrease in this once abundant and economically important species. Better statistics are required to gain a true understanding of the local status of this iconic and much admired fish.

Capture Technique: A popular target for many boat and shore anglers. The passive Conger Eel is best targeted during night time hours using larger baits compared to most CI species. The use of 150+ lb monofilament to an 8/0 hook is common practice. Heavy beach casters paired with large multipliers should be used from shore with mainline being 30 lb or above for most eeling situations. Congers lives in rocky, broken ground and can be caught all year round but the most effective time has traditionally been autumn. Large specimens are often caught from breakwaters and piers, especially after a period of unsettled weather. Boat fishing will find the largest specimens and is most productive over reefs and wrecks and, if deep enough, Congers can be caught throughout daylight hours. The darkest of nights over new moons or a high percentage of cloud cover is preferred. When landing Conger Eels, gaffs should be avoided unless the fish is going to be eaten.

Bait Preference: Mackerel and cuttlefish tend to be the most popular baits although many others can still prove productive such as Pouting, Garfish, Rockling, Launce and Squid. Conger Eels are more likely to come across demersal and benthic dwelling species and can therefore offer an advantage when using them as bait.

Allis Shad

Alosa alosa

Flyie

Max Length: 60 cm

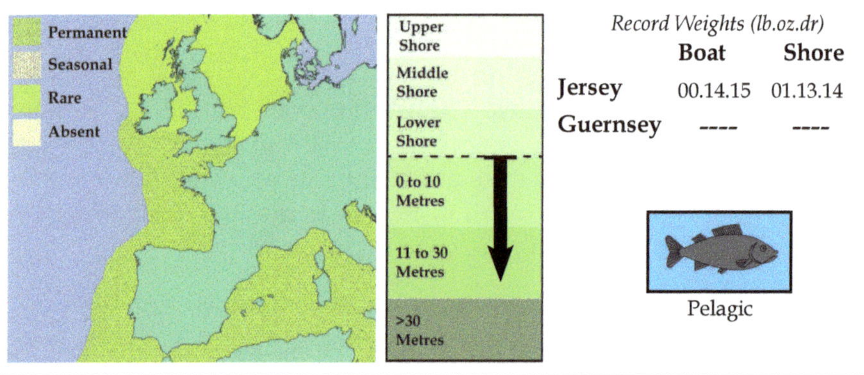

Record Weights (lb.oz.dr)

	Boat	Shore
Jersey	00.14.15	01.13.14
Guernsey	----	----

The Allis Shad and Twaite Shad are similar looking animals that are occasionally caught by anglers and netters around the Channel Islands. Both species have complex life histories which include the need to move from the sea into rivers to spawn. Pollution, overfishing, estuary barriers and habitat destruction have had a serious effect on both species and they are currently prohibited as commercial landings in the EU. Although populations are believed to have stabilised recently, these two fish species remain of concern in Northern Europe.

The Allis Shad was regarded as an occasional visitor to the islands in Victorian times and is historically less commonly recorded than the Twaite Shad. However, their visual similarity might lead to confusion between the two species. As a non-commercial fish, it is possible that both the Allis and Twaite Shad are under-recorded in the islands.

An Allis Shad at Gorey, Jersey, in 2017.

Twaite Shad

IUCN: LC

CI Status: Occasional

Alosa fallax

Flyînte; Minister

Max Length: 50 cm

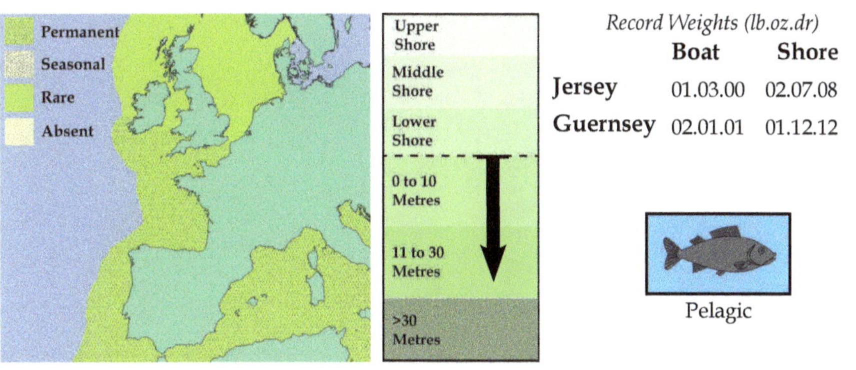

Record Weights (lb.oz.dr)

	Boat	Shore
Jersey	01.03.00	02.07.08
Guernsey	02.01.01	01.12.12

Pelagic

Much of what was written about the Allis Shad (see opposite) can be applied also to the Twaite Shad. This fish most obviously differs from the Allis Shad by the series of dark spots that run down its flank. It is most commonly encountered in the spring, summer and early autumn and is probably more common than the handful of known reports suggest.

The oldest record is from the 1840s when the Twaite Shad was described as being a rare visitor to Guernsey waters although regional reports from the start of the twentieth century suggest it was commonly caught by fishing boats. However, by the 1970s reports are rare, including in scientific surveys, and at present it is infrequently reported usually by recreational anglers. Like the Allis Shad, this fish is regarded as threatened in Europe and is scheduled to become legally protected in Jersey. If individuals from either species are caught then they should be released again and a report made to a biological record centre.

Herring

Clupea harengus

Héthan; V'nîse [juvenile]

IUCN: LC

CI Status: Occasional

Max Length: 40 cm

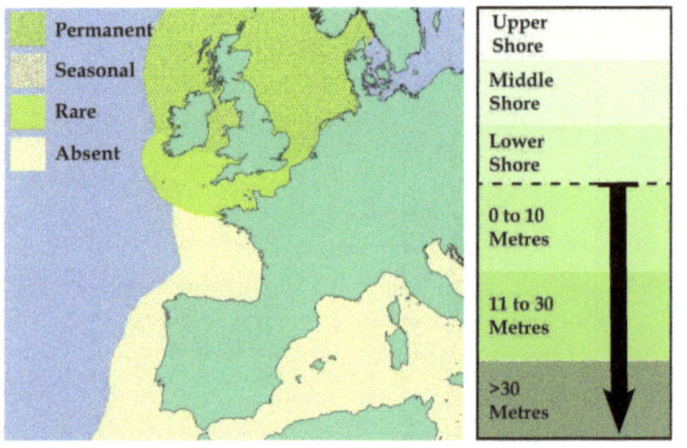

Record Weights (lb.oz.dr)

	Mini Species
Jersey	00.09.08
Guernsey	00.12.13

Pelagic

There are only a handful of Herring records from the Channel Islands and the species seems to have had little economic importance locally although small commercial catches have been recorded. This is in contrast to other parts of the Bay of Granville where the Herring seems to have been heavily fished in the summer months during the nineteenth and early twentieth centuries although catches decreased during the 1980s. Specimens are caught by boat anglers in the Channel Islands but, as an open water pelagic species, it is rarely seen by divers or snorkelers. It is perhaps not uncommon in the islands but as a small fish with little recreational and commercial value, the Herring is rarely reported. The species can be confused with the Pilchard.

False Herring

Harengula clupeola

Max Length: 18 cm

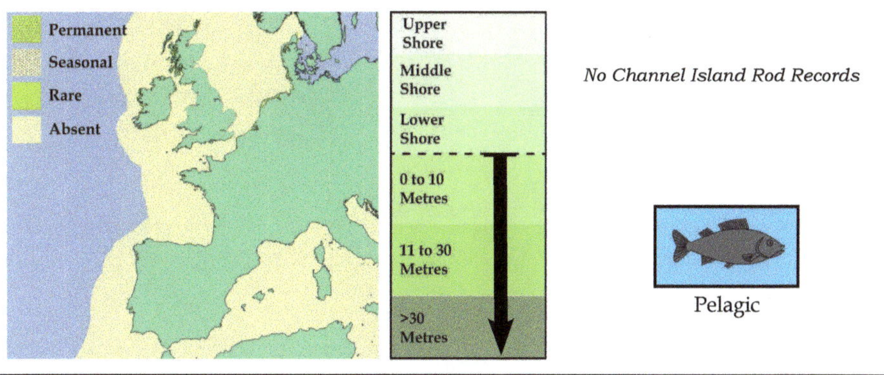

This is a tropical species from the western Atlantic that is highly unlikely ever to have been caught in Channel Island waters. The only local record comes from a list of fish species published in 1862 and it is probable that this represented a printing or identification error.

Sardine

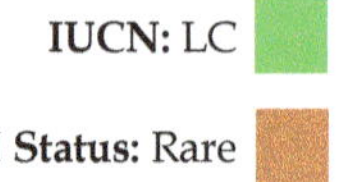

Sardina pilchardus

Pilchard; *Sardinne*

Max Length: 25 cm

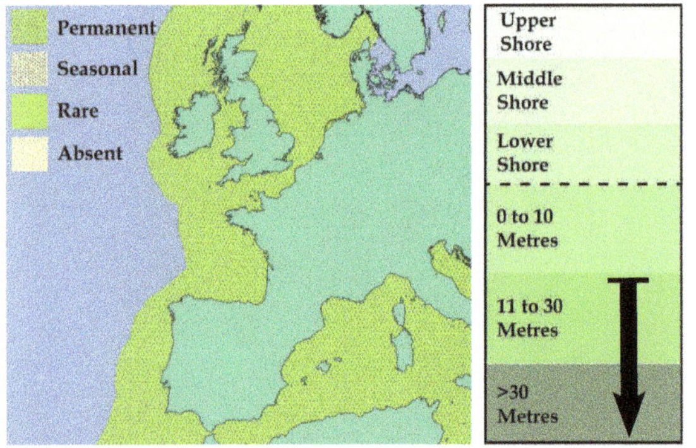

Record Weights (lb.oz.dr)

	Mini Species
Jersey	00.07.03
Guernsey	00.06.06

Pelagic

The Sardine (also known as the Pilchard) is a southerly species which is more common in the Mediterranean and Iberian waters but whose range reaches north to the British Isles. It is a shoaling species that lives in the water column and is fished heavily by some European fleets and is locally fished in the Bay of Mont St Michel. There are just two nineteenth century records of Sardines from the Channel Islands but it occurs commonly (sometimes abundantly) in parts of the Normano-Breton Gulf and has been found in abundances over offshore sandbanks. Locally the Sardine may have been confused with the Herring as the two fish are similar in appearance. This is probably a seasonal visitor to the Channel Islands particularly in the summer months when shoals migrate north from southern Europe.

Sprat

Sprattus sprattus

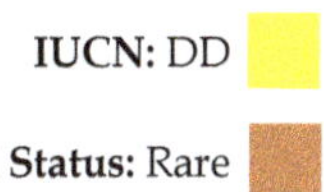

Êprot; V'nîse [juvenile]; *P'tit hethan*

Max Length: 16 cm

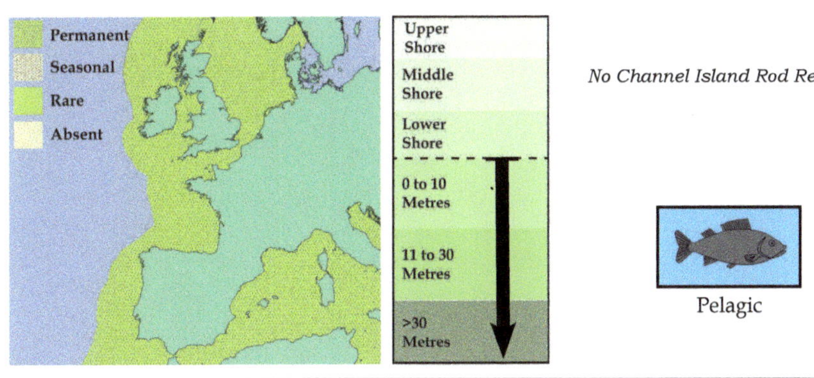

The Sprat is a pelagic species with a wide geographic distribution. It is heavily fished in northern Europe and is primarily caught through netting and trawling. At the beginning and middle of the twentieth century both Joseph Sinel and Ronald Le Sueur noted that the Sprat is 'of erratic occurence' in Channel Island waters. There are no official fishing records but it was recorded in trawl surveys made in 2006, 2010 and 2011 albeit rarely. The Sprat appears to be an occasional visitor to local waters and can sometimes be caught inside harbours. The species is associated with estuarine waters and is common in the Bay of Mont St Michel.

European Anchovy

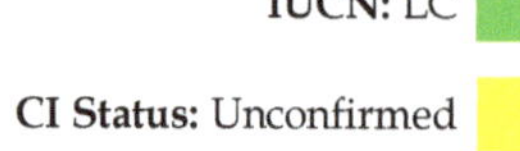

Engraulis encrasicolus

Anchouais

Max Length: 20 cm

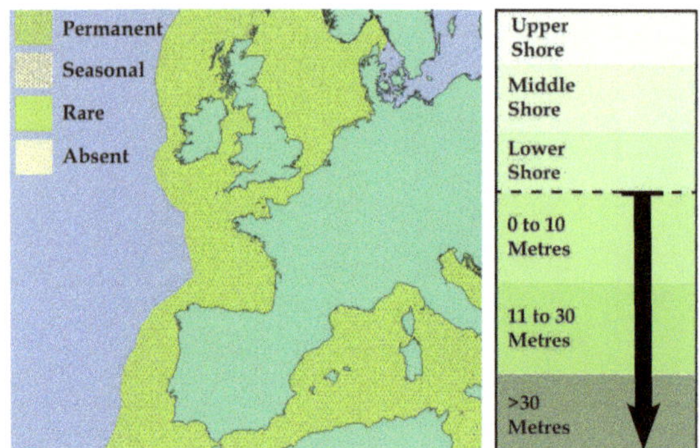

No Channel Island Rod Records

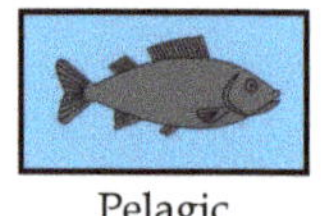

Pelagic

The European Anchovy is a seasonal visitor to the English Channel but there is just one historical record from the Normano-Breton Gulf in 1862. It does not feature in any local fishing records and has not been found in any of the many scientifc trawl surveys undertaken in the Channel Island region. This is probably not a species that occurs in the islands.

Coho Salmon

Oncorhynchus kisutch

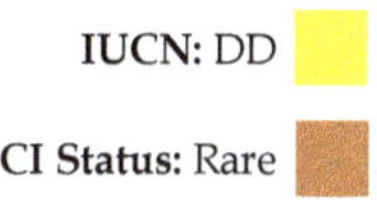

Max Length: 96 cm

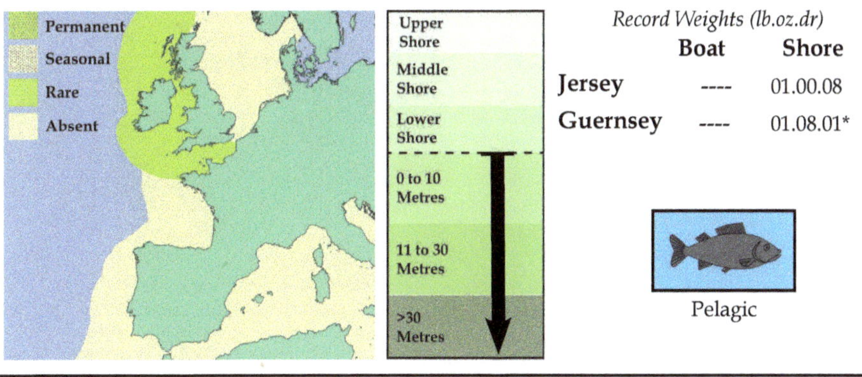

Record Weights (lb.oz.dr)

	Boat	Shore
Jersey	----	01.00.08
Guernsey	----	01.08.01*

The Coho Salmon is native to the Pacific Ocean but has been farmed extensively in Europe including in Normandy. A Channel Island specimen was caught off St Sampsons, Guernsey, in 1977 and was a British weight record. A second specimen was afterwards caught off Jersey but, beyond its weight of just over 450 grams, no other details are known.

Between 1973 and 1974 an estimated 50,000 Coho Salmon escaped from fish farms in Normandy leading to individual fish being caught in several rivers. It is probable that the Guernsey specimen was an escapee from a Normandy fish farm. It is not currently thought to be resident in Channel Island waters.

Salmon

Salmo salar

Saumon

IUCN: LC

CI Status: Rare

Max Length: 120 cm

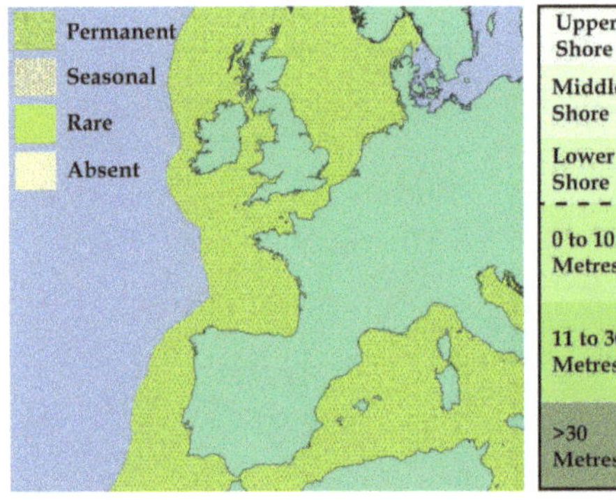

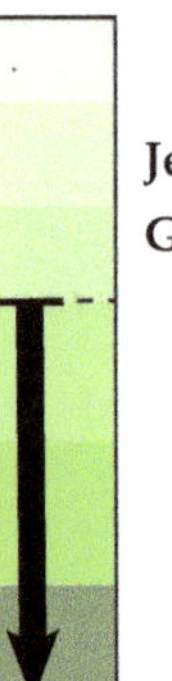

Record Weights (lb.oz.dr)

	Boat	Shore
Jersey	04.11.12	08.09.11
Guernsey	06.02.00	05.08.06

Pelagic

Salmon move from marine to fresh waters in order to return to their river spawning grounds but the population has suffered heavily from overfishing, pollution and the building of dams, weirs and other obstacles along rivers and streams. Most commercially sold Salmon comes from fish farms which can themselves present a threat to the wild animals through disease and eutrophication. The Salmon is rarely caught in the Channel Islands and, with no rivers to breed in, is probably an occasional visitor to local waters. Salmon do breed in some Normandy rivers and there was once a small fishery there. With the wild Salmon population in decline, reports from local waters are liable to be rare and erratic.

Stan Vaudin with the Guernsey shore caught record Salmon (5 lb 8 oz 6 dr).

Sea Trout

Salmo trutta

Érnard; R'nard

Max Length: 100 cm

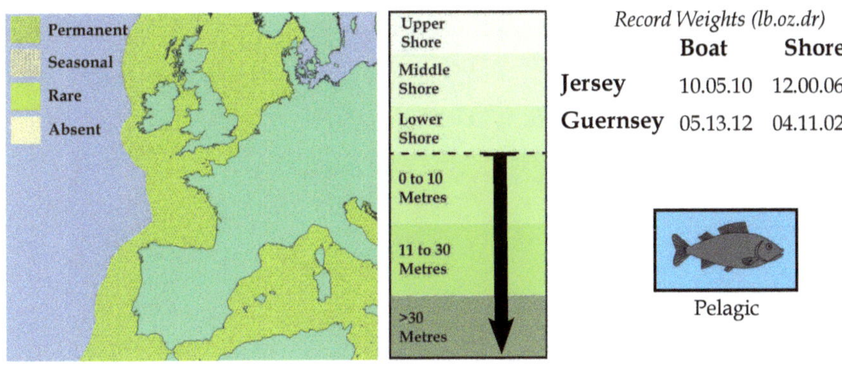

Record Weights (lb.oz.dr)

	Boat	Shore
Jersey	10.05.10	12.00.06
Guernsey	05.13.12	04.11.02

Sea Trout are pelagic fish that spend most of their life at sea but, as with the Salmon, will migrate into freshwater to breed. This is not a common fish in the Normano-Breton Gulf and there are just a handful of Channel Island records starting in the late nineteenth century. Fishing records suggest that a few specimens are caught annually which makes it probable that this is an occasional visitor to the islands. In other parts of Europe declines in wild Sea Trout have led to restrictions on their fishing, including closed seasons.

European Smelt

Osmerus eperlanus

IUCN: LC

CI Status: Unconfirmed

Max Length: 45 cm

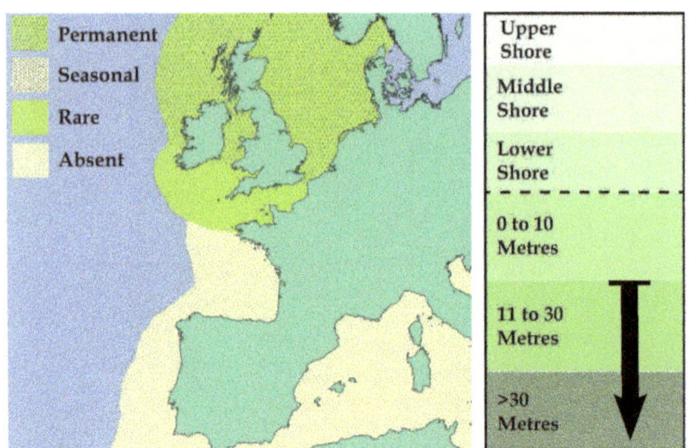

No Channel Island Rod Records

Pelagic

Only recorded from commercial catch landings made in Guernsey between 1979 and 1982, the European Smelt is an unexpected fish for local waters as it is a coastal species that is often found in estuaries and even freshwater areas. Its range normally does not include the western English Channel but was probably historically wider until overfishing and estuarine pollution took their toll. Even so, a lack of any other records from the Bay of Granville area suggests that this was probably not common enough to produce the commercial landings seen in the early 1980s. The European Smelt should be considered an unconfirmed Channel Island species until actual specimens are caught and verified.

Small-headed Clingfish

Apletodon dentatus

Max Length: 4 cm

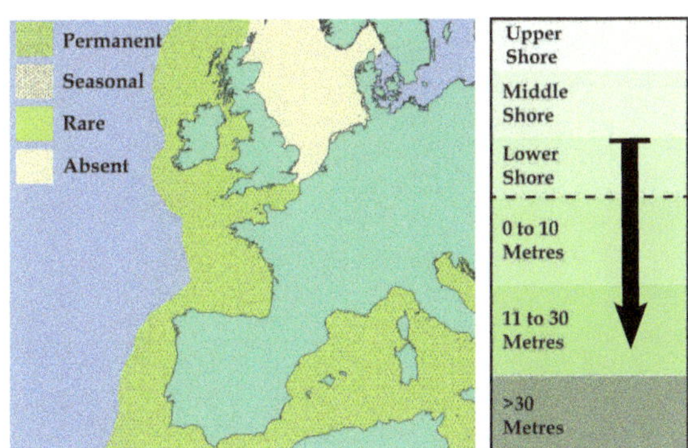

No Channel Island Rod Records

Mixed Ground

Rough Ground

Depending on your point of view, there is either one distinct or two very similar species (*A. dentatus* and *A. microcephalus*) that go under the name of Small-headed Clingfish. There are Channel Island historical records for both species but *A. microcephalus* has recently been synonymised with *A. dentatus* and so all recent records have been placed under this name. At just a few centimetres in length the Small-headed Clingfish is easily overlooked and is certainly not caught by anglers. It is, however, sometimes seen in rock pools where it hides under stones and in weed. When disturbed it will sometimes lie still for a short while providing an opportunity to examine or photograph it.

A Small-headed Clingfish in a rock pool on Jersey. The white band between the eyes is often present in this species.

Two-spotted Clingfish

Diplecogaster bimaculata

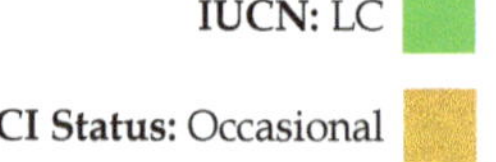

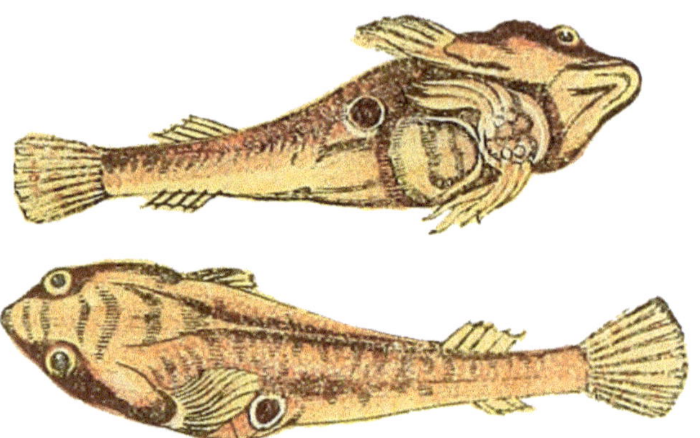

Max Length: 6 cm

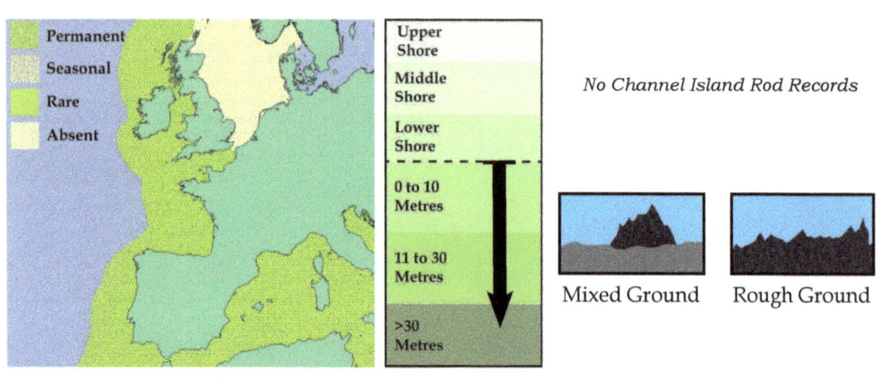

The Two-spotted Clingfish was first recorded from the Channel Islands in the 1880s from a specimen captured in Guernsey. It is mostly an offshore species, is small and can be confused with other clingfish species, especially the Small-headed Clingfish. For this reason most of the Channel Island records have been made during scientific surveys including several specimens taken north and east of Guernsey between 2008 and 2011 and west of Les Minquiers in 2006. Some casual rock pool records also exist and this is probably a reasonably common species that is rarely observed. Locally it may have a preference for important seabed habitats such as maerl (species of coralline seaweed) beds.

Connemara Clingfish

Lepadogaster candollei

Max Length: 6 cm

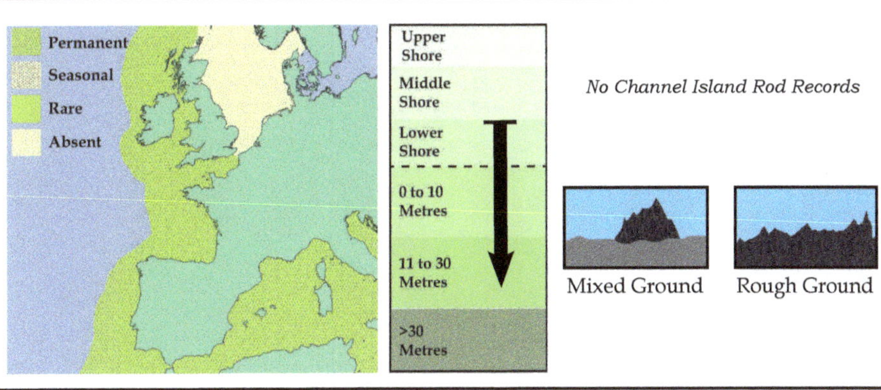

The Connemara Clingfish is a small and enigmatic fish that is encountered in rock pools and shallow marine rough seabeds. It is easily confused with other small clingfish species and so may be under-reported locally although there are established records from late Victorian times onwards. It is a rocky shore species that primarily lives under boulders but which is occasionally seen by divers or brought up with lobster and crab pots. Although rarely reported locally and regionally, the Connemara Clingfish is reasonably common on the lower shore but is difficult to spot and identify which has led to it being overlooked by naturalists.

A Connemara Clingfish photographed on Jersey's west coast where it is reported to be common in rock pools.

Cornish Sucker

Lepadogaster purpurea

Ocellated Clingfish

IUCN: LC

CI Status: Common

Max Length: 7 cm

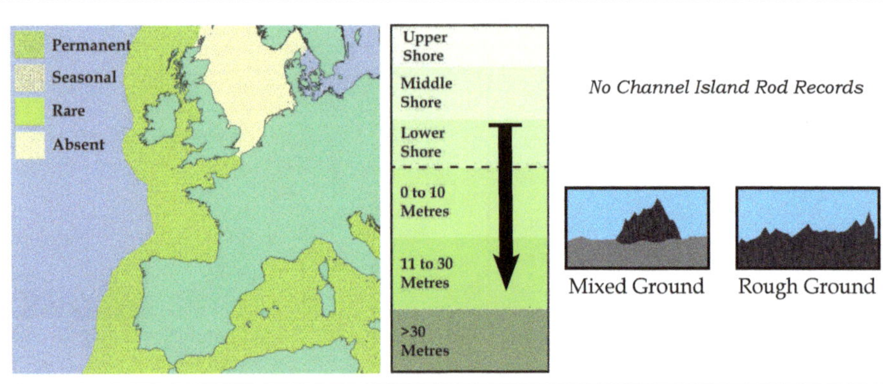

The Cornish Sucker can be easily mistaken for another species, the Crescent Clingfish (*L. lepadogaster*), and as both species have been reported locally, there has been historical taxonomic confusion. However, the northern range of the Crescent Clingfish stops in the Bay of Biscay and so all local reports have been corrected to the Cornish Sucker.

The Cornish Sucker has many Channel Island records going back to the 1860s. It is frequently encountered on the lower shore, usually under stones, to which it will cling for a few seconds before dropping into the water. The Cornish Sucker is particularly common in the winter months and may have a preference for more exposed coasts. There is no evidence that this species is in decline or threatened locally.

A Cornish Sucker in a rock pool on the coast of Guernsey.

Deep-sea Angler

Ceratias holboelli

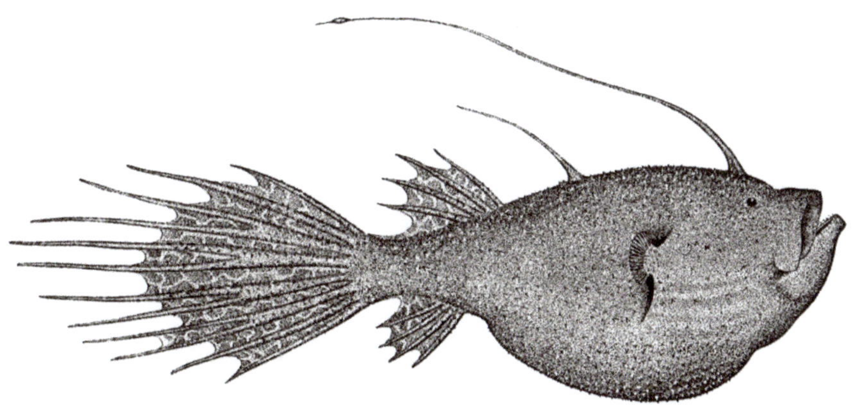

Max Length: 120 cm (female); 16 cm (male)

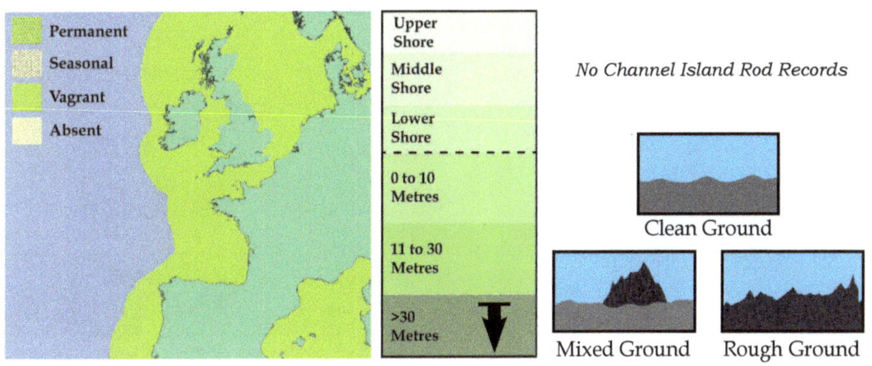

The Deep-sea Angler is a highly distinctive and large fish which belongs to an exotically-named family called the sea devils. As the name implies, the Deep-sea Angler generally lives several hundred metres below the surface but individuals have been caught at a variety of depths, including in shallow water. The only known regional record was made during a CEFAS scientific trawl survey in 2009 from the France-Jersey border just south of Les Minquiers. The species is highly sexually dimorphic with the females being large with a dangling lure (illustrated above) while the males are tiny in comparison. When a male finds a female he will attach himself to her body permanently and eventually becomes absorbed into her body. The Deep-sea Angler is a very rare fish and the discovery of a reliable record from the Channel Islands was unexpected; it is unlikely to be encountered regularly.

Angler Fish

Lophius piscatorius

Fishing Frog; *Paîsson à pouchettes; Raînotte dé mé; Scolpîn*

Max Length: 200 cm

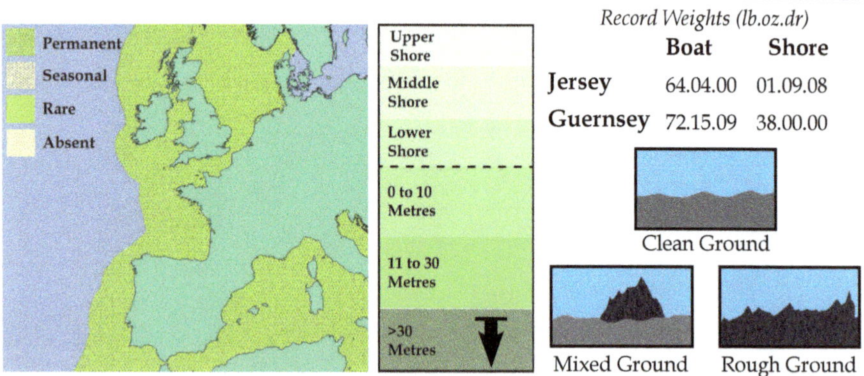

Record Weights (lb.oz.dr)

	Boat	Shore
Jersey	64.04.00	01.09.08
Guernsey	72.15.09	38.00.00

In 1904 the Jersey marine biologist Joseph Sinel wrote that 'it is doubtful if even a naturalist would call the angler-fish beautiful'. With a reputation for looking ugly and aggressive, the Angler gets its common name from a long, thin adapted dorsal fin which dangles a fleshy growth just in front of the fish's head. This acts as a lure, drawing small fish towards the Angler's broad, toothed and upward facing mouth. This can be opened and shut with remarkable speed, grabbing prey before it has a chance to react.

Historical records suggest that the Angler Fish was not common in the Channel Islands during the nineteenth and early twentieth centuries and that it was considered to be 'ill-favoured' as a commercial species. It was so unusual that several Victorian newspaper articles detailed local captures of Angler Fish, sometimes under the local name of Toad Fish.

Each one highlighted its wide mouth, size and ugliness. A specimen caught in 1870 was found to contain a bass and 7 kg mullet. It seems to have been considered as something of a curiosity rather than a potential food fish.

However, the Angler Fish became commercially targeted after World War I following a protracted wave of European fish stock collapses which rendered other more traditional large benthic species, such as the Skate and Monkfish, scarce. To encourage its consumption the unappealing sounding Fishing Frog was rebranded and sold as Monkfish or scampi. This is an early example of where a scarcity in traditionally fished species forced commercial boats to target previously ignored ones.

The Angler is generally caught by trawling and, although not locally rare, landings have declined both within the islands and elsewhere in the English Channel. Concerns over its population has resulted in the EU placing a minimum landing weight of 0.5 kg on Angler Fish. This is a species that prefers sedimentary seabeds but which may be found on a variety of substrates from just offshore to very deep waters. It is sometimes taken by recreational anglers but is rarely seen by divers. Most records are from commercial fishing, often to the west of the islands. The distinctive jawbones, which are full of fierce-looking teeth, will occasionally wash up and can be mistaken for those of sharks. The odd shape of this fish makes it difficult to impose a minimum landing size but, as per EU recommendations, specimens below 0.5 kg in weight should be released alive.

Mike Peel with the Jersey boat caught Angler Fish record (64 lb 4 oz).

Codfish

Codfishes are a diverse group of fishes that belong to the Order Gadiformes with the main families being Gadidae (Cod, Pollack, Pouting, Whiting and Haddock), Merlucciidae (Hake), Phycidae (Fork-beards) and Lotidae (Torsk, Ling, Rocklings). They are almost exclusively marine species with a preference for cold or temperate waters which is why they tend to be more common in northern latitudes such as the North Atlantic. Most juvenile codfishes are found inshore but will migrate into deeper water with age although some bottom-dwelling species, such as rocklings, will spend their whole lives in shallow waters.

Many of the codfishes are important commercial species that have been at the centre of historical fishing industries for decades or even centuries. In some areas, such as the North Sea, species such as Cod and Haddock form dense shoals offshore and the advent of mechanical trawling made catching vast numbers of fish relatively easy. Many species of codfish have been heavily fished, especially in European waters, leading to severe stock declines and, in some circumstances, near population collapses. This has led to codfishes being subject to strict European fisheries measures, conservation campaigns and sustainability audits. The commercial fishing of codfishes in the Channel Islands is relatively light and, as the most important species are either rare or do not form dense shoals. Of those fish that are landed, most have been caught as bycatch.

As with most fish groups the Channel Islands contain a mixture of northern European species, such as the Northern and Four-bearded Rocklings and Haddock, and southern European ones, such as the Shore Rockling, Blue Whiting and Fork-beard. It may be that warming seas will have an effect on the presence or abundance of some of the local codfishes species although the common ones, such as Pouting and Whiting, will probably be unaffected.

Cusk

IUCN: LC

Brosme brosme

CI Status: Rare

Torsk; Tusk; Moonfish

Max Length: 120 cm

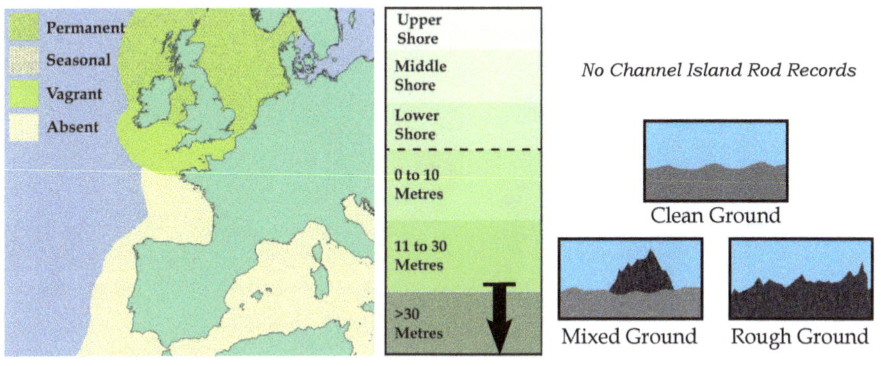

The Cusk is known from the Channel Islands via two specimens that were caught off Guernsey during the late nineteenth century. This is a cold water species that generally lives at depth and as such the Normano-Breton Gulf is not within its usual geographical or environmental range. With no subsequent reports, it is unlikely that the Cusk is resident in the Channel Islands and it is probable that the historical catches represent vagrant specimens.

Northern Rockling

Ciliata septentrionalis

Max Length: 20 cm

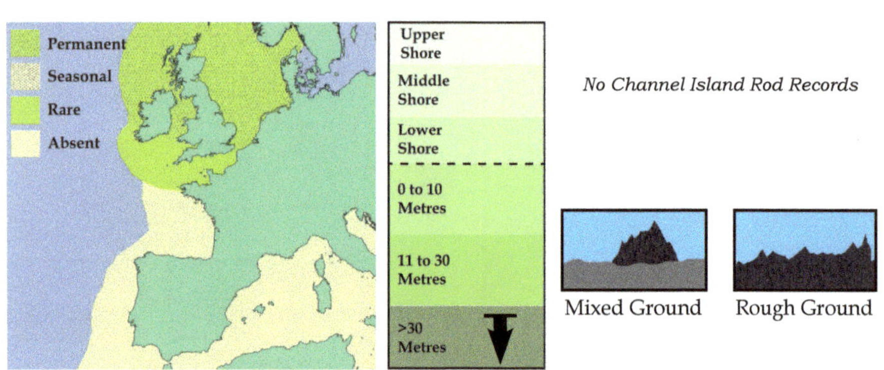

The Northern Rockling has a preference for colder waters which means that the Channel Islands lie at the southern fringe of its range. There are just two local records one from the west of Guernsey and the other south of Les Minquiers. Both were recorded during a 2018 CEFAS beam trawl survey of the English Channel.

The Northern Rockling lives on rocky or mixed seabeds in shallow marine areas but may migrate closer inshore during the winter months. It is very similar to the Five-bearded Rockling with the key difference being fleshy lobes on the Northern Rockling's upper lip. This fish is not targeted by anglers which might explain why there are no historical records. The Northern Rockling is probably a rare fish in Channel Island waters.

Five-bearded Rockling

IUCN: LC

Ciliata mustela

CI Status: Common

P'tite louoche

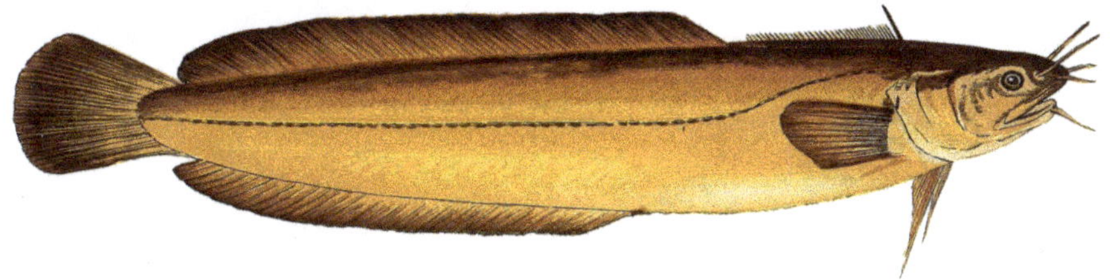

Max Length: 25 cm

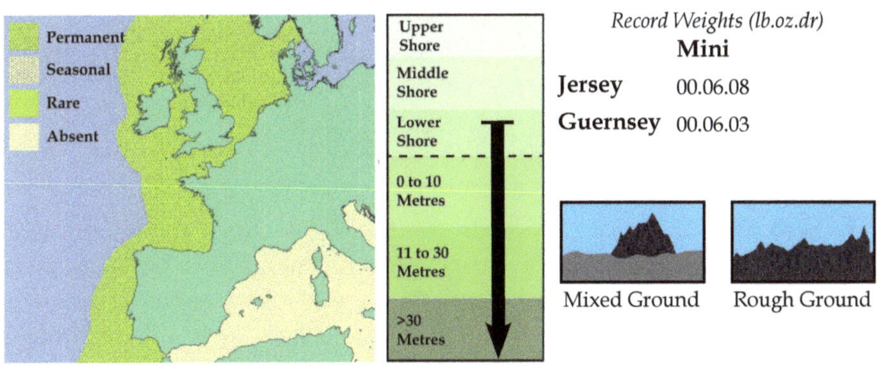

The Five-bearded Rockling was described as being 'very abundant' and 'very common' in the Channel Islands by writers in the late nineteenth and mid-twentieth centuries. Although perhaps not abundant today, this fish may often be seen in lower shore rock pools where its size and five 'beards' (barbels) make it easy to see and identify. It is sometimes caught by anglers but is not a commercial species and is not thought to be threatened. Offshore trawl survey work between 2006 and 2018 produced a number of specimens, mostly to the south-west of Guernsey but also south of Jersey and north of Alderney. It seems to be reasonably common around all the Channel Islands.

Shore Rockling

Gaidropsarus mediterraneus

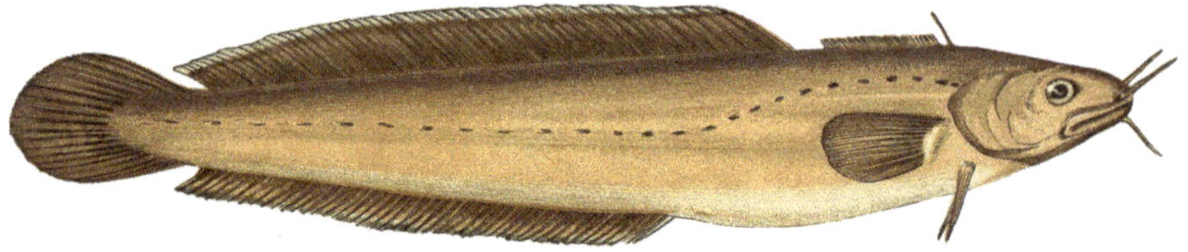

Max Length: 40 cm

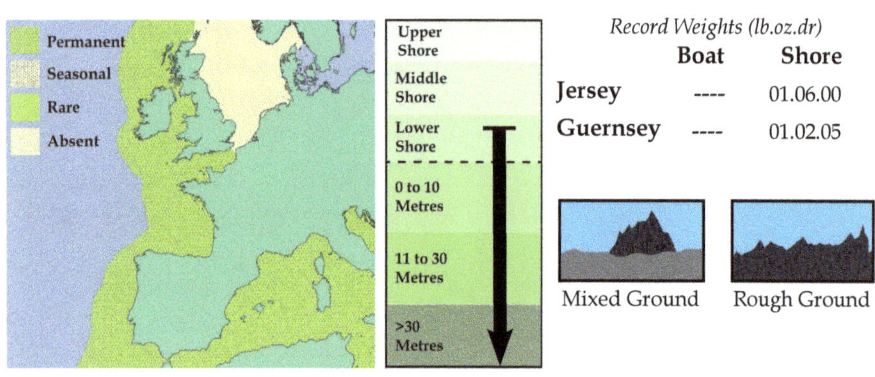

Record Weights (lb.oz.dr)

	Boat	Shore
Jersey	----	01.06.00
Guernsey	----	01.02.05

There are no regional records for the Shore Rockling before 1926, when a specimen was found by French biologists at Les Minquiers. Currently this fish is not uncommon on the lower seashore amongst rocks and boulders, often along more exposed coasts where there is muddy sand. The absence of historical records is curious and may be due to confusion with the Three-bearded Rockling although competent naturalists such as Joseph Sinel should have been able to separate the two species. Another possibility is that this is one of those southern European species that is a relatively recent arrival to the Channel Islands and which has become more common with time.

Ollie Handley with the Guernsey record Shore Rockling (1 lb 02 oz 05 dr).

Three-bearded Rockling

IUCN: LC

CI Status: Frequent

Gaidropsarus vulgaris

Grande Louoche; R'naud

Max Length: 60 cm

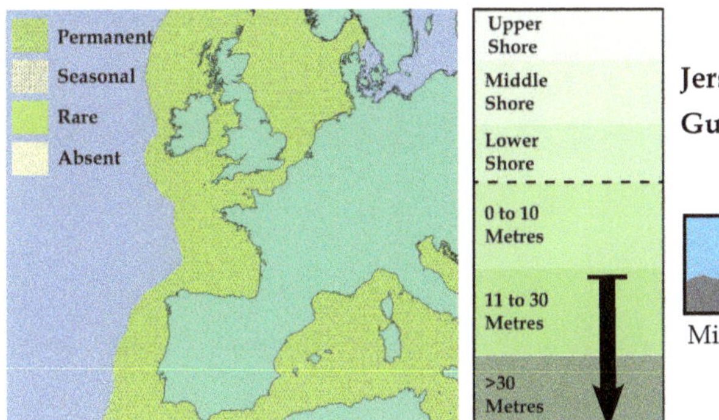

Record Weights (lb.oz.dr)

	Boat	Shore
Jersey	01.09.07	02.11.10
Guernsey	01.11.08	03.07.09

Mixed Ground

Rough Ground

The Three-bearded and Shore rocklings are similar to one another but the former is larger and generally a shallow marine species that is rarely seen onshore. The earliest Channel Island records are from the 1860s and reports since have been regular but sporadic. Being subtidal and a non-commercial species, most recent records are from scientific trawl surveys west of Guernsey and recreational angling. The species was historically considered to be 'very good for the table' and remains the commonest rockling species caught from the shoreline. It is possible that the Shore Rockling (which could be a relatively recent arrival) is competing with the Three-bearded Rockling for space in shallow marine habitats around the Channel Islands.

A Three-bearded Rockling from a lobster pot off Jersey, 2018.

Four-bearded Rockling

Enchelyopus cimbrius

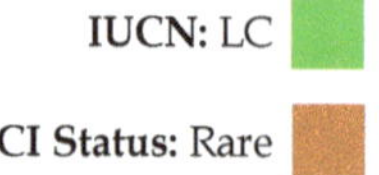

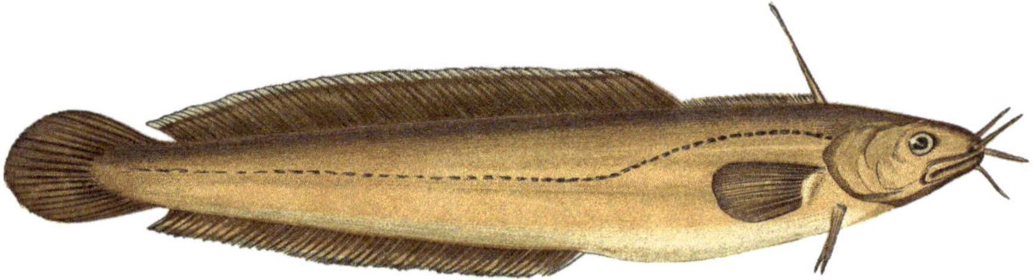

Max Length: 40 cm

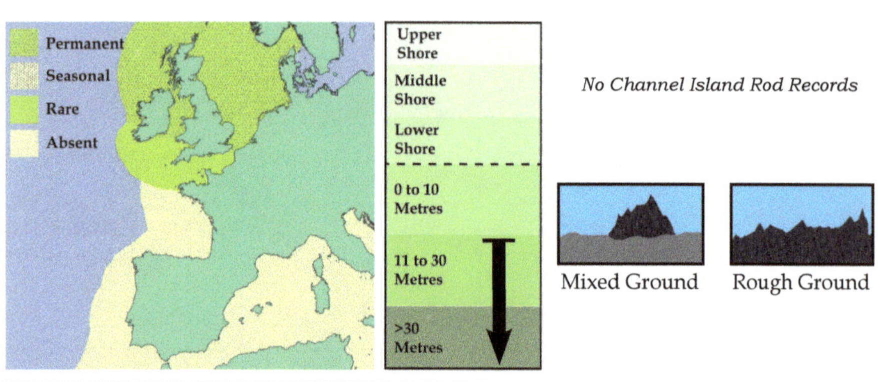

There are just three records for the Four-bearded Rockling within the Normano-Breton Gulf. The oldest comes from an 1862 list of Channel Island fish species while the other two are from scientific trawl surveys in 2006, west of Les Minquiers, and 2009, west of Les Casquets reef. The Four-bearded Rockling is predominantly a colder water species and the Channel Islands are near its southerly limit. Until the capture of the 2006 specimen it was thought that the Victorian report could have been a recording error. However, it seems as though this species may simply be a rare visitor to the islands although, with warming seas, it is unlikely to become more common in the future.

Ling

IUCN: DD

CI Status: Occasional

Molva molva

Lîn

Max Length: 200 cm

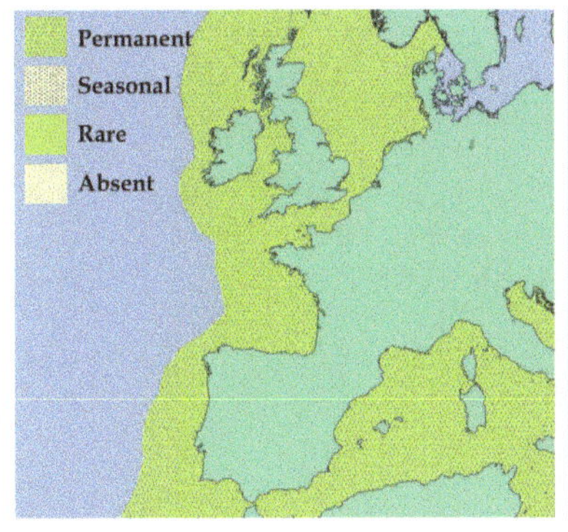

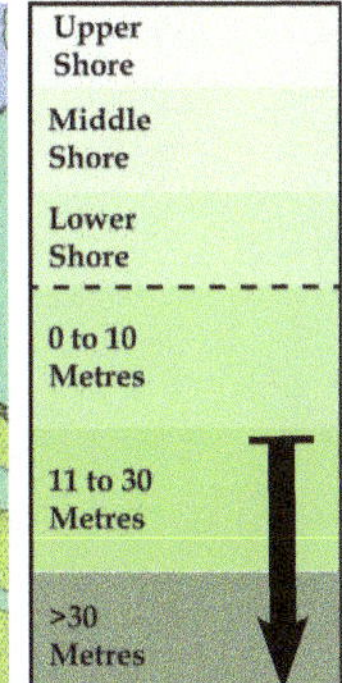

Record Weights (lb.oz.dr)

	Boat	Shore
Jersey	32.12.00	19.04.00
Guernsey	36.14.00	14.02.08

Mixed Ground

Rough Ground

The Ling is a deep-water fish that is known for its love of shipwrecks. It is a large and powerful fish that is popular with recreational boat anglers but which is sighted by divers too. Larger Ling tend to be found in waters that are deeper than those around the Channel Islands but juveniles will live in shallower areas offshore especially on rough or boulder strewn seabeds where there are plenty of holes to use as cover. The need for hiding places of the sort that are often found on deeper water shipwrecks and boulder fields which is why most recreational catches are from boats.

The Ling has at times been an important commercial fish to Channel Island boats. It was regularly fished in the nineteeth century and was popular at local fish markets where it was consideresd to be a summer fish by the traders. Ling was still being targetted in the late 1990s when up to 35 tonnes a year was being landed across the islands although this has since declined to just one or two tonnes annually. Historical records suggest that its population has probably remained steady over the past century.

Capture Technique: The Ling is a deep water fish that is almost strictly a boat anglers' species. Generally large fish baits will tend to be most productive but the Ling is also regularly caught on large pirks, with baited pirks being a favourite. Wrecks are the main target areas for boat anglers and 20+ lb boat outfits paired with heavy monofilament hook lengths should be used. This is due to the Ling having small and sharp teeth. Drift fishing tends to be most productive for this species. Braided mainline of 30 lb or above is best to ensure the angler feels what is going on with the bait and when bites are occuring. The Ling is another fish that shows high post-release mortality due to a blown swim bladder. As with Pollock, more information is needed on whether venting these fish helps their survival rate, if released. Once sufficient Ling are caught for your needs, fishing for them should cease.

Bait Preference: Mackerel and Pouting are two great options for catching ling due to their abundances, often in the same areas as where Ling are targeted.

Greater Fork-beard

Phycis blennoides

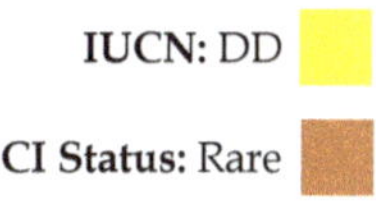

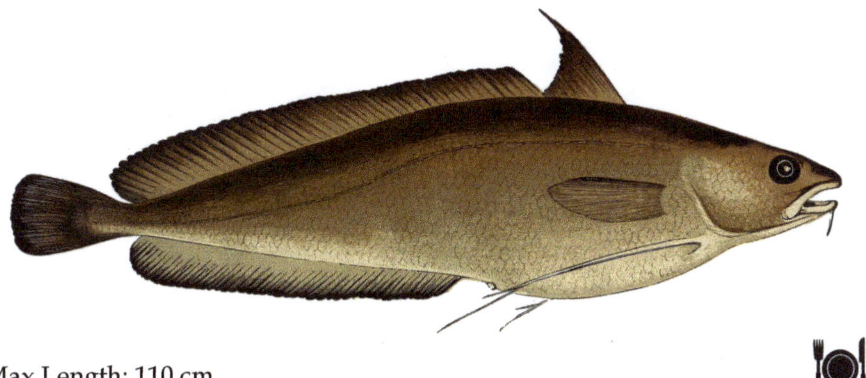

Max Length: 110 cm

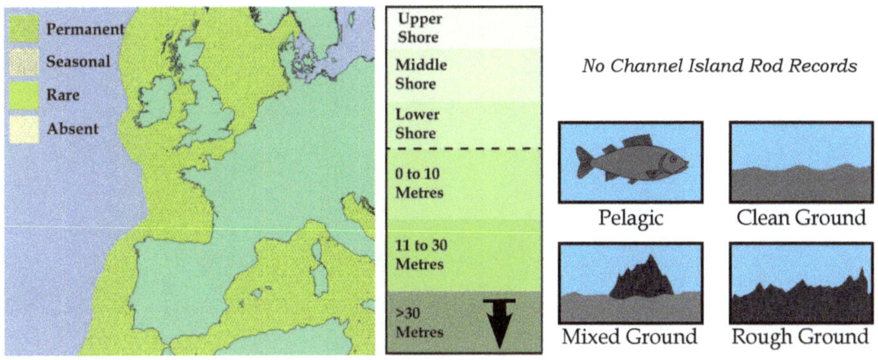

There are just two regional records for the Greater Fork-beard both from the 1860s. One is from a fish species list printed in 1862 which has known inaccuracies with its wildlife records. However, the other record has more credibility and comes from a compendium of British fish written by Francis Day in late Victorian times. This record refers to a specimen caught north-west of Guernsey in August 1866 which, at 47 cm, would have just been an adult.

As a deeper water species that generally lives below 100 metres, the Greater Fork-beard is unlikely to be a common visitor to the Channel Islands. However, younger specimens are said to have been captured in shallower waters and this is what the historical records may represent. With no recent records, this is considered to be a historic species that may no longer be present locally.

Fork-beard
Phycis phycis

Max Length: 65 cm

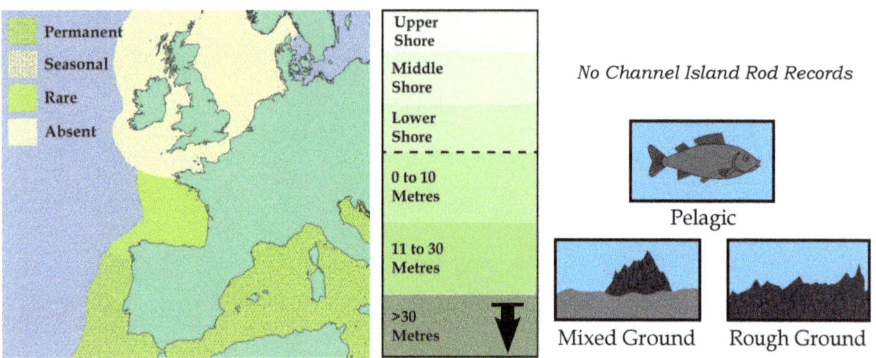

The Fork-beard has just two Channel Islands records. The first was in a fish list published in 1862 and the second was caught off Guernsey in December 1877. This is a southern European species whose range reaches north into the Bay of Biscay but which is generally listed as being absent from the English Channel. Several other Biscay fish species have been caught in the Channel Islands so it is possible that the Fork-beard could have been caught in local waters. However, a lack of modern records suggests that it is a very rare vagrant in the English Channel.

Tadpole Fish

Raniceps raninus

IUCN: LC

CI Status: Rare

Max Length: 30 cm

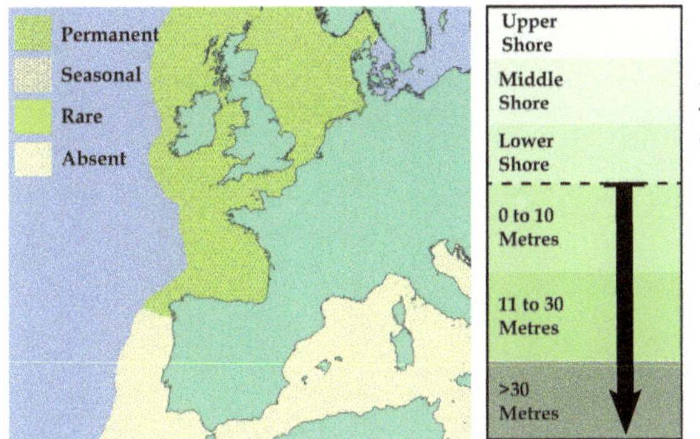

Record Weights (lb.oz.dr)

	Mini
Jersey	00.15.00
Guernsey	00.15.08

Rough Ground

The Tadpole Fish is rarely reported within the Channel Islands but its solitary, nocturnal nature and lack of commercial value may mean that is more common than the available evidence suggests. The oldest report was during the 1840s from Guernsey, after which there was just one report until the capture of two specimens at St Catherine's Breakwater, Jersey, from the same month in 1956.

Since the 1970s the Tadpole Fish has been intermittently reported including from one of the marinas in St Peter Port, Guernsey. There are some regional reports between 2006 and 2009 in trawl surveys and it is probably occasionally caught by recreational anglers. As a generally northern European species whose range just reaches into the Bay of Biscay, its range may contract northwards as sea temperatures rise. Any captures or sightings should be made to a local records centre.

A Tadpole Fish caught by Mark Le Huquet.

Cod

Gadus morhua

Mouothue; Laûdgi [male]; *Mouorue; Mouosue*

IUCN: VU

CI Status: Occasional

Max Length: 200 cm

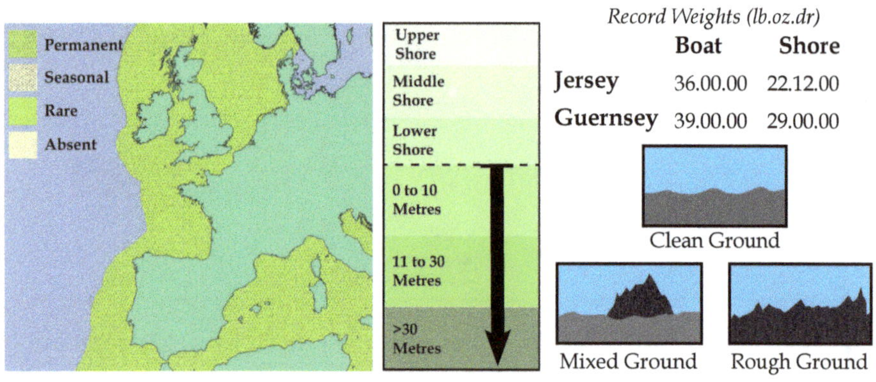

Record Weights (lb.oz.dr)

	Boat	Shore
Jersey	36.00.00	22.12.00
Guernsey	39.00.00	29.00.00

The Cod's relationship with the Channel Islands comes mostly via the local boats that travelled to the Gaspé coast, Canada, in the mid-nineteenth century to fish on the Grand Banks. However, the Cod is usually landed in the Channel Islands as bycatch. In 1877 the Cod was said to be 'making a regular appearance' by local fish merchants and in 1880 the capture of a 6.8 kg specimen at La Rocque, Jersey, was newsworthy. Cod were recorded as being 'constant but of small size' in 1904 but the Cod has been severely overfished right across Eurpope and, as elsewhere, it is probably less common in the Channel Islands now than before World War II.

Martin Turner with the current boat caught Jersey Record (36 lb 4 oz).

Haddock

Melanogrammus aeglefinus

Héthique

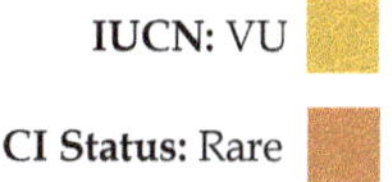

Max Length: 75 cm

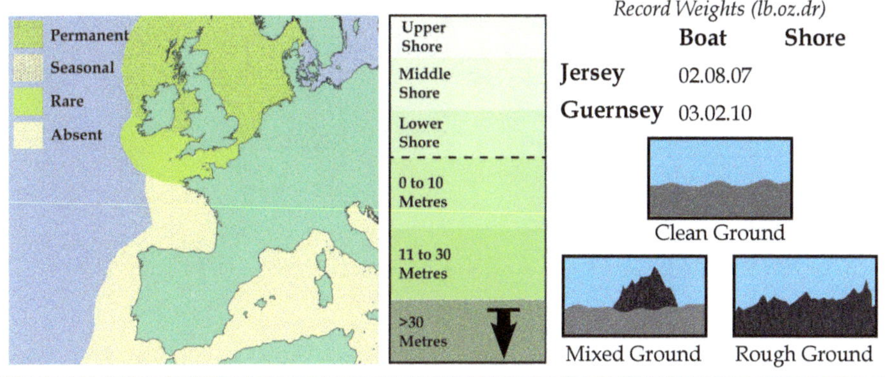

The Haddock is a cold and deep water species that is rarely seen in the English Channel. There are a handful of Channel Island records from the mid-nineteenth century to the modern day including small annual commercial landings (generally under 100 kg) in the late 1990s. It is an important commercial species that has been heavily fished in the north Atlantic leading to stock decreases. The IUCN lists the Haddock as being 'vulnerable' but the Channel Islands are at the southern edge of its range and, even allowing for overexploitation, it occurs only occasionally with there being just one specimen taken during the many scientific trawls around the islands between 2006 and 2018. Warming seas could make it even rarer in the future.

Whiting

Merlangius merlangus

Bideau; Gris Lieu; Lieu; Lieutîn [small]; *Liotîn* [small]

Max Length: 70 cm

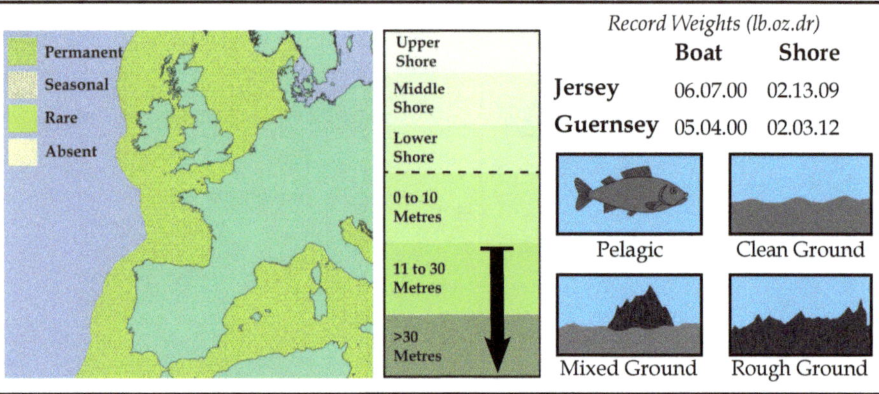

Record Weights (lb.oz.dr)

	Boat	Shore
Jersey	06.07.00	02.13.09
Guernsey	05.04.00	02.03.12

The Whiting is a relatively common fish around the Channel Islands and is commercially fished at low levels by local trawlers with catches usually averaging one or two tonnes a year. There has been a more intensive fishery in France where landing figures suggest that the Whiting is common in the Normano-Breton Gulf. It is not often targeted by recreational fishers but is caught by rod anglers and in offshore set nets. Although there is a historical track record of the Whiting in Channel Island waters back to the 1840s, there are relatively few records. This suggests that it is one of those background species that, while apparently common, is rarely recorded. There is little evidence concerning the status of the local population and, although local commercial landings have declined slightly in recent years, this may be due to a reduction in effort rather than stocks. Whiting can be confused with small Pollock.

Blue Whiting

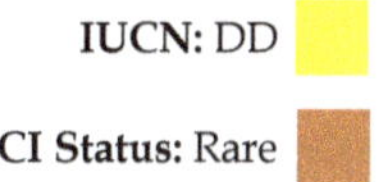

Micromesistius poutassou

Poutassou

Max Length: 50 cm

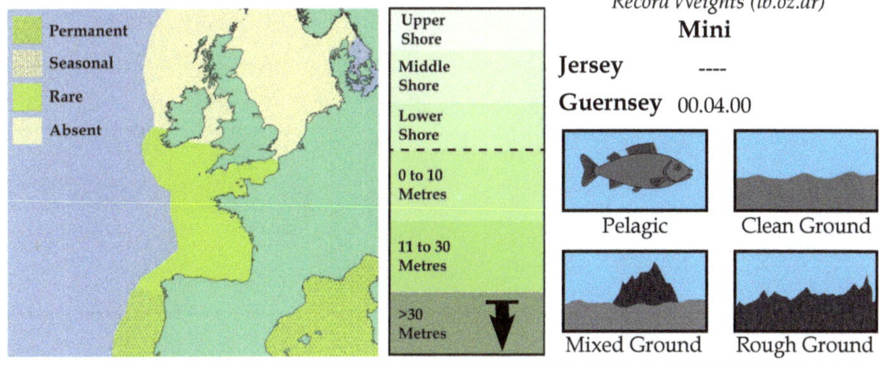

The Blue Whiting is a deep-water fish species that forms shoals below about 300 metres although juvenile fish will migrate closer inshore. It is a southern European species that is rare in the English Channel especially in the shallow waters around the Channel Islands. The only local records are from commercial landings by trawlers in the late 1990s, from a recreational record off the Great Bank in Guernsey in 1980 and a single specimen taken in a scientific trawl survey north of Alderney in 2011. The status of the species locally is unknown but the Blue Whiting is unlikely to be common across the islands and its population is in decline in other parts of Europe. Further information about this species is desirable and captures should be reported to a local records centre.

Pollack

IUCN: LC

CI Status: Common

Pollachius pollachius

Lythe; *Lieu; Vidan; Jaune Lieu*

Max Length: 130 cm

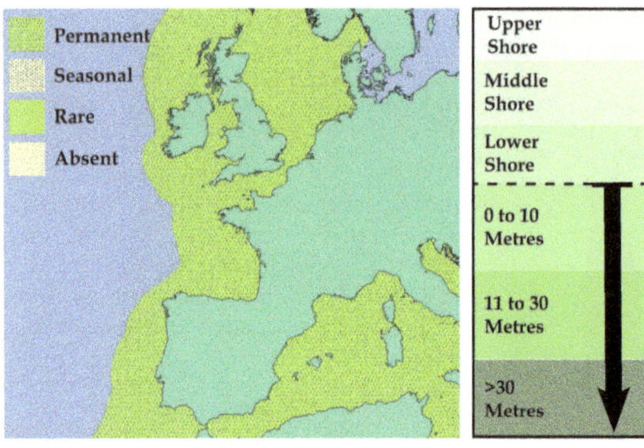

Record Weights (lb.oz.dr)

	Boat	Shore
Jersey	21.14.12	15.03.03
Guernsey	25.12.00	16.01.06

Mixed Ground

Rough Ground

The Pollack is a common, perhaps abundant, species that is well known to recreational anglers and divers. It tends to be found close to seabed features that offer cover such as kelp forests, seagrass beds, shipwrecks and undersea topographic features such as mounts and pinnacles. Juveniles will range closer inshore than adults so the largest individuals will generally be seen and caught offshore. There is an abundance of local records for Pollack across all the islands and anecdotal reports suggest that the population has remained stable since Victorian times. The fish has previously been regarded as so common among recreational anglers that it is said: 'if you take away the Pollack then there wouldn't be much else left to catch'.

A solitary nature and preference for rough seabeds will keep the Pollack out of the way of most commercial fishing vessels but it is nonetheless a commercial fish with several tens of tonnes being landed in the Channel Islands annually. Much of this will be either as bycatch from trawling, netting and line fishing as it is rarely directly targeted by the commercial fishing fleet.

Oliver Heart with the Jersey boat caught Pollack record (21 lb 14 oz 12 dr) in 1999.

Capture Technique: Pollack fishing is popular especially amongst boat anglers. The largest specimens are caught offshore on deep reefs and wrecks. Live sandeel and deep spinning will produce Pollack of all sizes but they can also be taken on bottom fishing gear. Weighted traces can be used on deeper marks to get the live bait or artificial lure to the demersal zone where most pollock are caught. Lighter tackle can still be used with the use of braided line and heavy jigs. Jigs ranging in size from 60 to 300 grams can be extremely effective and offer great sport.

Sustainable fishing practices should be thought of when targeting Pollack, especially from deep water. Many Pollack caught in deep water will show signs of a ruptured swim bladder. Signs include the stomach coming out of the mouth and intestines coming out of the anus. This is due to gas over-expanding inside the fish's swim bladder due to vast pressure differences in the water column. If released in this condition, it is likely the fish's buoyancy will keep the fish near the surface. A slow retrieve can reduce mortality rates when releasing pollock but the best practice is to stop fishing when the angler has caught what is needed to eat. Venting the fish's swim bladder can make a dramatic difference in the way a fish is released and the health of that fish. However, scientific research is needed in order to understand the post release mortality of these vented fish. Venting should be performed with a sharp needle like object one to two inches behind the pectoral fin to release the built up gases.

Bait Preference: If fishing for Pollack with the use of natural bait, the most successful baits tend to be sandeel, especially Launce. This is normally fished live for the largest specimens.

Coalfish

Pollachius virens

Coley; Saithe; *Colîn; Nièr Lieu*

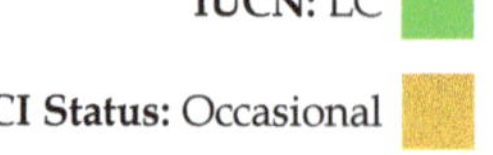

Max Length: 130 cm

Permanent
Seasonal
Rare
Absent

Upper Shore
Middle Shore
Lower Shore
0 to 10 Metres
11 to 30 Metres
>30 Metres

Record Weights (lb.oz.dr)

	Boat	Shore
Jersey	25.00.00	09.09.00
Guernsey	26.03.12	11.08.10

Pelagic
Clean Ground
Mixed Ground
Rough Ground

Coalfish look similar to Pollock but is a colder water species which has the Channel Islands near the southerly edge of its geographic range. This, and the adults' preference for deeper water, means there have been few regional reports although the recreational and commercial records (the latter being as bycatch) that do exist suggest it is irregular in its occurrence within the islands.

Within the Channel Islands Coalfish do not form the sort of dense shoals that make the species attractive to trawlers elsewhere within its range. A 1904 description noted that the Coalfish is 'sometimes, but by no means frequently, brought to market' in Jersey. As a colder water species, the geographic range of the Coalfish may move northwards with rising sea temperatures increasing its rarity locally.

Pouting

Trisopterus luscus

Bib; Flobber; *Bouothé; Fliabeu*

IUCN: DD

CI Status: Common

Max Length: 40 cm

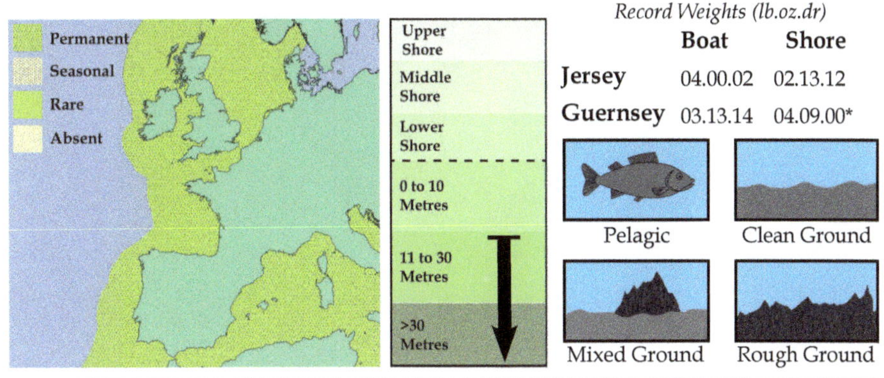

Record Weights (lb.oz.dr)

	Boat	Shore
Jersey	04.00.02	02.13.12
Guernsey	03.13.14	04.09.00*

Known locally as Flobber, the Pouting is a distinctive and common species that congregates around wrecks and other seabed features that provide suitable cover. The Pouting is frequently caught by recreational anglers but is sometimes regarded as a nuisance species that steals bait. It is not directly targeted by commercial fishers with annual weights being under four tonnes although there was a brief period after 2000 when up to 14 tonnes a year were landed.

Local records stretch back to the 1840s and suggest that the Pouting was, and remains, common around all the islands and that the population is stable. In recent years it has been particularly reported by divers around shipwrecks and reefs where shoals of Pouting will tuck themselves into shaded or overhanging areas. Adult fish will generally live in deeper water during the winter and come into the shallows during spring to breed. They are a short-lived fish that can reach sexual maturity at the end of their first year.

Poor Cod

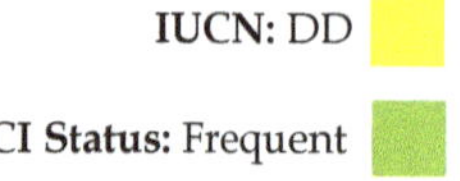

Trisopterus minutus

Bouosé; Tabûle

Max Length: 20 cm

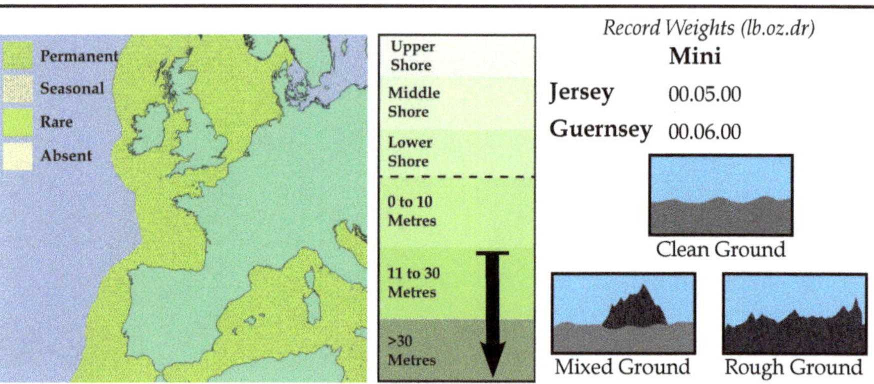

The naturalist Joseph Sinel described the Poor Cod as being abundant across the Channel Islands. The records made by divers' and trawlers over the past decade suggest that this is still the case. The Poor Cod looks similar to the Pouting and shares many of the same habitats such as shipwrecks, rocky seabeds and overhangs. The Poor Cod is not targeted by recreational or commercial fishers locally but is often taken as bycatch. Like the Pouting, it is fast-growing and usually breeds in its second year. There is a curious paucity of historical local records with just four known reports before 2008 but this is not uncommon with fish species that are not valued by recreational or commercial fisheries.

Hake

Merluccius merluccius

Mèrluche

Max Length: 140 cm

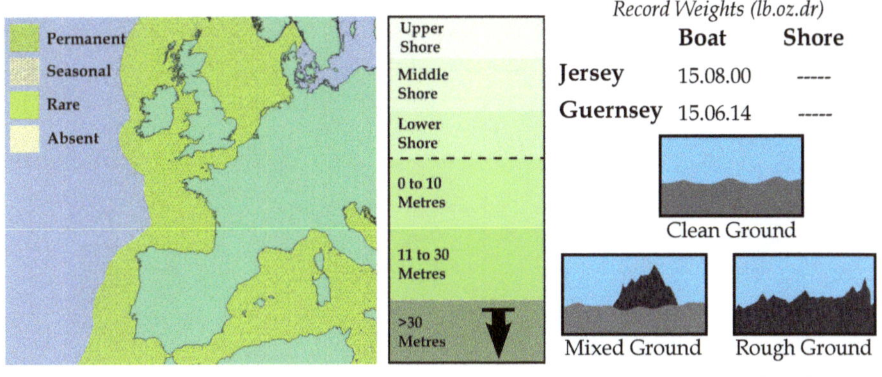

Record Weights (lb.oz.dr)

	Boat	Shore
Jersey	15.08.00	-----
Guernsey	15.06.14	-----

There are only a few Hake records for the Channel Islands including small quantities that have been landed by commercial fishing boats, although these could have been caught outside the region. The Hake was listed as rare in the Channel Islands during the 1840s and as occasional off Normandy in the 1890s. There are no twentieth century records until 1984 when a recreational fisherman caught a specimen off Jersey and again in 1987 when another was caught west of Guernsey. The Hake generally lives in deep water and is probably an occasional visitor to the relatively shallow waters around the Channel Islands. Elsewhere in the world it is an important commercial species that is heavily fished.

Atlantic Flying-fish

Cheilopogon heterurus

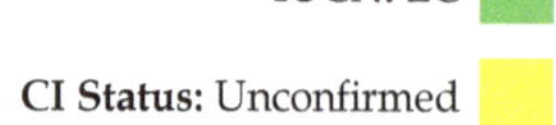

Max Length: 40 cm

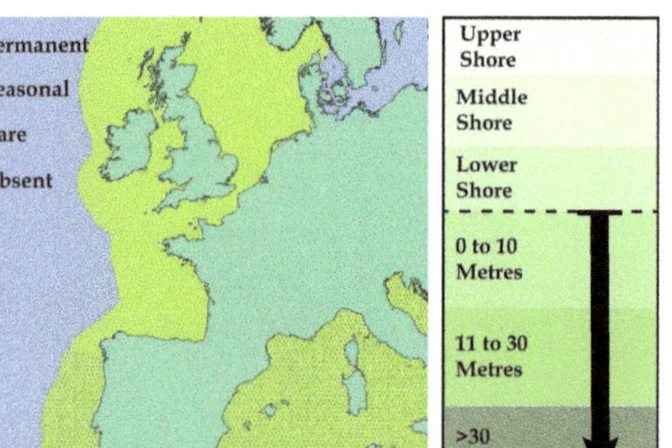

No Channel Island Rod Records

Pelagic

The Atlantic Flying-fish has no records from the Channel Islands but a specimen was caught in neighbouring waters in 1956 near St Servan, Brittany. This unusual animal is more commonly found in southern Europe but there are historic and modern records from the English Channel and even the North Sea. As the name suggests, this fish can take to the air by leaping clear of the water and gliding for short distances using adapted pectoral fins. This is usually done in response to danger and in other parts of the world they can sometimes be seen skipping across the water ahead of boats. With the Atlantic Flying-fish yet to be confirmed from the Channel Islands, any sightings or specimens should be reported to a local biological records centre.

Atlantic Saury

Scomberesox saurus

Max Length: 50 cm

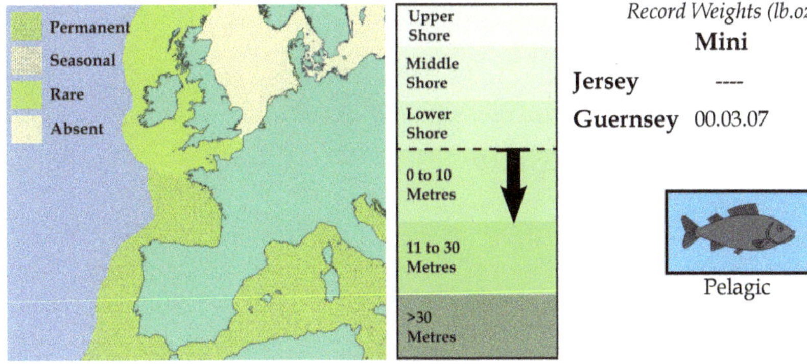

Record Weights (lb.oz.dr)

	Mini
Jersey	----
Guernsey	00.03.07

This is a fish with a mainly southern European distribution that is becoming common in the English Channel. The oldest British record was from Guernsey in November in 1860 but the next local record was not until 2007 when a specimen was caught north of Alderney. Since then the Atlantic Saury has been caught most years by recreational anglers, suggesting that it may be one of those warmer water species that is visiting the Channel Islands area more frequently. It is a surface dweller that migrates northwards in the summer months and is frequently taken by boat anglers targeting mackerel.

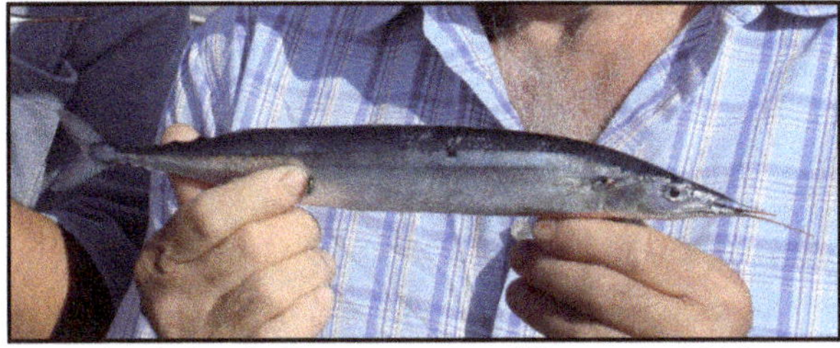

An Atlantic Saury caught off Jersey in 2010.

Snipe

Belone belone

Garfish; *Orfi*

IUCN: LC

CI Status: Frequent

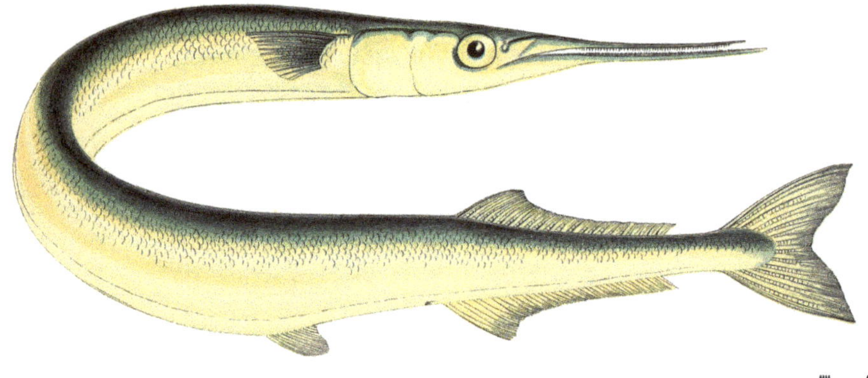

Max Length: 80 cm

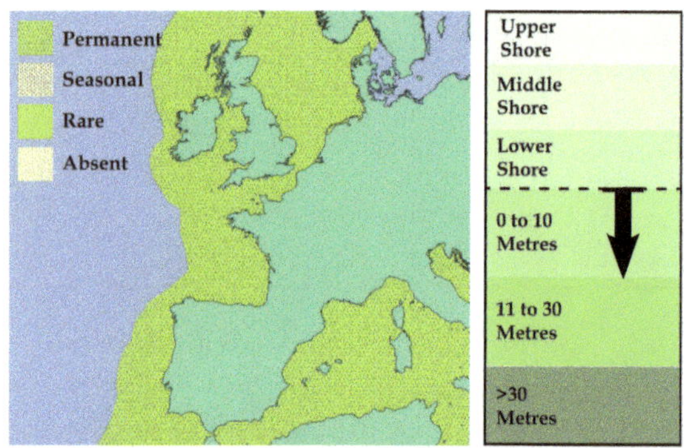

Record Weights (lb.oz.dr)

	Boat	Shore
Jersey	02.07.00	02.01.00
Guernsey	02.12.05	02.11.11

Pelagic

Once very popular in Channel Island fish markets, the Snipe (or Garfish) is now rarely eaten but is frequently caught by recreational anglers often as bycatch when targeting mackerel. Distinctively eel-like with a pointed rostrum, the Snipe is fast-swimming and often found within shoals of mackerel although they will also hunt as individuals. In the English Channel the Snipe used to migrate into coastal waters during the spring and summer but in recent years Channel Island anglers have been reporting catches from across the winter months too.

Although not often eaten domestically in the British Isles (its green bones are said to be off-putting), there is a small commercial market for Snipe in Europe with Channel Island boats usually landing between one and two tonnes annually. Aside from having green bones, the Snipe is also well-known for being able to leap clear of the water when disturbed or being chased by predators. It swims within a few metres of the sea surface and will sometimes shadow snorkelers and divers at a distance. Historical records start in the 1840s when it was regarded as plentiful and there have been plenty of sightings since, suggesting that the Snipe remains common across all the Islands.

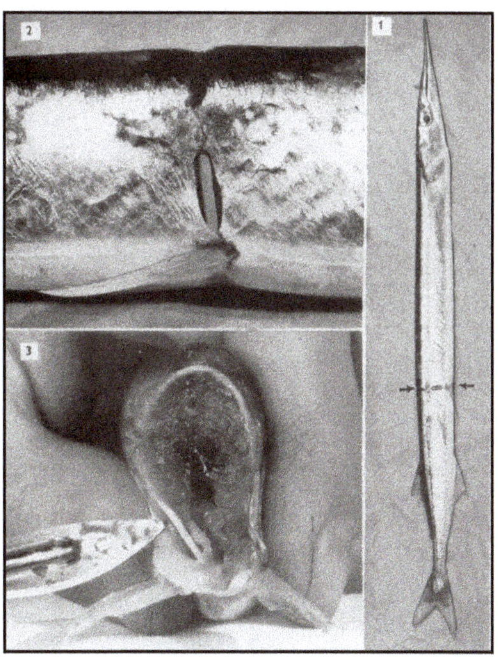

In May 1960 a Snipe was caught off the coast of Jersey that had a rubber band embedded in its body (see opposite). The rubber band had been there since it was a young fish as the animal's body had grown around it. Banding was not something practiced by either anglers or scientists but in the 1960s does suggest that the fish had been caught and released earlier in its life.

Svetovidov's Garfish (*B. svetovidovi*) may also be present in the region. It was only discovered by science in the 1970s and can only be identified by subtle differences in the gill cover and pre-orbital bone.

Capture Technique: The main capture method when targeting the pelagic Snipe is float fishing. Float fishing tends to be best around features such as submerged reefs and breakwaters that break up the main tidal flow. Floats of different sizes can be used depending on the level of current with depths usually set between 3 to 15 ft. Light tackle should be used with this species as most captures will be around one pound or below in weight. Hooks should be small (size 8 to 2) and very sharp due to the Snipe's hard beak often resulting in the hook not setting. Smaller hooks tend to hook more fish allowing the bait to travel further down the beak into the fish's mouth. A float stop is best practice as this can easily be moved up and down the mainline as the angler is able to find where the Snipe are feeding. Lure fishing is another successful method with the use of small metals. This species is known to regularly take feathers.

Bait Preference: Two of the most successful baits when fishing for Snipe are small strips of mackerel and small sandeels. A chum (shirvy) can be used to entice shoals of Snipe into an area and they can often be seen feeding off the water surface.

Sand Smelt

Atherina presbyter

Grasdos

Max Length: 20 cm

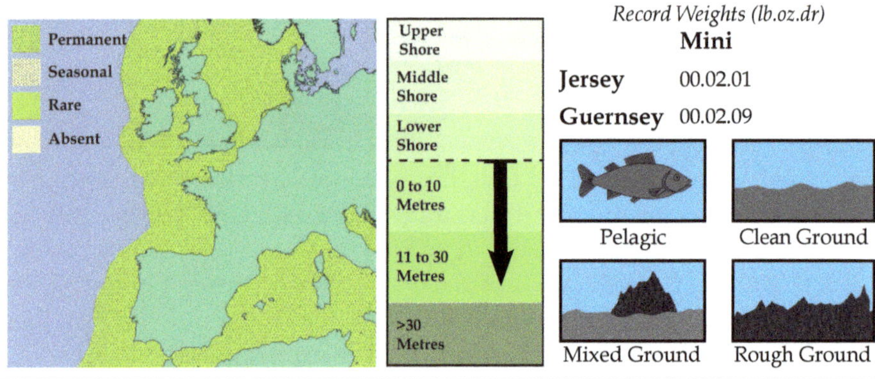

Common inshore, especially in sheltered sandy bays, the shoaling Sand Smelt (or *Grasdos* in Jèrriais) was once so heavily targeted by local seine netters (for whitebait) that by the turn of the twentieth century its population was thought to have decreased by nearly half. However, its popularity declined after World War II and it is now rarely targeted by either commercial or recreational fishers. Dense shoals are common and may sometimes be seen along the water's edge where they will swim slowly past bathers and snorkelers as a seemingly endless stream of small fish. Historical records begin in early Victorian times and are infrequent but, as with many of the smaller inshore fish species, this probably represents under reporting rather than scarcity.

Sand Smelt in a rock pool, Bonne Nuit, Jersey.

Big-eyed Sand Smelt

IUCN: LC

CI Status: Rare

Atherina boyeri

Big-scale Sand Smelt; Black Sea Silverside; Boyer's Sand Smelt

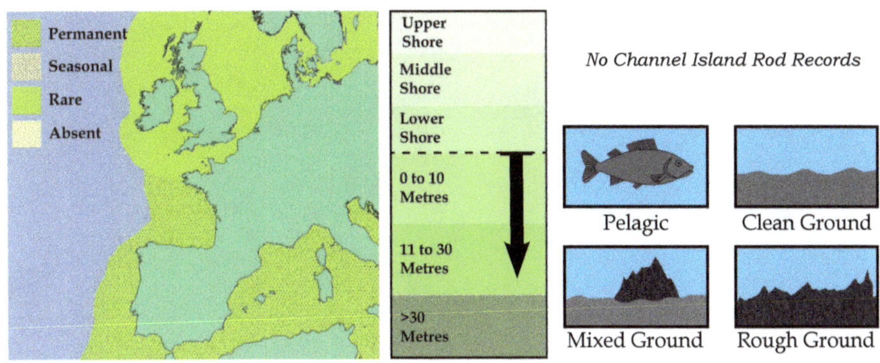

The Big-eyed Sand-smelt is a Mediterranean species whose presence in the English Channel was considered doubtful until recently when specimens were confirmed from the English Channel, North Sea and Wales. There is possibly a gap in its reported geographic range covering the Atlantic coast between Iberia and southern Brittany which is difficult to explain.

There are only two records of the Big-eyed Sand Smelt from across the Normano-Breton Gulf. These are from Herm and Guernsey where they were found by members of a Porcupine Society during a survey in September 1994. Increasing regional sea temperatures may favour warmer water species such as the Big-eyed Sand Smelt but its small size and similarity to the native Sand Smelt (see opposite) means that it may go unnoticed in local waters. Any Channel Island specimens are of scientific interest and should be reported to one of the local record centres.

John Dory

Zeus faber

Dorée; Douothée; Jean-Doré

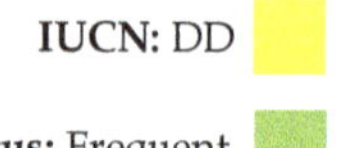

Max Length: 90 cm

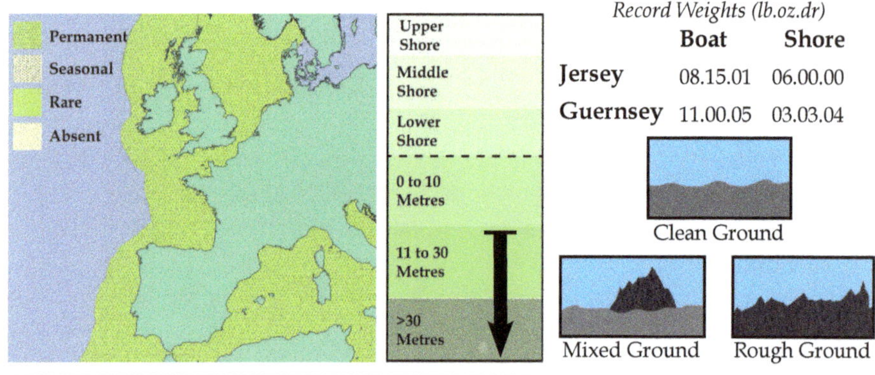

Record Weights (lb.oz.dr)

	Boat	Shore
Jersey	08.15.01	06.00.00
Guernsey	11.00.05	03.03.04

A favourite of underwater photographers, the John Dory is a large and unmistakable fish that can be found around rocky reefs and overhangs in relatively shallow waters. The fish has a characteristic black spot in the middle of its body which is said to be the thumbprint of St Peter. It is this that provides the French name of *St Pierre*. The John Dory is irregularly caught by anglers and sometimes landed commercially in the islands. It is much more heavily fished in France where annual catches may be 100s of tonnes.

Within the Channel Islands the John Dory was described as being 'frequent' in the nineteenth and early twentieth centuries. However, there were few individual reports until around 2010 when local Seasearch divers began to sight them regularly around all the islands. The John Dory is normally encountered singly or in pairs with the largest specimens being female. The species is thought to have defined spawning grounds which, as far as is known, probably does not include the Channel Islands. Although not abundant, the John Dory may be found offshore around all the islands and will sometimes stray into relatively shallow water. It is considered a delicacy in many parts of Europe and is still eaten locally. Dead specimens will occasionally be found washed up along the strandline.

Paul Wheaton with the Jersey boat caught record for a John Dory.

Silver Dory

Zenopsis conchifer

Max Length: 80 cm

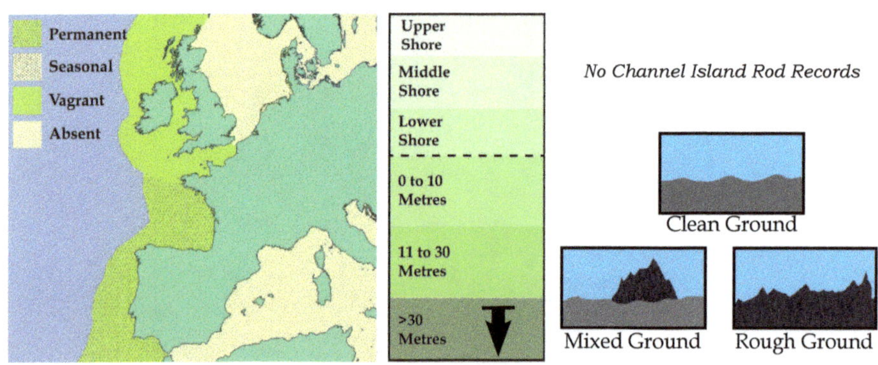

The Silver Dory is a southern European species which has been steadily expanding its range northwards along the Atlantic coast. It was first recorded from the Bay of Biscay during the 1980s and the English Channel during the 1990s. There is just one regional record from May 2012 when an angler off Sark retrieved a snagged net which had a single specimen in it. Strangely, the same net also contained a lobster, a John Dory and a hand grenade.

There have been reports of the Silver Dory having been caught as far north as Ireland and it is probable that other Channel Island specimens have been caught but not recorded. Any captures are of scientific interest and should be reported to one of the local records centres.

Boar Fish

Capros aper

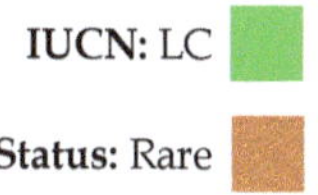

Max Length: 30 cm

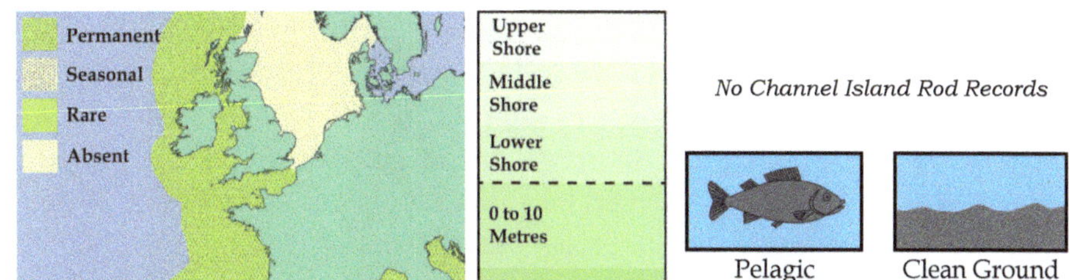

The shape and bright colour of the Boar Fish makes it easy to identify. It was said to be an 'occasional visitor' around Jersey in the nineteenth century with Joseph Sinel reporting that people would often catch a dozen at a time off Herm. He also noted the fish's peculiar habit of deliberately beaching itself including an occasion when hundreds were stranded on the seashore following a storm. However, there were no reports at all made between the turn of the twentieth century and 2002 after which time three reports were made in Guernsey and Jersey. The Boar Fish is normally a deep water dweller but it can occur at all depths, including in rock pools. It is probably a rare visitor to the Channel Islands.

Sticklebacks, Seashores and Pipefish

Sticklebacks, pipefish and seahorses are distinctive and iconic fish that belong to the families Gasterosteidae (sticklebacks) and Syngnathidae (seahorses and pipefish). They are masters of camouflage and use their body shape and colours to hide or blend into dense patches of seaweed and seagrass. However, once seen they are relatively easy to identify to species level with key features being size, body outline, colour and, in pipefish, the snout. Although they are relatively easy to catch in nets and buckets (and often come up with lobster pots) they do not like being handled and should be photographed for identification purposes and then immediately released.

Most sticklebacks live in fresh or brackish water and only the fully marine Sea Stickleback is common locally. There are several species of pipefish recorded from the Channel Islands, four of which are relatively common in lower shore rock pools or shallow marine areas. There are two species of seahorse (Short and Long-snouted) both of which were assumed to be rare although recent records suggest that they may be more common and may live deeper offshore than previously expected. Most naturalists and divers will associate pipefish and seahorses with seagrass (*Zostera marina*) habitats such as are found on most of the main Channel Islands. However, while the large species of pipefish are certainly associated with seagrass, reports of seahorses in seagrass are rare locally and systematic searches are largely unsuccessful. Records from trawl surveys and commercial lobster pots suggests that seahorses may be more common in water deeper than about 10 metres and that they are attracted to lobster pots, perhaps because they can cling on to the netting with their tails.

The rigid nature of the bodies of pipefish and seahorses means that they can be preserved through desication. Their mumified bodies will occasionally be found among seaweed on the strandline and are usually well-preserved enough to allow for an identification. In some countries there is a tourist trade in seahorses that have been killed and dried. Although decorative, all seahorse species are covered by the CITES agreement which means that their trade is subject to restrictions and monitoring. Please do not be tempted to buy mummified seahorses (or other marine life killed for the tourist trade) as it may be breaking customs' regulations.

Sticklebacks, seahorses and pipefish are regarded as indicators of climate change and are of scientific interest. Any specimens should be photographed (ideally without handling them) and the records submitted to a biological records centre (see page 277).

Three-spined Stickleback

Gasterosteus aculeatus

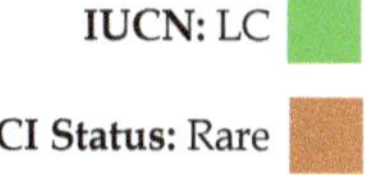

Max Length: 11 cm

Permanent
Seasonal
Rare
Absent

Upper Shore
Middle Shore
Lower Shore
0 to 10 Metres
11 to 30 Metres
>30 Metres

No Channel Island Rod Records

Pelagic
Clean Ground
Mixed Ground
Rough Ground

In the 1860s the Three-spined Stickleback was reported to be abundant in Guernsey in a large brackish pond that once existed on the north of the island. It was similarly said to be common in the estuarine channels around Mont St Michel, Brittany. This preference for lower salinity waters is typical of the Three-spined Stickleback although it can be found in fully marine coastal waters too. The lack of large brackish water bodies and estuaries within the Channel Islands means this is a rare fish locally but it is common regionally where rivers exit along the French coast. The last confirmed Channel Island report was in 2009 from Jersey.

Sea Stickleback

IUCN: LC

CI Status: Occasional

Spinachia spinachia

Fifteen-spined Stickleback; Sea Adder; *Êpinnoche*

Max Length: 15 cm

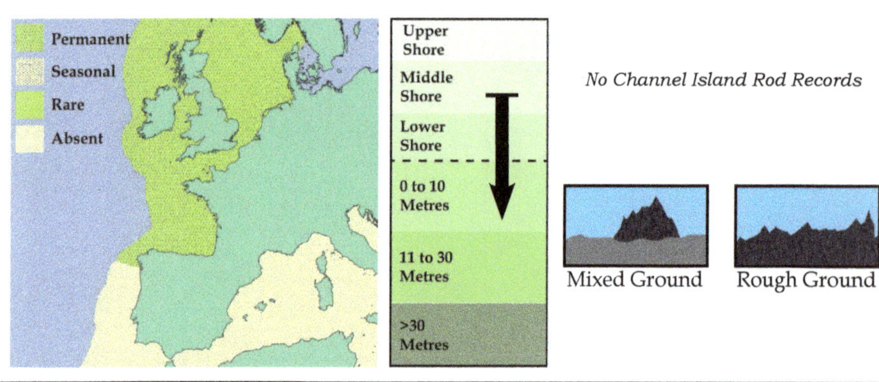

This is a distinctive, arrow-shaped fish that is not uncommon around all the Channel Islands. Although generally a shallow marine species, searching through rock pools will occasionally produce a Sea Stickleback hiding in amongst dense seaweeds or seagrass on the lower shore. They are also seen by sharp-eyed divers and may sometimes be seen swimming beneath pontoons in the islands' harbours and marinas. The Sea Stickleback is an unusual fish which builds nests from cemented seaweed fronds in which the female lays her eggs, leaving the male to guard them. When seen underwater they are often unafraid of cameras and can be highly photogenic.

A Sea Stickleback (and its reflection) in St Helier Harbour, Jersey.

Short-snouted Seahorse

IUCN: DD

Hippocampus hippocampus

CI Status: Occasional

J'va d'mé

Max Length: 16 cm

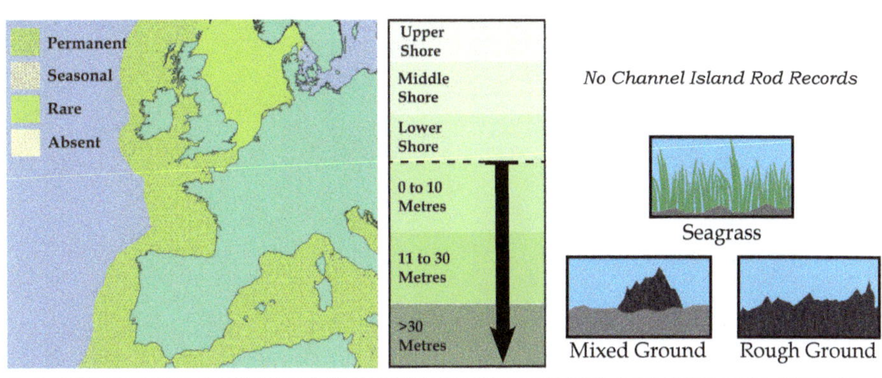

The Seahorse is an iconic fish whose familiar shape adorns products and hotel logos across the globe. Recorded as being of 'frequent but erratic occurence' in 1904, the Short-snouted Seahorse is currently considered to be vulnerable across many parts of its range. This is due to it having been historically fished for tourist souvenirs, for the aquarium trade and because one of its key habitats, seagrass, has been severely depleted due to development, pollution, dredging etc. In 1999 the Seahorse Trust was founded in the UK (with assistance from Channel Island naturalists) to campaign for the conservation of these species and the enhancement of their habitats.

The status of the Short-snouted Seahorse in the Channel Islands is difficult to assess. Survey work by divers in the 1990s and 2010s suggests that it is not common, even within seagrass areas off Guernsey and

Jersey. However, a majority of recent seahorse records have come from commercial fishers where they are brought up clinging to lobster pots.

This has happened regularly enough to suggest that: (a) the Short-snouted Seahorse is not as rare as was first thought; and (b) that its range of habitats is wider than just seagrass. Many of the lobster pots have been retrieved from 20 to 30 metres of water with the north coast of Jersey being where they are most commonly seen. This pattern was also seen in scientific trawl surveys between 2006 and 2018 where specimens were caught in deep water (>35 metres) off Guernsey and Jersey.

In the 1990s a colony of Short-snouted Seahorses was found to be living in Elizabeth Marina, St Helier, by local naturalist Sue Daly. A recent survey of the marina by divers did not find any animals although a juvenile was found under one of the pontoons in 2017 which suggests that they are still in residence. If seen, seahorses should not be handled or disturbed, especially in Jersey waters where they are scheduled to become legally protected. This is a species of national scientific interest and any reports should be made to a local records centre.

Left: *A pregnant male seahorse (*H. hippocampus*) found in a lobster pot off Bouley Bay, Jersey, in 2017.* Right: *A juvenile seahorse (possibly* H. guttulatus*) that was trapped in a plankton net during a 2014 survey off Les Écréhous, Jersey.*

Long-snouted Seahorse

Hippocampus guttulatus

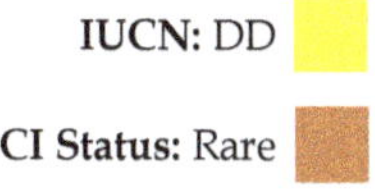

Max Length: 22 cm

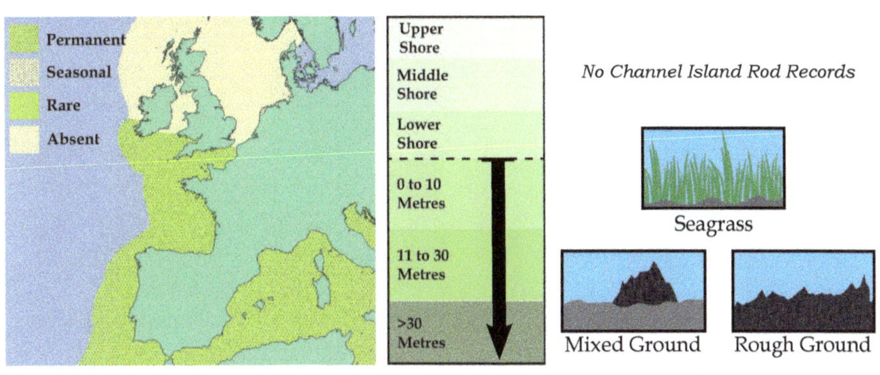

The Long-snouted Seahorse is one of Britain's rarest fish species and the Channel Islands (especially Jersey) have been cited as being a particularly good place to view them.

This fish may be a relatively recent arrival to the islands as the oldest local record is from 1957 when a seagull regurgitated several freshly dead specimens onto a road in Jersey. Subsequent reports are sporadic but this species is observed by divers and fishers from time to time plus four specimens were taken in scientific trawls between 2006 and 2011. As with the Short-snouted Seahorse, the trawled specimens were from deeper water, suggesting that there may be offshore populations that are only irregularly encountered. All seahorse species are notable because it is the father that incubates the eggs in a special pouch and so is the one that gives birth to the young (see image on the page opposite).

Worm Pipefish

Nerophis lumbriciformis

Longnez

Max Length: 15 cm

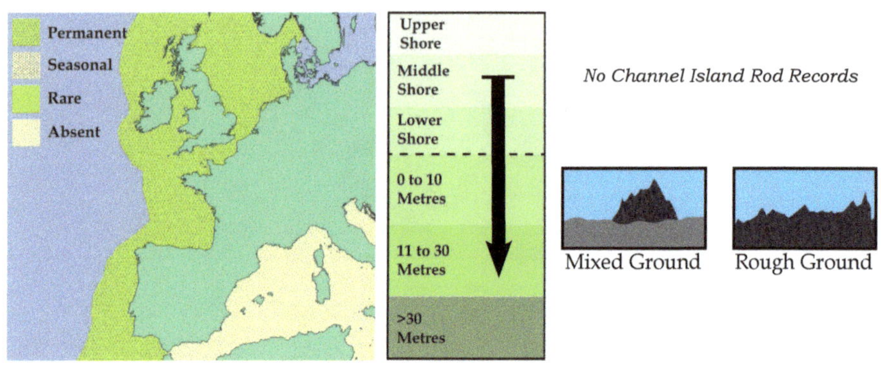

The smallest of the pipefish species, the Worm Pipefish may be commonly found underneath rocks and amongst seaweed from the middle shore downwards. It is dark, thin and rigid and can resemble loose pieces of seaweed making it hard to spot. The Worm Pipefish was first reported from the Channel Islands during the 1860s and has been consistently described as being common or abundant ever since. It remains common on rocky shores and in shallow rock pools from the middle shore downwards. It is particularly fond of shallow gravel-floored rock pools with clear water.

A Worm Pipefish in a rock pool at Gorey, Jersey.

Straight-nose Pipefish

Nerophis ophidion

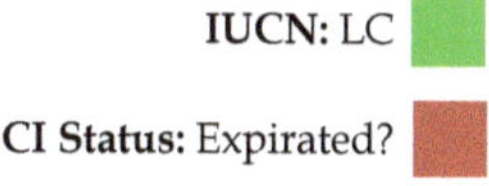

Max Length: 30 cm

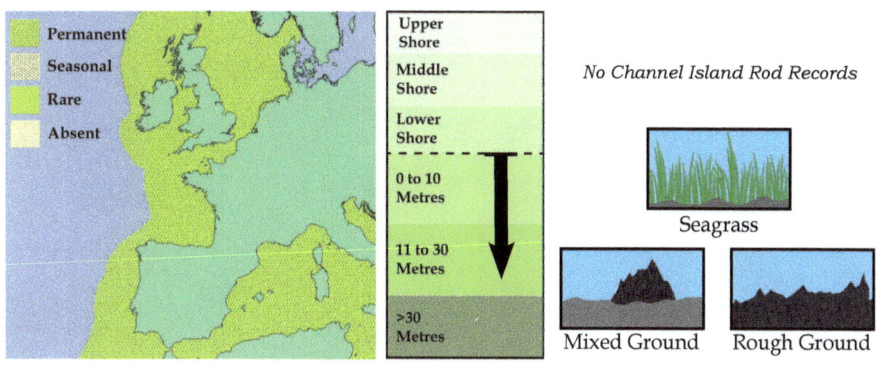

The Straight-nosed Pipefish was said to be common in Guernsey and Jersey between the 1860s and early 1900s but has not been reported since. This fish likes to live in seagrass habitats and in the 1960s Ronald le Sueur speculated that the severe decline in seagrass areas across Europe in the 1930s (due to a fungal infection) might have led to a local decline in this species. (Note: studies of aerial photographs by the Société Jersiaise suggests that seagrass beds in Jersey shrank by over 90% between 1933 and 1944 which would probably have had a serious impact on local marine biodiversity.)

Although possibly very rare or locally extinct in the Channel Islands, Straight-nose Pipefish specimens are still occasionally reported from the Normandy coast and Chausey, usually in seagrass beds. A recent (and unexpected) expansion of seagrass beds in Jersey since 2006 may warrant a systematic survey in the islands for this and other pipefish species.

Black-striped Pipefish

Syngnathus abaster

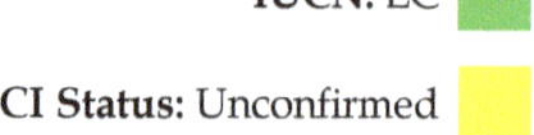

Max Length: 21 cm

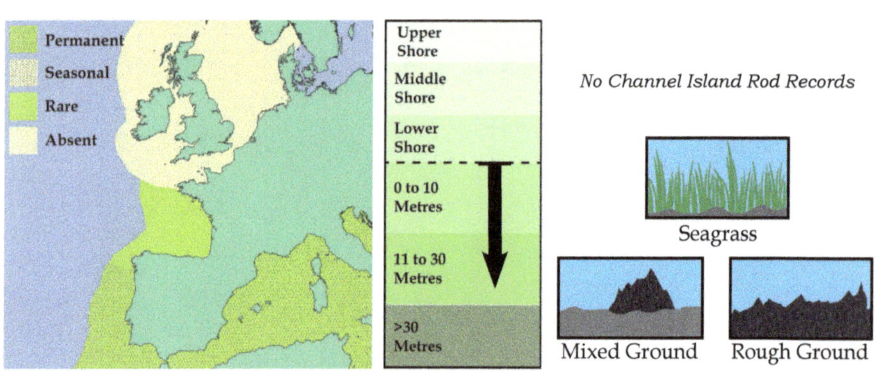

The Black-striped Pipefish is a Mediterranean species whose range stretches to the northern part of the Bay of Biscay. Two reports were made of this species in 1996 within seagrass beds in the Bay of Mont St Michel but has not been recorded since. In his 2009 survey of regional fish species, Patrick Le Mao acknowledges that these reports are highly unusual and that they may represent a misidentification of the similar Nilsson's Pipefish (*q.v.*). The species is not known from the Channel Islands and, without further proof, the records from the Normanno-Breton Gulf must be treated with caution.

Greater Pipefish

Syngnathus acus

Long-snouted Pipefish; Common Pipefish

Max Length: 45 cm

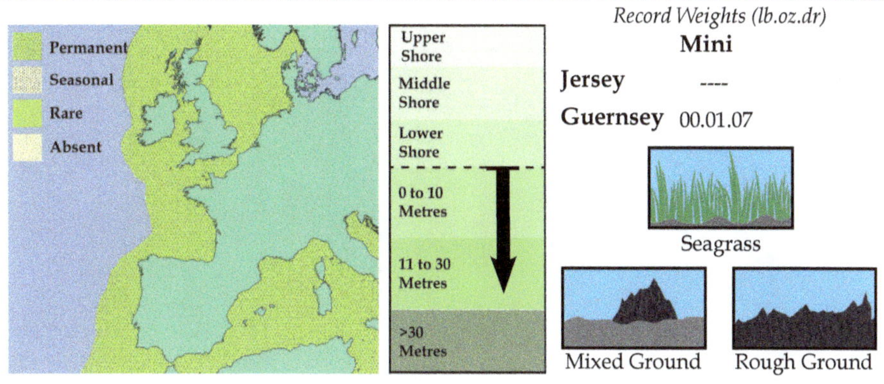

This robust and large species seems to be common in the Channel Islands and wider region. It is often associated with seagrass meadows but may sometimes be found in lower shore rock pools, especially at low water on large spring tides. Individuals may also be seen by divers lying on the seabed among seaweeds but have also been hauled up in lobster pots or more rarely, caught offshore, usually in trawls or dredges. As with the seahorses, it is the male pipefish that broods the eggs in a pouch in its stomach. Historical records begin in the 1860s and are constant through to the current day and, while only infrequently reported, it is probably not uncommon across the islands.

A Greater Pipefish taken from a lobster pot off Jersey in 2018.

Nilsson's Pipefish

Syngnathus rostellatus

Lesser Pipefish

Max Length: 17 cm

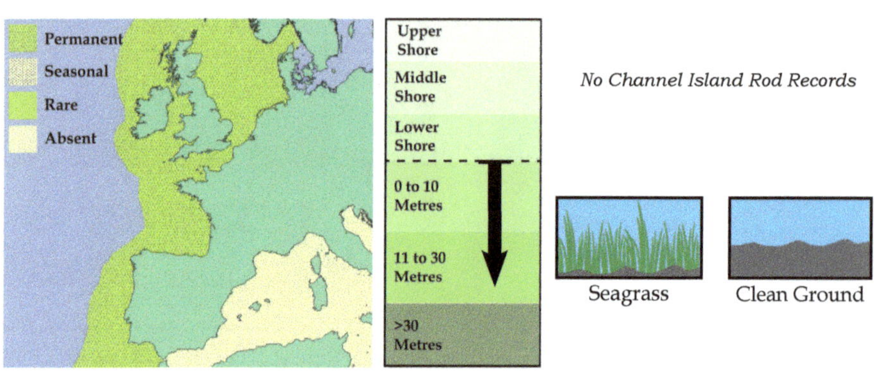

There are no local or regional records of Nilsson's Pipefish prior to the 1980s and yet this fish is currently reported as being common along the coasts of Jersey, Herm and Guernsey and also in the Bay of Mont St Michel. This suggests that this species may either have been overlooked historically (perhaps due to confusion with the Deep-snouted Pipefish) or it is a relatively recent arrival in the area. Nilsson's Pipefish does not feature in many historic fish identification guides suggesting that knowledge of the species may not have been available to the islands' pioneering naturalists. In 2010 sweep net surveys among the seagrass meadows on the east coast of Jersey produced a large number of specimens.

Nilsson's Pipefish at Anne Port, Jersey.

Deep-snouted Pipefish

Syngnathus typhle

Broad-nosed Pipefish; High-snouted Pipefish

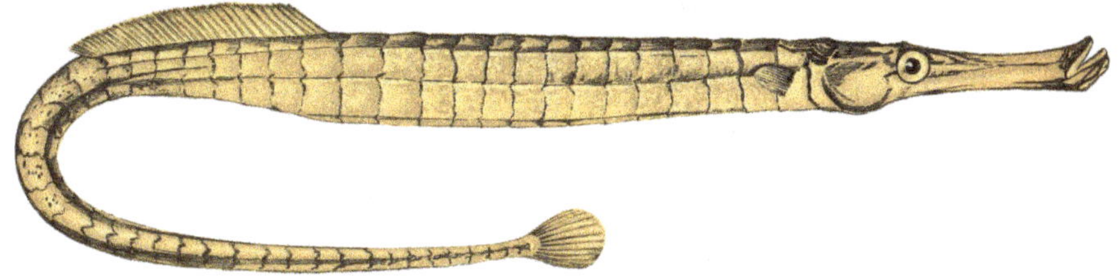

Max Length: 25 cm

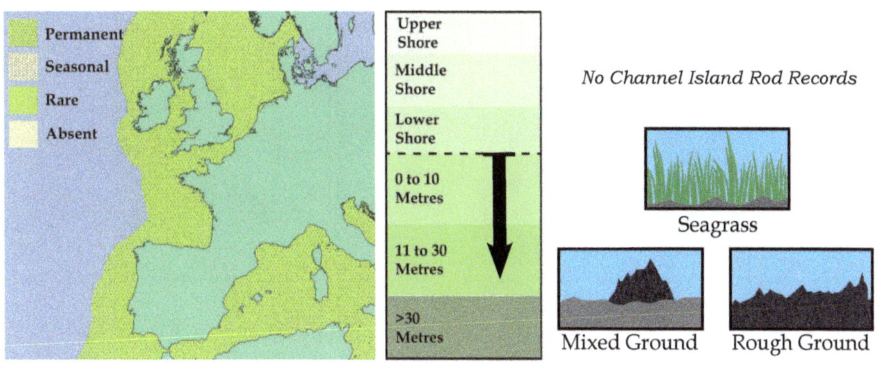

This is another species of pipefish species that is closely associated with seagrass meadows and which has a long but sporadic track record of reporting in the Channel Islands. It was described as being common in Victorian times and, despite only a handful of local records since, it can still be found around the modern Jersey coast and probably also the other islands. Most regional reports are from May onwards which could be due to its annual migration into shallow water to breed during the spring and summer. The Deep-snouted Pipefish has been caught regularly in surveys of seagrass made along the Normandy coast and is probably present but rare in all the Channel Islands.

Snake Pipefish

Entelurus aequoreus

Max Length: 60 cm

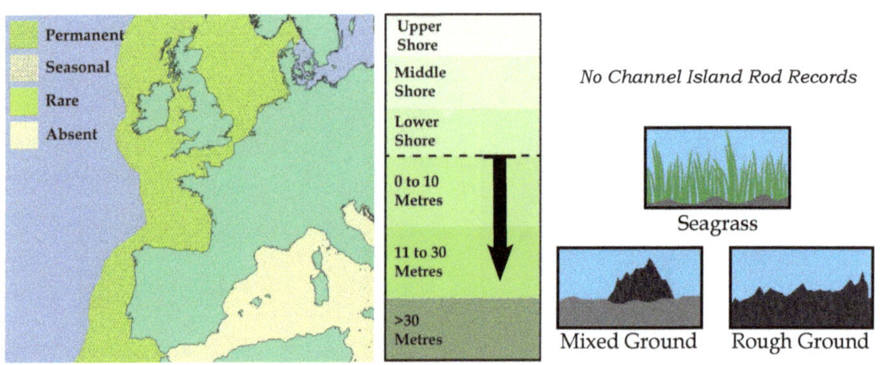

Notable for its size and colourful patterning, the Snake Pipefish is considered to be a nuisance in some parts of Europe where it has been blamed for the starvation of seabirds. The theory is that the overfishing of sandeels has forced seabirds to mistakenly feed upon the Snake Pipefish which is tough to digest and nutritionally low. There are, however, no reports of this occurring locally. This fish can be found on the lower shore, usually in rock pools, and amongst seagrass and they may become stranded on the beach by the retreating tide.

A Snake Pipefish left stranded at Ouaisné, Jersey.

Scorpionfish, Gurnard and Sea Snails

The Scorpaeniformes (scorpionfish, gurnards and sea snails) are a diverse order of fish that are characterised by a robust body shape and defensive features such as spines and bony plates. Their armour means that they are rarely targeted by predators and some species, such as the Scorpionfish, are venomous. An exception is the enigmatically named 'sea snails' which have no obvious spines but do retain the rigid cheekbones that help define the morphology of this order of fish.

Most species of Scorpaeniform are bottom-dwelling with the smaller ones hiding in rocky, seaweed dominated areas while the larger ones may be found in a wider variety of habitats, usually in the shallow marine or offshore. Several species (such as the Pogge, Bull Rout and sea snails) prefer cold water which means that the Channel Islands lie near the southern limit of their geographical range. These species may become rarer if sea temperatures rise as predicted (see page 279) although at present they remain a common part of the local marine fauna.

The four Scorpaeniforme families found locally are the Cottidae (bullheads and sea scorpions), Scorpaenidae (scorpionfish), Triglidae (gurnards); Cyclopteridae (lump fish) and Liparidae (sea snails). Of these, it is only the gurnards that have a commercial fishery as they are used for bait in the crab and lobster industry and, in France, as a food fish. In the 1990s landings were around 20 to 35 tonnes annually but this has steadily declined to under ten tonnes.

There is a fishery for the Lumpsucker in Scandinavia but this fish is approching its southern limit in the English Channel and is not common enough locally to permit a commercial fishery although there was interest in this possibility around a decade ago. At the time of writing, the Lumpsucker is scheduled for legal protection under Jersey's wildlife law as there are concerns that its population may be declining locally.

Some of the small species of scorpaeniforme fish (such as sea snails, bullheads and sea scorpions) will be found in rock pools at low water or may be caught in prawn nets during autumn low water fishing. Most species are robust and will cope with gentle handling/examination. However, in the spring months some species could be guarding eggs (generally visible as a yellow/orange on the underside of stones) and so should not be picked up or moved from where they are found.

Gurnards and Lumpsuckers will sometimes be seen by divers or snorkelers and will often remain still enough on the seabed for photographs to be taken. None of the common gurnard species are targeted by anglers although they may be taken as bycatch.

Blue-mouth

IUCN: LC

CI Status: Rare

Helicolenus dactylopterus

Blackbelly Rosefish; Blue-mouth Redfish; Jac

Max Length: 46 cm

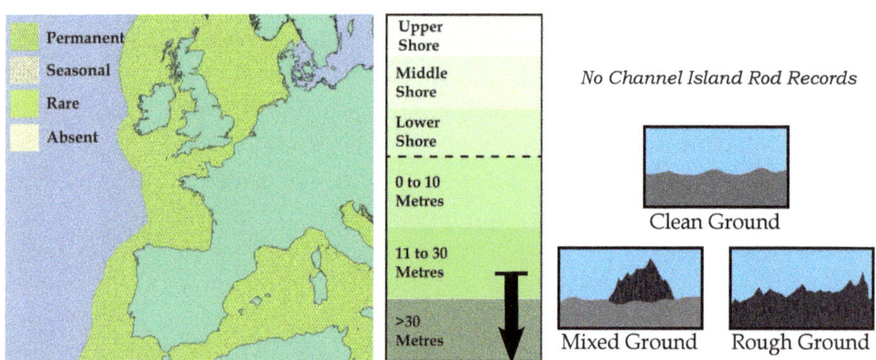

There is just one regional record of the Blue-mouth when a single specimen was taken in 1997 by a trawler about eight miles to the west of Guernsey. This is generally a deep water fish although in recent years there has been an increased number of catches from shallower waters off the western UK coast. With no other reports, it is hard to judge the status of this species locally but its absence in any of the scientific trawl surveys undertaken regionally suggests it is probably a rare visitor to the area. Any captures should be reported to the local biological records centres.

Scorpionfish

Scorpaena scrofa

Max Length: 50 cm

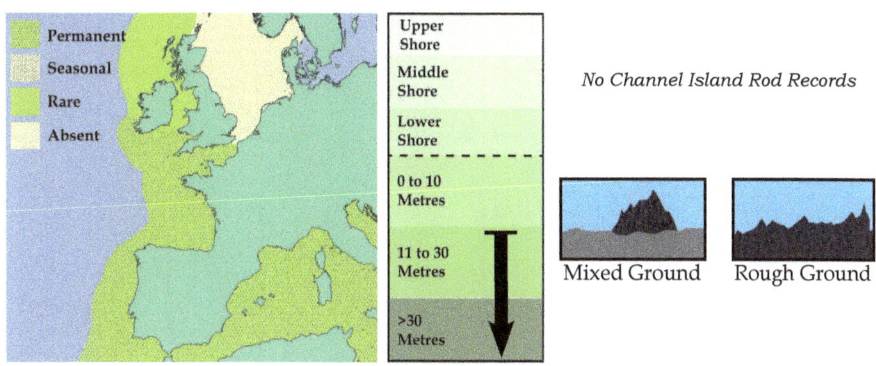

The Scorpionfish is an entirely different species to the similar sounding and more commonly seen Sea Scorpion (*Taurulus bubalis*). The Scorpionfish is a southern European species which occasionally travels far enough north to reach the English Channel or Irish Sea. It is known locally from just one record taken in 2010 by a commercial fishing boat operating about 12 miles west of Guernsey. The Scorpionfish is normally a deeper water species but it can sometimes be found in relatively shallow water. It is probably a rare visitor to local waters and, as it is only likely to be encountered in trawls and dredges, may be under reported regionally. The Scorpionfish has highly venomous spines and is considered to be one of the most dangerous species within its family of fish.

Red Gurnard

Chelidonichthys cuculus

Rouoget

IUCN: LC

CI Status: Frequent

Max Length: 50 cm

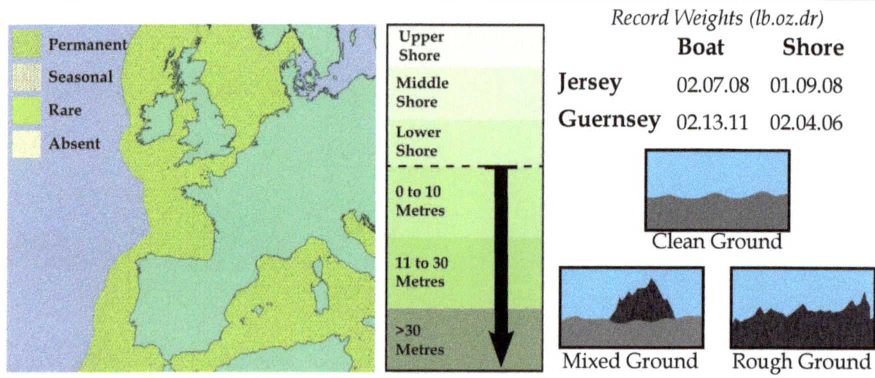

Record Weights (lb.oz.dr)

	Boat	Shore
Jersey	02.07.08	01.09.08
Guernsey	02.13.11	02.04.06

Red Gurnards are most often seen on the decks of commercial fishing boats where they are widely used as bait for lobster pots. This fish is spectacular especially when seen by divers resting on its 'fingers' (actually adapted pectoral fins). More peculiar are the Red Gurnard's underwater grunting noises which are believed to play a social role between individuals. They are generalists and can be found across a range of seabeds and depths including in shallow water.

Described as abundant in early Victorian times, by the end of the century local biologist James Hornell thought that all gurnards had been overfished. More recently they have been heavily targeted by local commercial boats with annual catches above 40 tonnes although they have been below a tonne since 2006. Red Gurnards are often caught by anglers but usually as bycatch. They can be confused with other species from its family so careful checking is needed for specimens.

Grey Gurnard

Eutrigla gurnardus

Grondîn

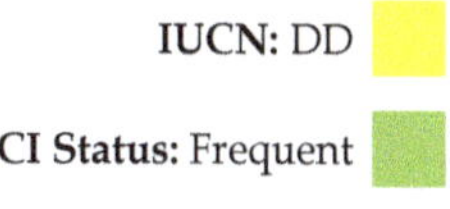

Max Length: 45 cm

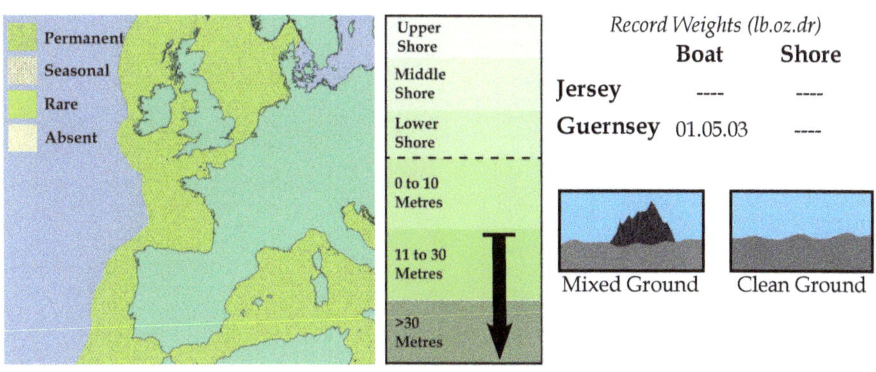

Record Weights (lb.oz.dr)

	Boat	Shore
Jersey	----	----
Guernsey	01.05.03	----

There is little information available on the status of the Grey Gurnard within the Channel Islands although it is probably not uncommon offshore. Arguably the least colourful of the local gurnard species, it lives on the edge of the depth range of recreational diving and is more likely to be caught by boat anglers than those fishing from the shore. Historical records go back to 1841 but are otherwise poor although anecdotal reports suggest it is currently widespread through the islands. In 1905 Joseph Sinel claimed that the juveniles were frequently seen within the seagrass beds that then fringed much of the south coast of Jersey.

Tub Gurnard

Chelidonichthys lucerna

Max Length: 70 cm

Permanent
Seasonal
Rare
Absent

Upper Shore
Middle Shore
Lower Shore
0 to 10 Metres
11 to 30 Metres
>30 Metres

Record Weights (lb.oz.dr)

	Boat	Shore
Jersey	07.08.03	02.08.00
Guernsey	08.03.02	05.09.01

Clean Ground

A large and striking fish when seen underwater, the Tub Gurnard can have an attractive and colourful red, blue and green patterning on its pectoral and dorsal fins. Although always regarded as common in the Channel Islands, it is a predominantly southern fish whose range has recently expanded northwards in the British Isles. The Tub Gurnard can come into quite shallow water and may even be seen by snorkelers, especially in seagrass areas where smaller specimens can hide themselves. Like other gurnards, there are not many reports for this species although it is probably common and widely distributed through the islands. This is certainly what is suggested by scientific trawling records although, unusually, all the specimens taken by CEFAS between 2006 and 2018 were in deeper water. The Tub Gurnard has little commercial or recreational value locally although with the decline of more traditional edible fish species, it is being more widely eaten on the continent.

Streaked Gurnard

Chelidonichthys lastoviza

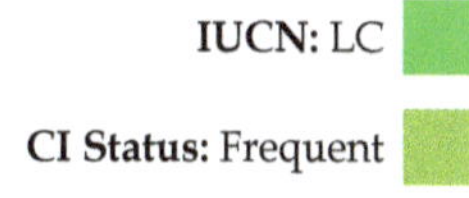

Max Length: 40 cm

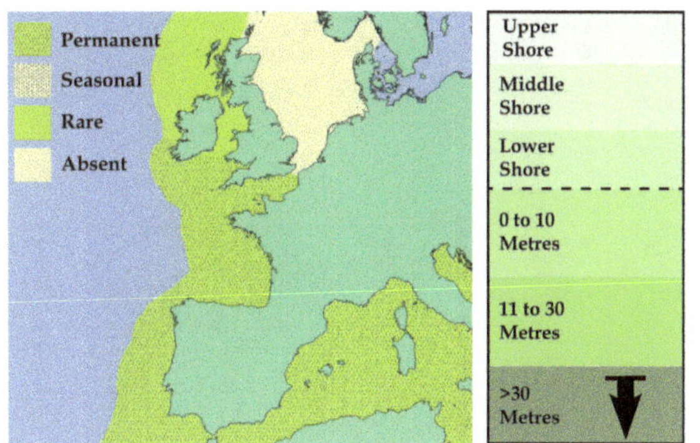

Record Weights (lb.oz.dr)

	Mini
Jersey	00.09.04
Guernsey	00.10.04

Clean Ground

Regarded as being an 'occasional catch' in 1862 and 1905, the Streaked Gurnard has just one twentieth century angling record when a specimen was caught off the Schole Bank, Guernsey, in 1993. Based on this it could be assumed to be a rare fish locally and yet scientific trawl surveys between 2006 and 2018 produced dozens of specimens from across the whole of the Channel Islands.

The English Channel is at the northerly end of the Streaked Gurnard's geographic range and, as the trawl data suggest, it generally prefers deeper waters with most records being below 30 metres. As a southern European species, it has been speculated that this fish could become more common in the UK if sea temperatures continue to rise. However, in the case of the Channel Islands it already seems to be a reasonably common but under-reported species.

Norway Bullhead

Max Length: 7 cm

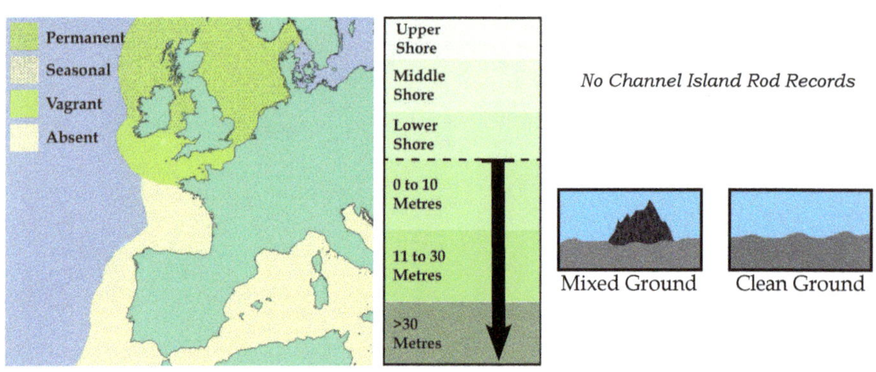

There is just one Channel Island record for this northern European species from when a specimen was caught in a 2018 beam trawl survey south of the Schole Bank, Guernsey. A second specimen was taken close to Alderney (but outside Channel Island waters) during a scientific survey in the 1970s. The Norway Bullhead is a subarctic species that has only been rarely found in the English Channel and then only historically. With increasing sea temperatures, it is unlikely to be found in the Channel Islands with any frequency and is probably rare within the region.

Bull Rout

Myoxocephalus scorpius

Shorthorn Sculpin; *Cabot du Dgiâbl'ye*

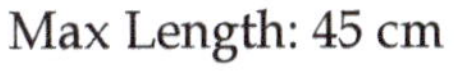

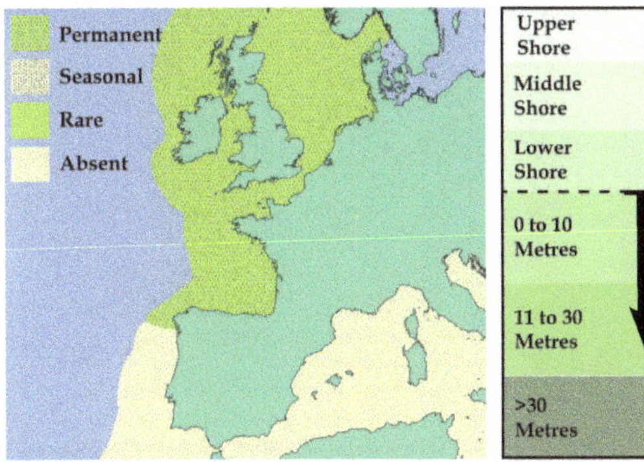

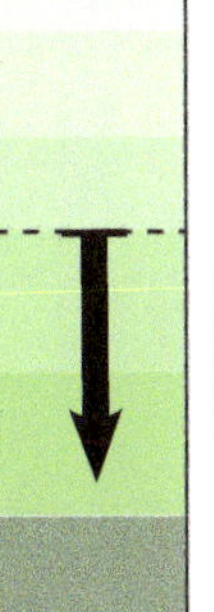

No Channel Island Rod Records

Mixed Ground

Rough Ground

The Bull Rout is common around the Channel Islands and has a long recorded local presence back to early Victorian times. The Normano-Breton Gulf is within the southern part of its range and specimens tend to be smaller here than in places such as Scotland and Scandinavia where it has been said to reach a metre in length. Generally found below the low water mark, the Bull Rout will usually be seen by divers and anglers but may rarely be found in rock pools or caught in nets when prawning. Although it and the Sea Scorpion (*Taurulus bubalis*) look aggressive, they are not poisonous although their spines are sharp.

Sea Scorpion

Taurulus bubalis

Long-spined Bullhead; *Crapaud d'mé*

Max Length: 20 cm

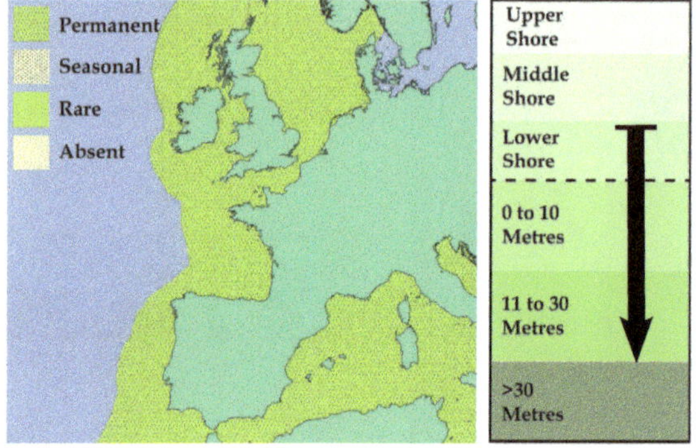

Record Weights (lb.oz.dr)

	Mini
Jersey	00.06.08
Guernsey	00.08.01

Smaller than the Bull Rout but of similar appearance, the Sea Scorpion is a common find on rocky shores where it can be seen in rock pools and under stones. From January onwards this fish may be found next to its distinctive orange egg mass and, even if disturbed may remain in place defending its nest. Shore specimens in the Channel Islands tend to be under 10 cm in length but they can grow to more than 20 cm. Although common locally the Sea Scorpion is a northern European species whose range only stretches south to the Iberian peninsula. The head spines are said to be venomous during the spring months.

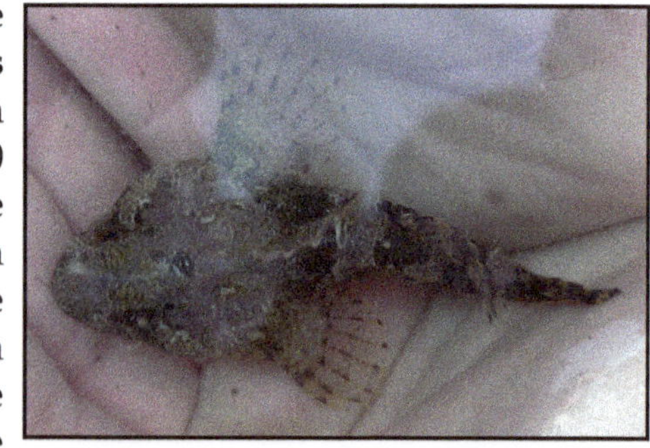

A Sea Scopion from a Guernsey rock pool.

Pogge

Agonus cataphractus

Hook-nose

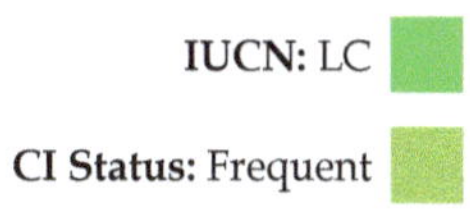

Max Length: 20 cm

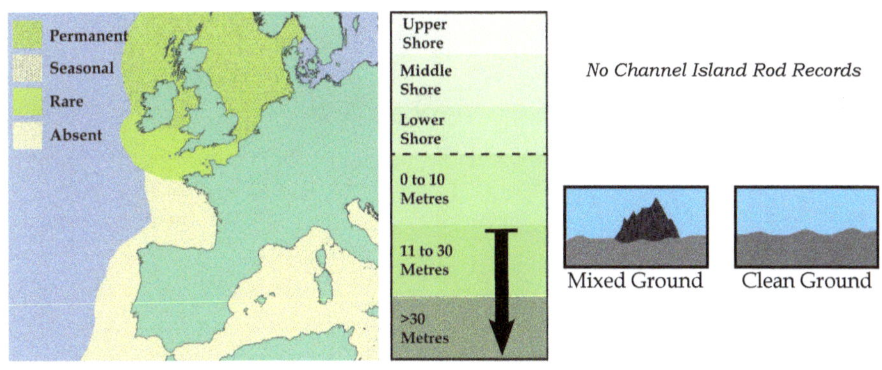

The English Channel marks the southern end of the Pogge's range and up until the 1960s there had been no regional records. However, since then specimens have turned up frequently in scientific surveys along the north Brittany coast while trawl surveys of 1991, 1992 and between 2006 and 2018 produced dozens of specimens from within the Channel Islands.

Although still only recorded from scientific surveys, current data suggest that the Pogge is actually not uncommon offshore. In other parts of Britain the Pogge is considered to be a shallow water species but all Channel Islands records are from deeper water (>20 metres) and almost all are from Jersey waters, the one exception being a single specimen from north of Alderney. The Pogge lives in fine to coarse sediment and is most likely to be seen by divers although there are yet to be any reports by this route. The lack of historical and casual records is unusual and any Channel Island sightings should be reported to a local biological records centre.

Lumpsucker

IUCN: NT

CI Status: Occasional

Cyclopterus lumpus

Lump Fish; *Paffot; Poule d'ieau; Poule d'ieau; Tambour*

Max Length: 40 cm

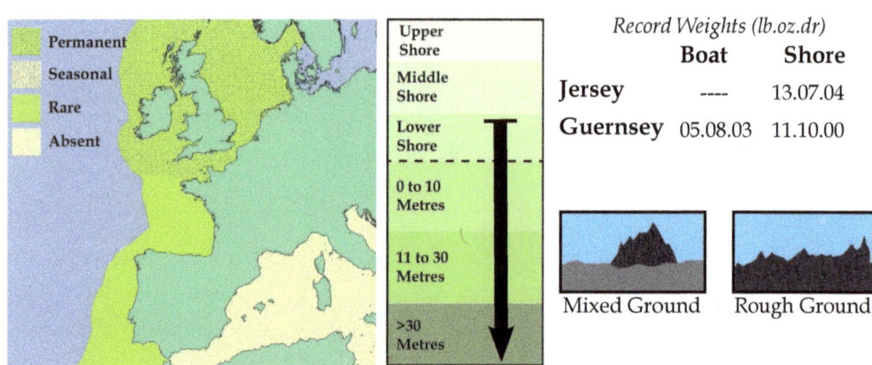

Record Weights (lb.oz.dr)

	Boat	Shore
Jersey	----	13.07.04
Guernsey	05.08.03	11.10.00

The Lumpsucker is an unmistakable fish that may be found guarding its eggs on the lower shore during the winter or spring months when it moves into shallow water to breed. At other times of the year it lives further offshore but is encountered by divers and anglers with large specimens sometimes reaching several kilogrammes in weight.

The Lumpsucker is vulnerable to commercial fishing in local waters and it may have declined since Victorian times when records suggest it was common. Nowadays it is rarely encountered on the seashore but is observed infrequently by snorkelers and divers. Some specimens have been known to remain in the same location for days or weeks. In other parts of Europe juvenile Lumpsuckers of a few centimetres have been reported clinging to *Laminaria* fronds in the spring months.

Striped Sea Snail

Liparis liparis

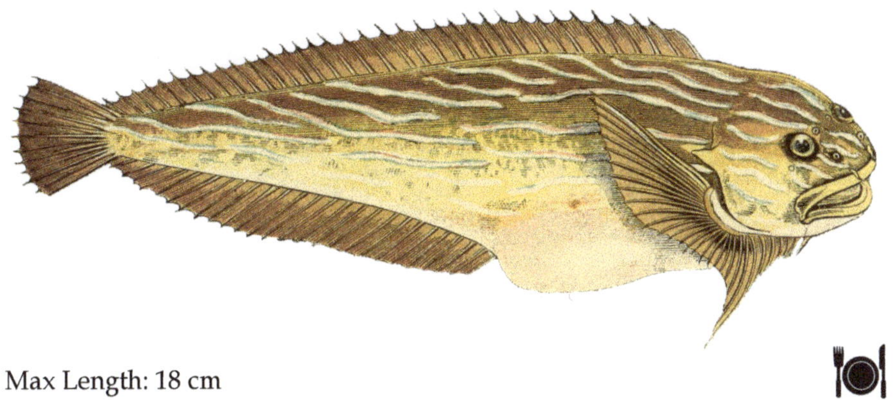

Max Length: 18 cm

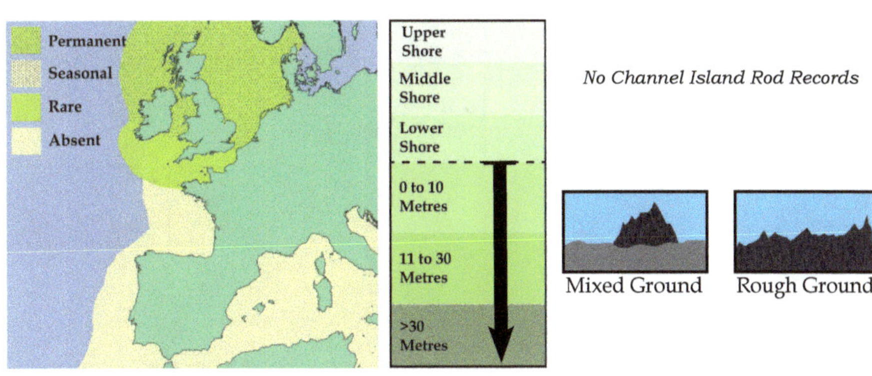

The Sea Snail has several records from the Normano-Breton Gulf between the 1960s to 1980s and one historical Channel Island report from an 1884 synopsis of British fish species. In April 2006 CEFAS scientific trawling produced two additional specimens from immediately north and south of Jersey but it has not been recorded since.

The Sea Snail is a cold water species and the Normano-Breton Gulf is right on the southern edge of its range. All known records seem to be concentrated into the period between December and April suggesting a winter seasonality to its occurrence. The regional pattern of records suggests that it may be a rare visitor to the islands but that increasing sea temperatures could preclude the Sea Snail from local waters as its range contracts northwards. It is easily confused with the Montagu's Sea Snail but generally lives in the shallow marine rather than the seashore.

Montagu's Sea Snail

Liparis montagui

Montagu's Sucker

Max Length: 7 cm

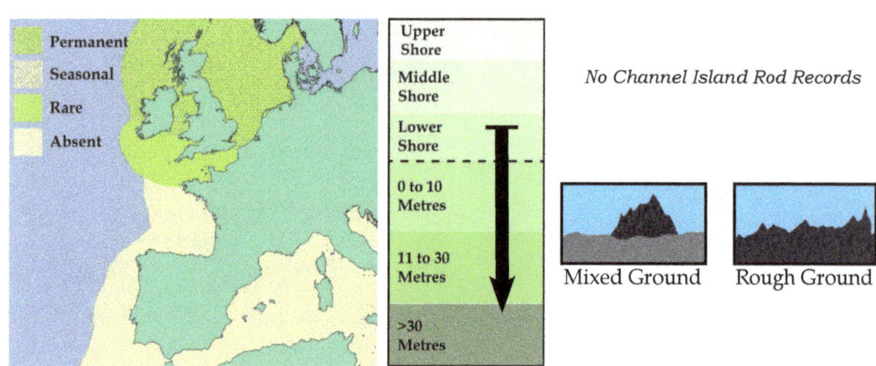

The Channel Islands are at the southern end of Montagu's Sea Snail's geographic range and the species is used in some parts of Europe as a climate change indicator. However, despite rising sea temperatures since the 1970s this fish has had more Channel Island reports in the past decade than in the previous century and a half. As a predominantly littoral fish, Montagu's Sea-snail is most common on the lower shore, particularly in the kelp zone and in pools on rocky shores. It is one of the Channel Islands' smallest fish and is easily overlooked. The curious name is probably ironic and perhaps comes from the species having first been described in an 1804 volume on British molluscs.

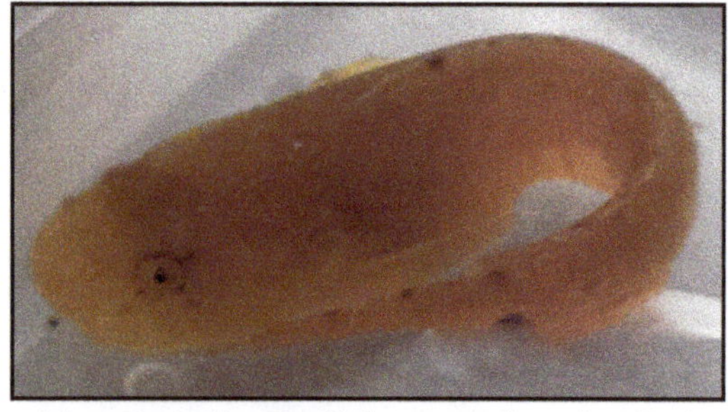

Montagu's Sea Snail from a rock pool at Petit Port, Jersey, in 2016.

Bass, Sea Perch and Wreckfish

The Perciformes is a large order of fish that includes a diverse range of families including familiar ones such as the bass, mackerel, mullets, gobies and sandeels. This is the most diverse order of fish within the Channel Islands and there are 89 species of perciformes fish reported locally, many of which are popular with commercial and recreational fishers.

This section deals with the families Serranidae (sea perches), Moronidae (seabass), Polyprionidae (wreckfish) and Echeneidae (remora). With the exception of the remora, which is a vagrant species known from just one record, the other species are large, powerful predatory fish that are popular with sea anglers. However, of all these species it is only the European Seabass that is commonly found in local coastal waters as the other species either live offshore (such as comber and wreckfish) or are rare/seasonal visitors to the region (e.g. Spotted Bass). The Spotted Seabass is, however, becoming more frequently caught by recreational anglers and may eventually become resident in the Channel Islands region.

The European Seabass is a prized sports fish and also has a high commercial value but in recent years northern European stocks have declined to a point where ICES (an organisation that monitors international fishing stocks) recommended a drastic reduction in commercial and recreational fishing effort. A 2015 survey of Jersey anglers estimated that between 5,000 and 8,000 bass were caught annually making it the second most retained fish by anglers, after mackerel. The same survey also asked anglers which fish populations they thought were in decline locally; the bass was the one most often cited as being in decline by respondents which may bear out the ICES findings.

In 2016 concern by ICES led them to advise that 'when the precautionary approach is applied, there should be zero commercial and recreational catch' for bass. This was not fully enacted in Europe until 2018 but a reanalysis of the data in July of that year led to a suggested one fish a day bag limit for recreational anglers. Given the fragile state of some bass populations, it seems probable that closed seasons, bag limits and other restrictions will be part of the fishery for some years to come while stocks recover. A conflict of opinion between scientists, regulators and fishers has made bass the most often talked about and controversial fish species in Channel Island waters.

Dusky Grouper

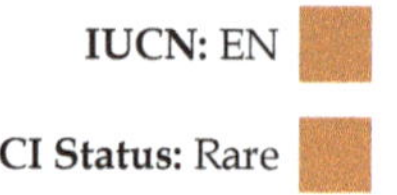

Epinephelus marginatus

Dusky Perch; *Pèrche*

Max Length: 150 cm

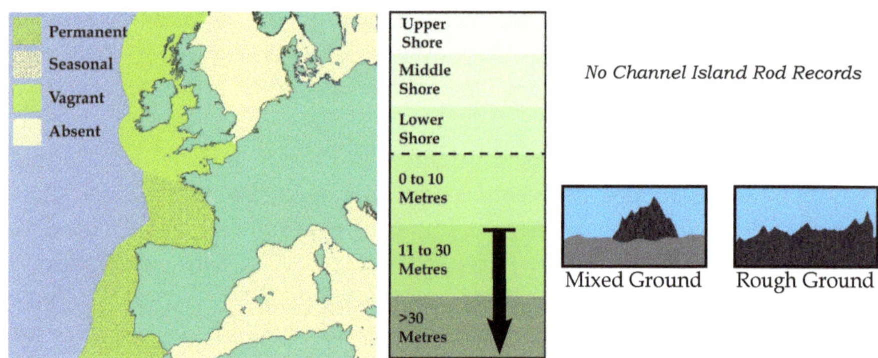

This is a large southern European species that may reach 1.5 metres in length. It is rare to find the Dusky Grouper north of the Bay of Biscay but some English Channel records exist including a Guernsey capture from the 1860s and a preserved Jersey specimen (88 cm long) which was on display in the Société Jersiaise museum until the 1980s and probably dated to the early twentieth century.

Overfishing has severely affected the Dusky Grouper and it is becoming rarer within its normal range let alone in more marginal areas such as the Normano-Breton Gulf. With no recent local or regional records, this is an historically recorded fish species that has the potential to reach the Channel Islands but which probably rarely does so. It lives in the shallow marine areas where there are boulders, crevices and overhangs to shelter around. As an endangered species, any caught specimens should be released alive.

Comber

Serranus cabrilla

Max Length: 40 cm

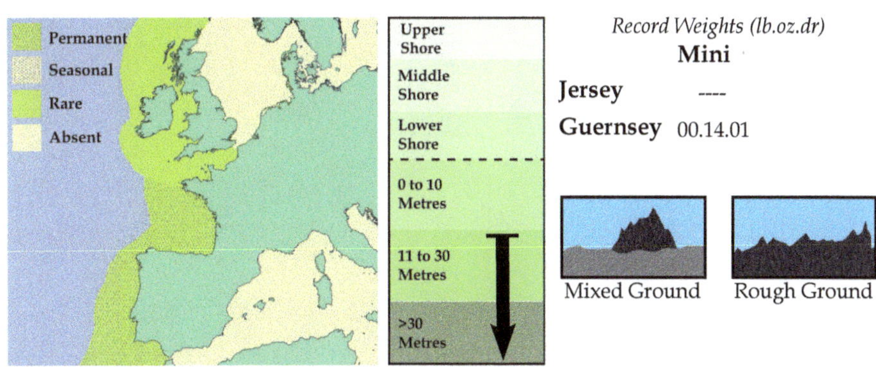

The Comber is a southern European species that is infrequently found in the English Channel and even more rarely in southern England and Wales. Local reports start in 1905 but are infrequent and mostly come from recreational anglers and includes a 0.4 kg specimen caught south of Guernsey in 1978. The Comber resembles a wrasse and has perhaps been misidentified and under-reported although a lack of records from divers and anglers suggests that it is probably a rare visitor. This fish has been known to breed in the English Channel and, with rising sea temperatures, has the potential to establish itself more widely within the Channel Islands area.

A Comber caught to the west of Jersey, 2018.

European Sea Bass

Dicentrarchus labrax

Bar; Bâsse

Max Length: 100 cm

Permanent
Seasonal
Rare
Absent

Upper Shore
Middle Shore
Lower Shore
0 to 10 Metres
11 to 30 Metres
>30 Metres

Record Weights (lb.oz.dr)

	Boat	Shore
Jersey	16.01.08	17.05.00
Guernsey	18.06.12	18.06.05

Pelagic
Clean Ground
Mixed Ground
Rough Ground

Of all the Channel Island fish species, the European Seabass (usually referred to simply as 'Bass') is probably the best known. Described as a 'cult fish' by Len Le Page, Bass are the favourite sport fish for recreational anglers and entire clubs and even industries have grown up around catching them. The Bass is also popular with diners and fetches a high commercial price. When combined with the fish's slow growth, late breeding, small legal landing size and position at the top of the food chain, this universal popularity eventually led to overfishing and a near collapse in northern European stocks. Severe restrictions were imposed on recreational fishing for Bass across northern Europe (as well as the Channel Islands) and commercial catches were limited to bycatch. The angling restrictions have been controversial as the recreational fishers feel, with some justification, that they are being penalised for historical overfishing and poor management from within the commercial sector.

Bass were historcially abundant around the islands and could reach a large size. For example, in 1876 a visiting biologist to Jersey commented that 'the Bass in these waters attain the finest possible development with examples weighing from 14 to 18 lb (6 to 9 kg) being common on the market stalls'. In 1907 a single fishing expedition from Le Hocq, Jersey, returned with 93 Bass, the smallest of which was 1.3 kg. In 1877 over seven hundred were netted by a single individual near Vazon, Guernsey.

Commercial catches were low until the early 1990s when they rose to between 20 and 30 tonnes annually in Jersey but peaked at nearly 200 tonnes in Guernsey due largely to pelagic trawling. A decline in local landings began soon afterwards and, by 2014, stocks in Europe were so dire that the EU was forced to take drastic measures. The minimum landing size was raised from 36 cm to 42 cm, bans and bag limits were imposed on various fishing sectors although arguably generous bycatch limits remained in place. Much to the chagrin of many commercial and recreational fishers, identical or similar measures have been in place across the Channel Islands. This means that those wishing to target Bass should first check what the local fishing regulations are. Ironically, much of the Bass sold by Channel Islands' restaurants is grown on fish farms in Mediterranean countries.

Capture Technique: The target species for anglers, Bass fishing has evolved hugely in recent times. Traditional shore methods involve beach fishing into the surf using baits such as lugworm. This is especially effective over the winter months. The modern era has brought along lure fishing. Lures can be cast and retrieved on the surface, subsurface, or weighted with a jig head to reach the desired depth. This method uses much lighter tackle than traditional methods and can be exceptional sport. Targeted areas usually include fast flowing water over reefs and sandbanks, especially during spring tides when the currents are at their strongest. Fishing is most productive from April to November. When water depth increases, heavier tackle is often used with weighted, long flowing, baited traces. Large or live baits can effectively be used on rock marks and inside harbours. This method is known to attract some of the largest solitary, scavenger Bass.

Bait Preference: Two of the most proven Bass baits are mackerel and sandeel whether fished live or dead. Worm baits can provide great fishing especially when beach fishing. This method can catch all sizes of Bass but there is a tendency of worm often attracting the smaller school Bass.

Spotted Sea Bass

Dicentrarchus punctatus

Bar Tacheté

Max Length: 70 cm

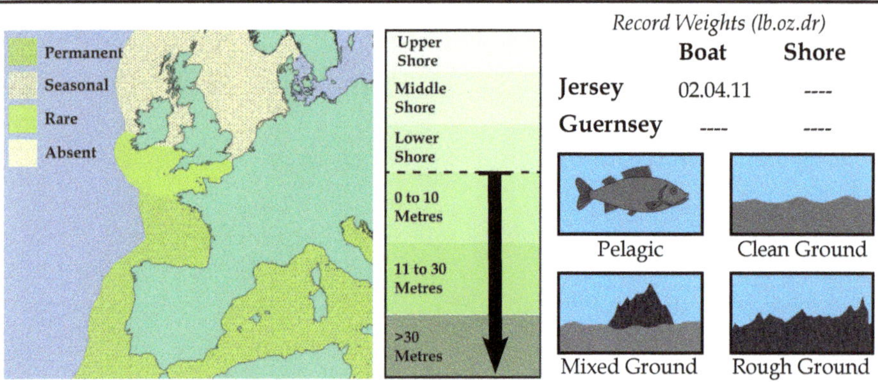

As the name suggests, the Spotted Sea Bass may be distinguished from its more common cousin (*D. labrax*) by a series of dark spots along its flanks. It is an occasional migrant from southern Europe but does have a regional presence back to at least 1897 when a summary of fish species in Normandy lists the Spotted Sea Bass as being 'very rare'. It remains so today with only a handful of local records, all of which were recreationally caught since 1996 from around Jersey. The Spotted and European Sea Bass share the same habitats and prey and at present the former is probably a vagrant species in Channel Island waters. However, as with many warmer water species, there is the potential for it to become more common or even resident. Any records should be made to a local biological records centre.

Atlantic Wreckfish

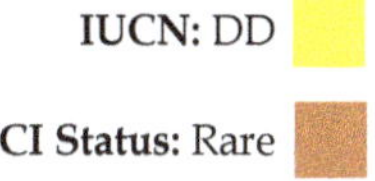

Polyprion americanus

Stone Bass

Max Length: 200 cm

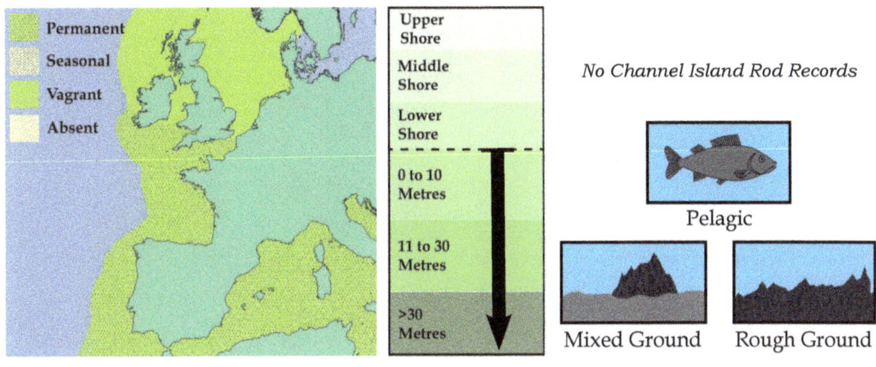

The Atlantic Wreckfish (or Stone Bass) is a large species of sea perch that is more typical of tropical or warm temperate waters although individuals do occur in the English Channel and even into the North Sea. As a deeper water fish that generally lives below 50 metres, the Normano-Breton Gulf is on the shallower end of its depth range. This, and its preference for southerly waters, means that the Atlantic Wreckfish is represented by just one regional record - a specimen caught off Guernsey in December 1841. Captures are infrequent but regular off south-west England and in the 1990s Jersey boats landed several specimens that had been caught some distance west of the island. With no recent reports it must be considered a very rare visitor to local waters. As the name implies, the Atlantic Wreckfish inhabits shipwrecks, mounts, caves and other prominant subtidal features.

Remora

Remora remora

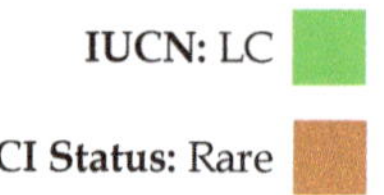

Max Length: 90 cm

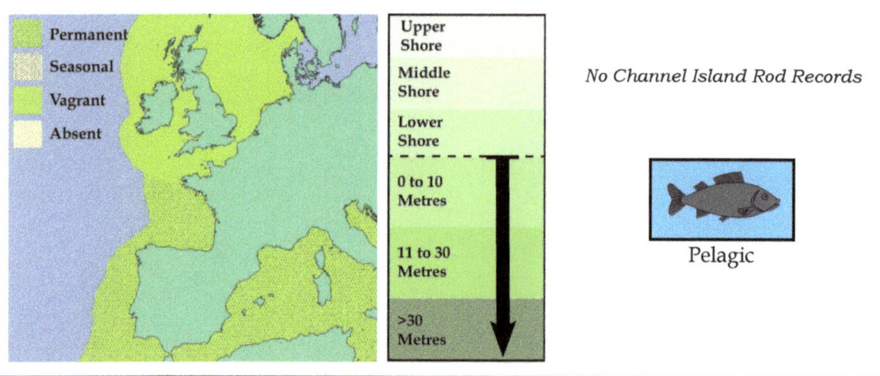

Remora are warm water pelagic fish which use an adapted pad on the top of their heads to suction themselves to the underneath of larger animals such as sharks, turtles and whales. Although primarily tropical and subtropical in distribution, specimens have been reported from as far afield as the North Sea. The lone Channel Island record comes from a fish caught in Guernsey some time prior to 1860 by a Madame Mauger. This specimen was preserved and later presented to the British Museum (now the Natural History Museum, London) where it still resides in their collections. No further specimens have been reported but with warming waters it is certainly possible that larger fish, such as sharks, will range further north, bringing Remora with them.

Scad, Jacks and Seabream

This section covers more families from the Perciforme order of fish some fo which are of particular interest to ichthyologists as they include southern European species that seem to have moved north into local waters during recent decades. Within this section are species from the families Carangidae (jacks and amberjacks), Bramidae (pomfret), Sparidae (seabream), Sciaenidae (meagre) and Mullidae (goatfish).

Of the 21 locally reported species in these families, 11 were either not recorded locally at all before the 1990s or were rare but have become more common since. This is particularly true of the jacks, amberjacks and seabream several species of which have recently arrived in Channel Island waters and are being caught in increasing numbers (e.g. Almaco Jack, Bogue, White Bream, Couch's Seabream). It is probable that rising sea temperatures (see page 277) may be permitting these coastal dwelling species to migrate north from the Bay of Biscay into local waters where some, such as Couch's Seabream, may have become permanently resident.

Being located on the southern side of the English Channel, the Channel Islands seem to be receiving these species marginally ahead of the UK. British angling records for several jack and seabream species are held in the Channel Islands and these records are continually being broken as the size of specimens increases. This northely migration may have begun over a century ago with species such as Gilthead Bream, Black Bream and Red Bream that, while historically common in the Channel Islands, have only recently become common in the UK.

As well as the species that are known from the region, there are several other species of jack and seabream that could find their way into local waters in coming years. As probable indicators of regional climate change, reports of jacks, amberjacks and seabream are of great interest scientifically. It is likely that reports of any newly arrived species will come from recreational and commercial anglers which places these groups at the forefront of citizen science when it comes to monitoring changes in local marine fish populations.

Gareth Mcmonagle with a Jersey shore record Gilthead Bream (7 lb 6 oz 1 dr).

Pilot Fish

Naucrates ductor

Max Length: 70 cm

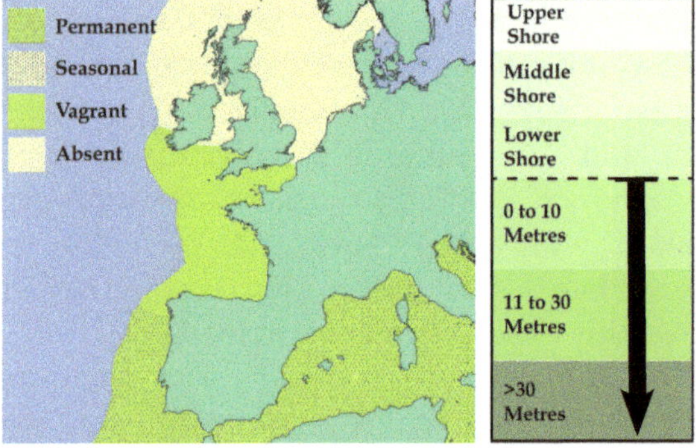

No Channel Island Rod Records

Pelagic

The Pilot Fish is a pelagic species that commonly associates itself with large oceanic sharks although, in the days of sail, it was known to follow ships for long distances too. Pilot Fish are primarily a warm water species but prior to the twentieth century reports of them from the English Channel were not unusual. This suggests that oceanic sharks may have been historically more common or perhaps that they were travelling north with sailing boats. There are two Channel Island records, one prior to 1836 from Guernsey and a second vague reference made in 1862. It is possible that both reports refer to the same specimen. Pilot Fish are currently rare in the English Channel although reports are still received, often of individuals that have come in during the summer on the Gulf Stream. As a vagrant, it is possible that Pilot Fish will occasionally find their way into Channel Island waters.

Guinean Amberjack

Seriola carpenteri

Max Length: 73 cm

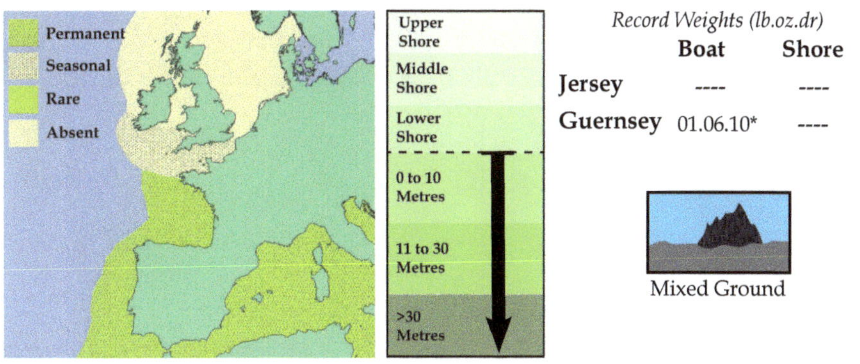

Record Weights (lb.oz.dr)

	Boat	Shore
Jersey	----	----
Guernsey	01.06.10*	----

The Guinean Amberjack is a relatively recent arrival in the Channel Island region with the first scientifically confirmed record coming from an angler off Herm in September 2000. Other reports followed from both Jersey and Guernsey and the species is currently considered to be an irregular visitor that is most commonly caught at the end of the summer. It should, however, be noted that the Guinean and Greater Amberjack are extremely similar to one another with the only secure means of identification being to count the number of gill rakes on the first gill arch. For this reason, specimens need to be carefully examined, ideally by a biologist, to secure a firm identification.

The Guinean Amberjack has also been caught further north in the English Channel suggesting that this may be a southern European species whose range is expanding with increasing sea temperatures. This is a species of local scientific interest and any caught specimens should be reported to one of the biological records centres so that they can be examined by an ichthologist to confirm the identification.

Greater Amberjack

Seriola dumerili

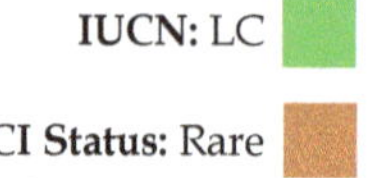

Max Length: 190 cm

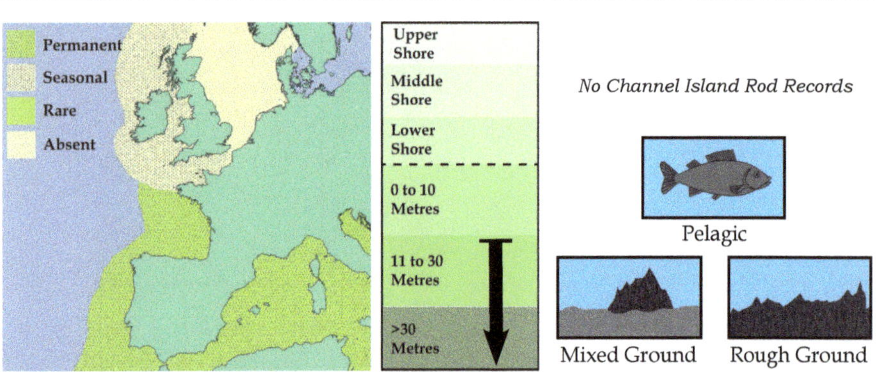

The Greater Amberjack is a large, powerful fish that has only recently started to be caught by anglers in the English Channel. The first Channel Island (and twelfth British) record was in December 2009 when a small specimen of 37 cm was caught by a recreational angler off Guernsey. There have been no further local records but the Greater Amberjack has continued to be infrequently caught off south-west England and, based on the pattern of other amberjack species, it seems probable that it will be caught again by Channel Island anglers. Like its close relative the Guinean Amberjack, this is a southern European species whose northerly range may have expanded to include the English Channel. Any specimens should be reported to one of the local record centres.

Almaco Jack

Seriola rivoliana

Longfin Yellowtail

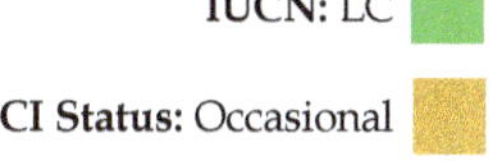

Max Length: 160 cm

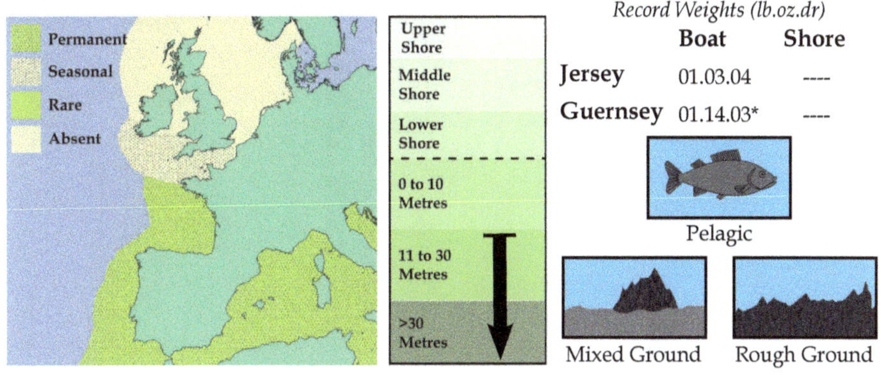

Record Weights (lb.oz.dr)

	Boat	Shore
Jersey	01.03.04	----
Guernsey	01.14.03*	----

The pattern of Channel Island reports for the Almaco Jack is similar to that of the Guinean and Greater Amberjack, which it closely resembles. The first local report was in December 2004 off Les Casquets and in the decade that followed further specimens were captured off Alderney, Guernsey and Jersey. Although pelagic, this fish prefers deeper waters below about 30 metres and is generally caught by boat anglers. It can occur as individuals or in shoals and may be distinguished from other jacks by its tall, crescent-shaped second dorsal fin.

It is probable that the Almaco Jack is a recent arrival to local waters and is currently a regular but rare visitor to our region. This is a species whose range could be expanding as the sea temperature rises and so it may be encountered more frequently in coming years. Any specimens should be reported to one of the local record centres.

Horse Mackerel

Trachurus trachurus

Scad; *Cârré*

Max Length: 50 cm

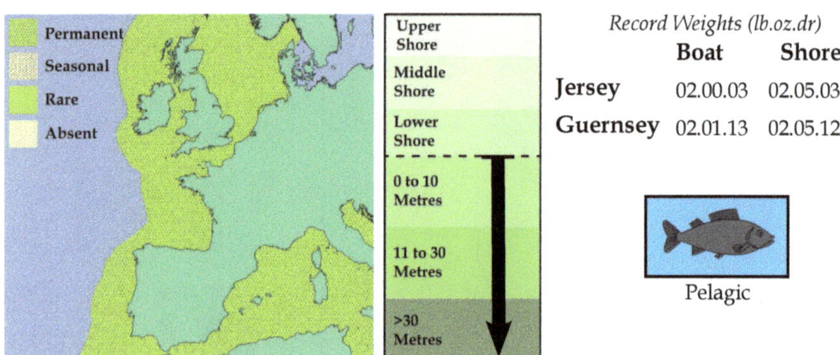

Record Weights (lb.oz.dr)

	Boat	Shore
Jersey	02.00.03	02.05.03
Guernsey	02.01.13	02.05.12

The Horse Mackerel is a bony fish that is rarely eaten by humans but is widely used as lobster pot bait in the Channel Islands. It is small, has spines on both its pectoral and anal fins and frequently taken as bycatch by both commercial and recreational fishers, the latter often while feathering for mackerel. Historical records begin in 1862 when they were said to be common in coastal waters although, as a spring migrant to the Channel Islands, later naturalists noted that their arrival and abundance could be erratic between years. 'It would seem,' wrote naturalist Joseph Sinel in 1904, 'that Jersey is a little out of the track of its migrations.'

Commercial catches were several tonnes annually until 2003 when they decreased to under a tonne. The Horse Mackerel is a mid-water pelagic fish that moves in shoals. Its status is difficult to estimate but anecdotally it seems to be common in the Channel Islands, especially during summer and autumn.

Blue Jack Mackerel

Trachurus picturatus

Max Length: 60 cm

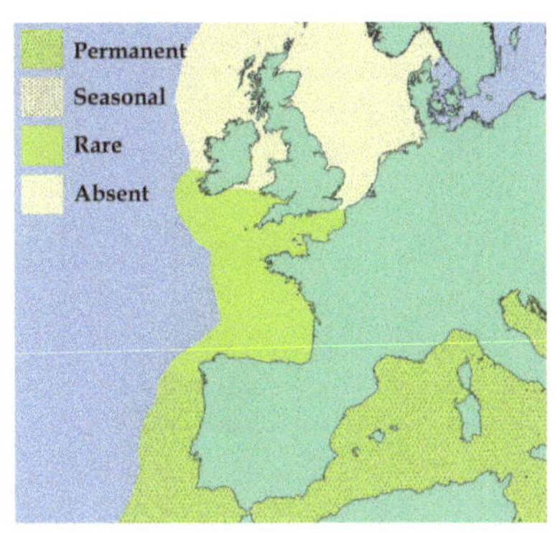

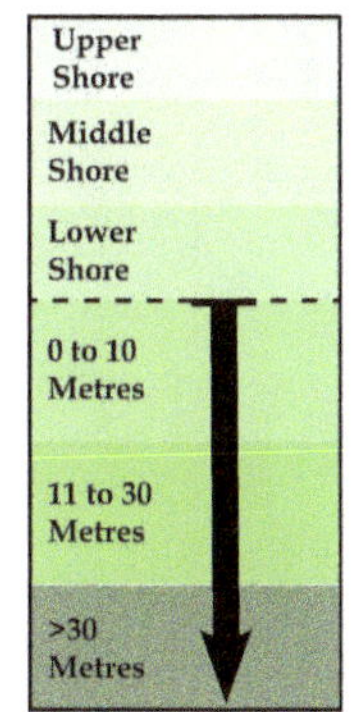

No Channel Island Rod Records

Pelagic

The Blue Jack Mackerel is a southern European species whose northerly limit is usually given as the Bay of Biscay. The authors can find no English Channel records for the species and its inclusion in this book is from a single commercial catch landed in Guernsey in 1991. Although several southern European fish species have started to regularly visit the Channel Islands in recent decades, a lack of other regional records suggests that the 1991 landing was either a misidentification (possibly of a Horse Mackerel) or that the fish were caught further south and landed in Guernsey. Without further evidence, this is an unconfirmed species for the Channel Islands.

Ray's Bream

Brama brama

Atlantic Pomfret

Max Length: 100 cm

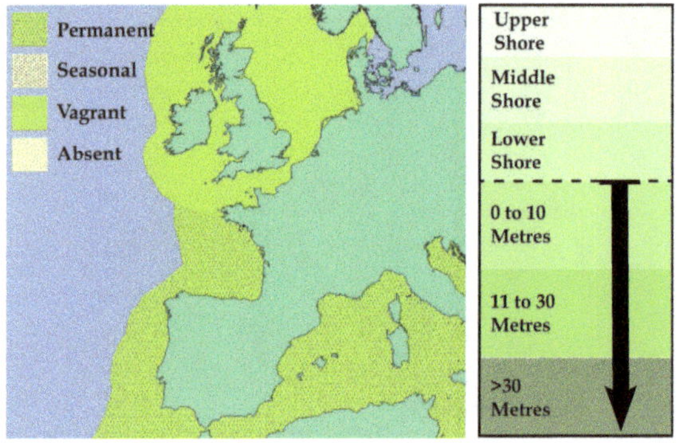

No Channel Island Rod Records

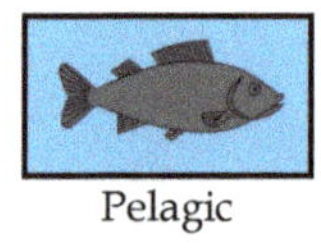

Pelagic

Ray's Bream are large and distinctive fish that generally live in deeper, warmer waters than are found in the English Channel. However, they can migrate for long distances and reports of Ray's Bream from around the UK (usually of stranded specimens) have become more common and even include some commercial catches off Scotland. Ray's Bream is named after the naturalist John Ray who found a specimen washed ashore near the Yorkshire coast in 1681 but outside Britain the fish is better known as the Atlantic Pomfret.

This is possibly one of those warmer water fish species whose range is expanding northwards with rising sea temperatures. There is just one known Channel Island record when a 46 cm specimen was washed up on St Brelade's beach, Jersey, in August 2007. Although a rare vagrant at present, Ray's Bream has the potential to become more common in the near future. It can grow up to 20 kg in weight.

Bogue
Boops boops

IUCN: LC

CI Status: Occasional

Max Length: 36 cm

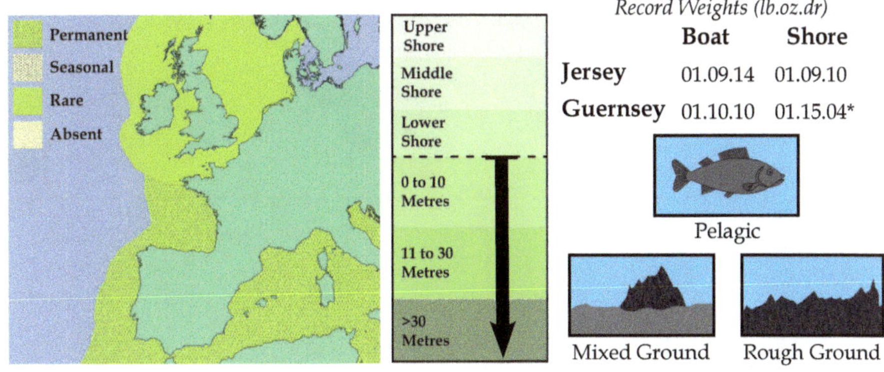

Record Weights (lb.oz.dr)

	Boat	Shore
Jersey	01.09.14	01.09.10
Guernsey	01.10.10	01.15.04*

The Bogue is another example of a southern European fish that has started to become more common in local waters. The oldest known report is of a angling capture from Guernsey in October 1915 but it was not until the 1980s that people started to report irregular captures of this species. By the turn of the twenty-first century the Bogue was being caught regularly in Channel Island waters with several specimens a year being taken by anglers from Guernsey and Herm. However, actual (as opposed to anecdotal) reports are sparse but this fish seems to be caught in the autumn and winter which suggests these may be individuals that have reached the region during their summer migration. The Bogue is currently a part of the local marine fauna but more reports are desirable and can be made via local records centres. Further south this species has a commercial value and is often shipped to the Channel Islands and used as lobster bait for commercial fishers.

White Bream

Diplodus sargus

Sargo

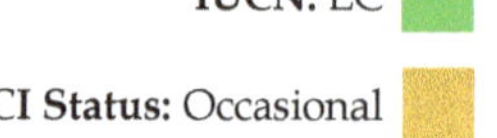

Max Length: 45 cm

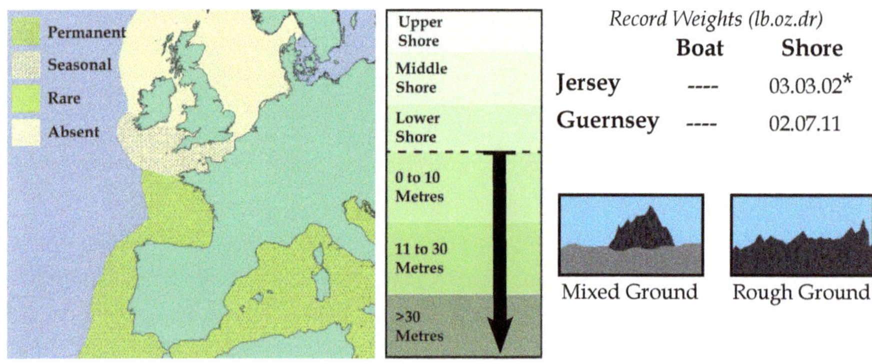

Record Weights (lb.oz.dr)

	Boat	Shore
Jersey	----	03.03.02*
Guernsey	----	02.07.11

The White Bream (or Sargo) is a southern European species that was unknown regionally until several fish became trapped in the marine bathing pool at St Malo, Brittany, in 1988. From 1999 the White Bream started to be caught with increasing frequency by anglers in Jersey, Guernsey and Sark, usually when fishing from the shore. As with other recently arrived bream species to the Normano-Breton Gulf, the White Bream is most often caught in the late summer or autumn. It is currently more common in the Channel Islands than the UK with Jersey at present holding the shore caught British record. This is a species of scientific interest so further reports are desirable and should be made to local records centres.

Two-banded Bream

Diplodus vulgaris

IUCN: LC

CI Status: Rare

Max Length: 45 cm

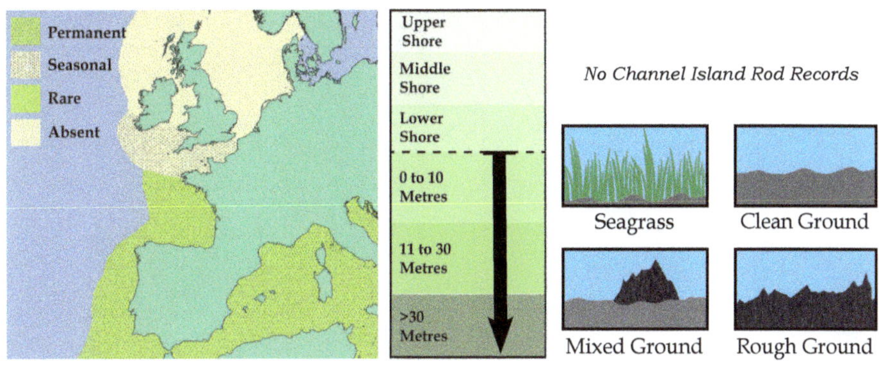

The Two-banded Bream is a shallow water species with a similar distribution to the White Bream (see opposite). Like other southern bream species, the Two-banded Bream is a relatively recent arrival in the Channel Islands and so the frequency with which it is caught is liable to increase. The earliest local records are from the mid-2000s and are anecdotal with the first confirmed specimens being caught in January and July 2009 from shore anglers in Guernsey. These were also the first British records for this species. There are unconfirmed reports from the other Channel Islands but as this species can easily be confused with other bream, it is probable that some specimens have been caught but misidentified. As with other recently arrived bream species, this is a fish of some scientific interest and anglers are requested to report any captures to a local records centre.

Annular Bream

Diplodus annularis

Max Length: 27 cm

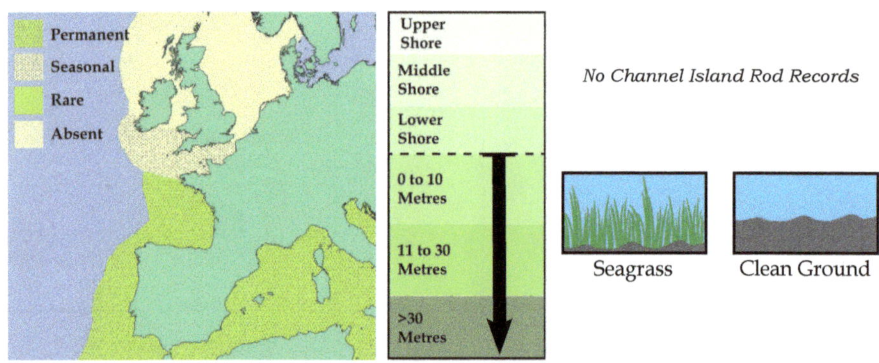

The presence of the Annular Bream has not been confirmed from Channel Island waters but there are two reliable reports. The first was in October 2001 from an angler on Herm and the second, a year later, by an experienced angler who was snorkelling off Guernsey. Without photographs or specimens these records cannot be validated but the northern range of the Annular Bream is the Bay of Biscay and, as with some other bream species (e.g. White Bream; Two-banded Bream), it is thought to be expanding northwards. The Annular Bream is a shallow water species with a preference for seagrass and seaweed cover. Anglers and divers are asked to report (with photographs) any Annular Bream specimens they encounter so that this species can be added to the local fish list.

Spanish Seabream

Pagellus acarne

Axillary Seabream

Max Length: 36 cm

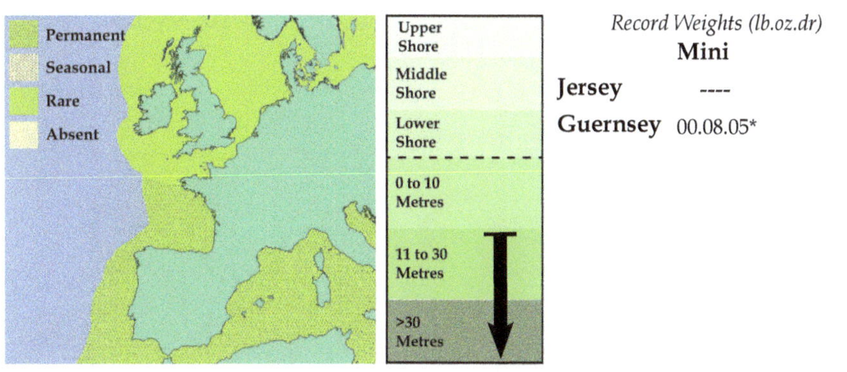

Record Weights (lb.oz.dr)

	Mini
Jersey	----
Guernsey	00.08.05*

There are just two Channel Island records of the Spanish Seabream both from Guernsey waters. The oldest is from 1983, when a 235 gram specimen was caught in St Peter Port Harbour, and the second was a slightly larger specimen caught from a wreck south-west of the island in October 1995. This is primarily a southern European species but specimens have recently been turning up in the English Channel and even the North Sea, suggesting that its range is expanding northwards. Although still a rare vagrant in local waters, the Spanish Seabream is a coastal fish that may become more common in the future. Any captured specimens should be photographed and reported to one of the local biological records centres.

Red Bream

IUCN: NT

CI Status: Frequent

Pagellus bogaraveo

Blackspot Seabream; *Brême Sarde; Sarde* [small]

Max Length: 70 cm

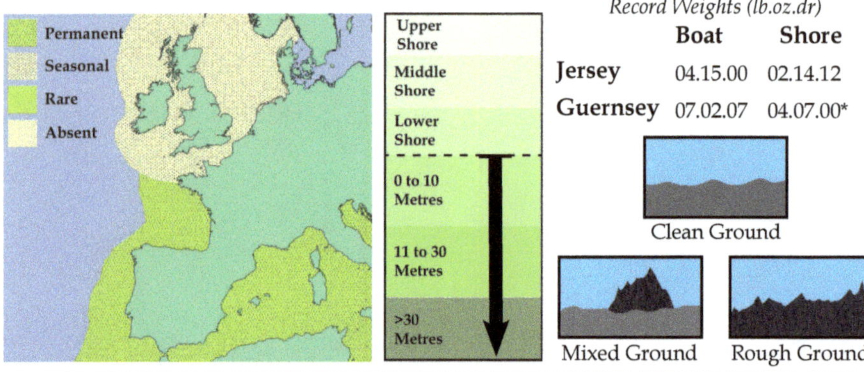

Record Weights (lb.oz.dr)

	Boat	Shore
Jersey	04.15.00	02.14.12
Guernsey	07.02.07	04.07.00*

The Red Bream has been fished commercially for many years and was said to be abundant in Victorian times. However, in 1897 local biologist James Hornell wrote that Jersey catches had declined by over forty percent. Guernsey angler Len le Page reported a steep decline in Red Bream catches between 1984 until 2006 since when they made a limited recovery. The fish's reproductive strategy includes a sex change from male to female which makes it vulnerable to overfishing. The Red Bream can grow up to 18 kg and is more commonly caught by boat anglers near deep structures such as wrecks.

Rob Green and the Jersey boat record (4 lb 15 oz).

Common Pandora

Pagellus erythrinus

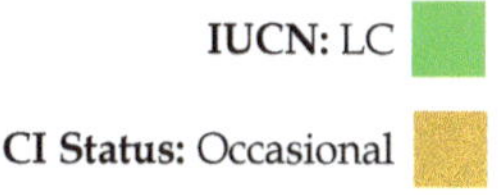

Max Length: 60 cm

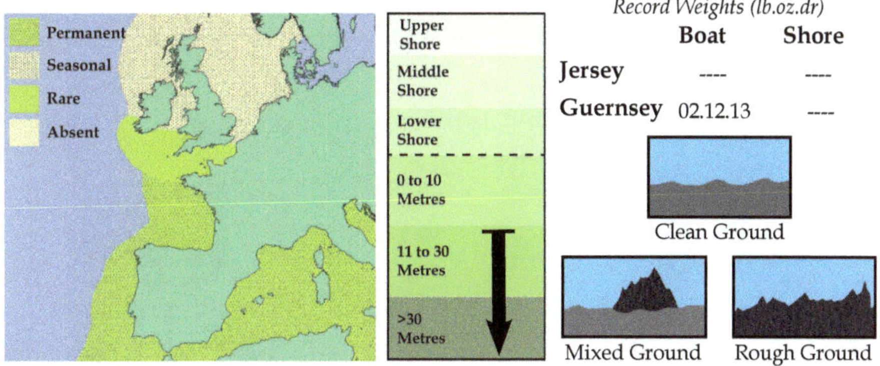

Record Weights (lb.oz.dr)

	Boat	Shore
Jersey	----	----
Guernsey	02.12.13	----

The Common Pandora used to be a rare visitor to the English Channel with its northern range usually finishing in the Bay of Biscay. There are, however, isolated Channel Island reports from the 1840s onwards and the Common Pandora is said to have been encountered more frequently by local anglers since 1997. There are few official Channel Island records to back this up but those that do exist (plus those from the southern UK) suggest that the Common Pandora is indeed on the increase. It is just one of several similar species whose geographic range may be shifting into the English Channel as the water temperature increases. This is a species of scientific interest and captured specimens should be reported to a local records centre.

Saupe

Sarpa salpa

Salema

IUCN: LC

CI Status: Rare

Max Length: 55 cm

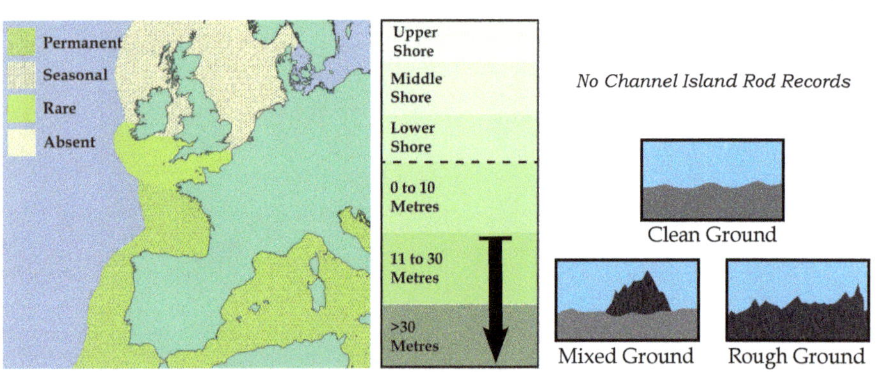

The Saupe is a large member of the bream family only known from a handful of records outside of the Bay of Biscay one of which was from an angler at Belle Grève Bay, Guernsey, in 1982. The previous British capture was from 1932 and the Guernsey specimen was such a rarity that it was presented to the Natural History Museum in London. There have been other UK captures since 1982 but none were from the Channel Islands. Distinguished by its yellow stripes and eye ring, the Saupe is a very rare vagrant into local waters but given the increased occurrence of other southern European species, future captures should not be ruled out. This is a species of scientific interest and any specimens should be photographed and reported to a local records centre.

Gilthead Bream

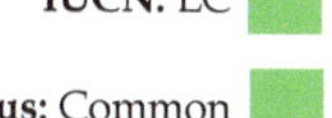

Sparus aurata

Rouoge Brême

Max Length: 70 cm

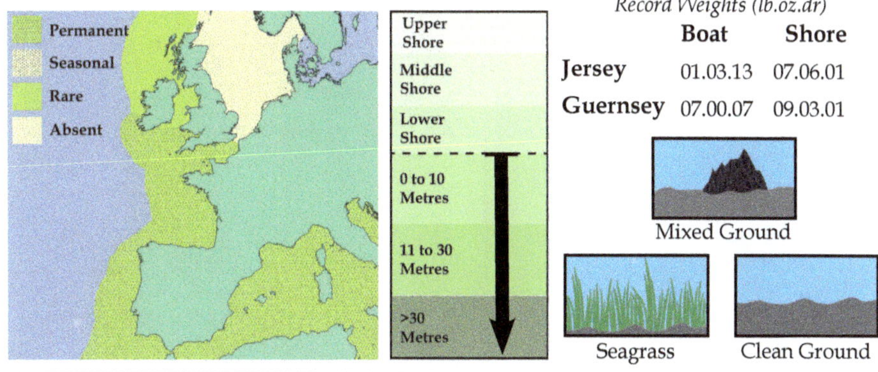

Record Weights (lb.oz.dr)

	Boat	Shore
Jersey	01.03.13	07.06.01
Guernsey	07.00.07	09.03.01

The Gilthead Bream is an inshore fish that is popular with anglers and whose British record is regularly held by the Channel Islands both from the shore and boat. It is a southerly species whose range is extending northwards from the English Channel and it is thought that larger fish are being caught locally because of increasing sea temperatures. The Gilthead Bream has been common in Channel Island waters from at least the early nineteenth century and anecdotal reports suggest that its local population remains healthy. Most shore caught specimens tend to be small to medium-sized but the species can reach over 4.5 kg in weight. As with some other bream species, Giltheads are born male but become female at about three years in order to reproduce. The species is not subject to widespread commercial fishing locally but is farmed as food in other countries.

Black Bream

Spondyliosoma cantharus

Old Wife; *Néthe Brême; Bliue Brême*

Max Length: 60 cm

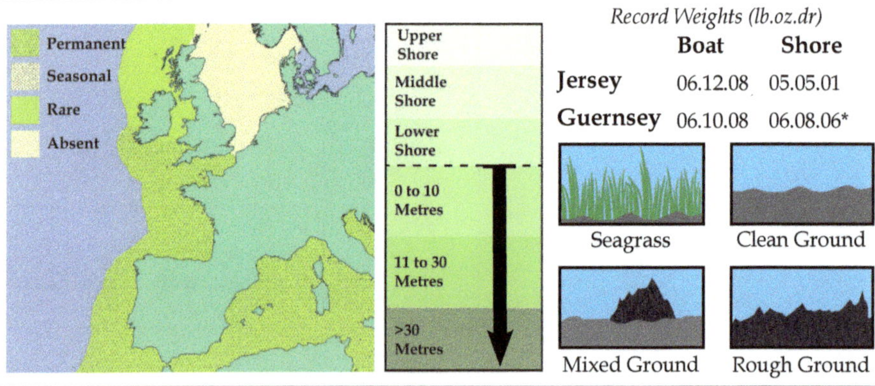

Record Weights (lb.oz.dr)

	Boat	Shore
Jersey	06.12.08	05.05.01
Guernsey	06.10.08	06.08.06*

The Black Bream is a popular fish with recreational anglers but is also an important commercial species. In the nineteenth century local fishers would prepare for the annual 'bream season' by making up the long and trot lines that would be baited with whelk ready for the arrival of the April shoals.

The Black Bream will winter in deep parts of the English Channel and then migrate into Channel Island waters during the spring. The arrival of the first Bream being greeted with joy by recreational anglers as the Channel Islands are regarded as one of the top locations in the British Isles for Black Bream fishing. However, this fish's abundance has varied markedly between years with the fluctuations first being noted during the 1890s and again from 2005 when intensive pair trawling around Guernsey is thought to have caused a drop in angling catches. Numbers recovered when commercial trawling lessened from 2009 but Black Bream are still heavily fished off Jersey and in the English Channel with thousands of tonnes landed annually.

Darren Braby with a previous Alderney Black Bream record: 5 lb 15 oz 11 drms.

The Black Bream is susceptable to overfishing because it builds nests on the seabed which are guarded by the male until the juvenile fish reach several centimetres. Nesting grounds may contain hundreds of bream and, once discovered, trawlers can remove a breeding population in a few days. This is alleged to have happened at several locations in Channel Island waters which, in combination with a minimum landing size that is widely regarded as being too short, means that the Black Bream population is being overfished. This has been recognised by local and national recreational fishing associations as well as marine conservation groups, some of whom have campaigned for an increased minimum landing size and a recommended catch and release policy for the male fish, which build and guard the nests. Although listed as 'least concern' by the IUCN, the Black Bream features on several 'fish to avoid eating' lists and could be vulnerable to commercial overfishing, locally and in the wider region.

Capture Technique: Black Bream are a shoaling fish that, once located, can be relatively easy to catch. It has a small mouth meaning that hooks should be size 1 or smaller. A paternoster is a typical bream fishing rig and the main rig body can be made extra long to increase the heights of the bait off the seafloor. This helps to avoid bycatch such as dogfish. Hook lengths should be 15 lb test or over but lighter line can be used with care. This species can offer superb sport on light tackle and responds well to shirvy. The shirvy can attract the Bream into an area higher up the water column where they can be caught on a light float set up. The largest specimens are caught offshore, this can be on habitats such as mussel beds and rough ground and are also known to shoal around large structures such as wrecks. Black Bream are also known to be caught on feathers and small metals. Again with a light set-up, great sport can be found.

Bait Preference: Mackerel, ragworm and sandeel will all catch Black Bream but the prefered baits tend to be squid and cuttlefish cut into strips.

Couch's Bream

Pagrus pagrus

Red Porgy

Max Length: 91 cm

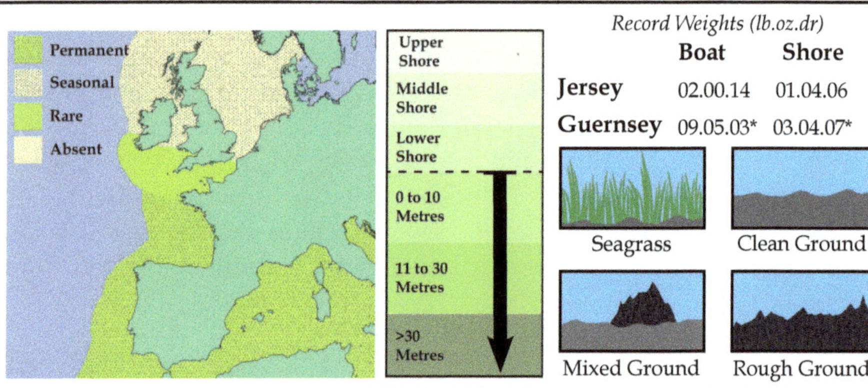

Record Weights (lb.oz.dr)

	Boat	Shore
Jersey	02.00.14	01.04.06
Guernsey	09.05.03*	03.04.07*

Couch's Bream was virtually unknown from north of the Bay of Biscay until 1993 when a specimen was caught in Soldiers Bay, Guernsey. This was the first British record but by the turn of the twenty-first century it was being regularly caught in Guernsey and Jersey. As well as increased catches every year, the size of specimens has grown and it is thought that the species is now breeding locally. Most reports are from Guernsey with the status in other islands being less well-known. Couch's Bream remains of scientific interest and captures should be reported to local records centres.

Richard Le Prevost with the Guernsey and British boat record.

Common Dentex

Dentex dentex

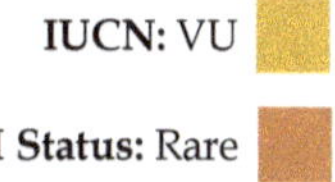

Max Length: 70 cm

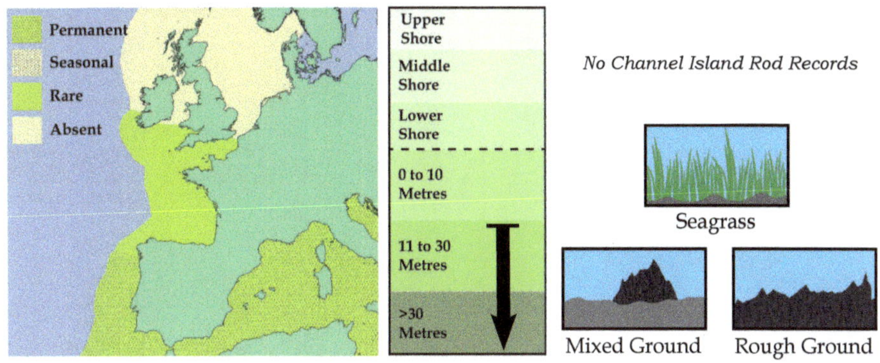

The Common Dentex is a subtropical fish that is rare north of the Bay of Biscay although there are isloated records from the English Channel and even as far north as Scotland. The only Channel Island records are from the end of the nineteenth century when specimens were caught off Jersey in 1873, 1875 and 1880. This bunching of records around the 1870s is unusual and there are no traceable local records before or after this time.

A high commercial value in combination with slow growth has made the Common Dentex vulnerable to overfishing and since the 1970s its population has decreased to the point where it has been classed as vulnerable by the IUCN. Although specimens could reach the Channel Islands from the Bay of Biscay, the lack of modern records suggests it is unlikely to be found locally.

Meagre

Argyrosomus regius

Croacher

Max Length: 230 cm

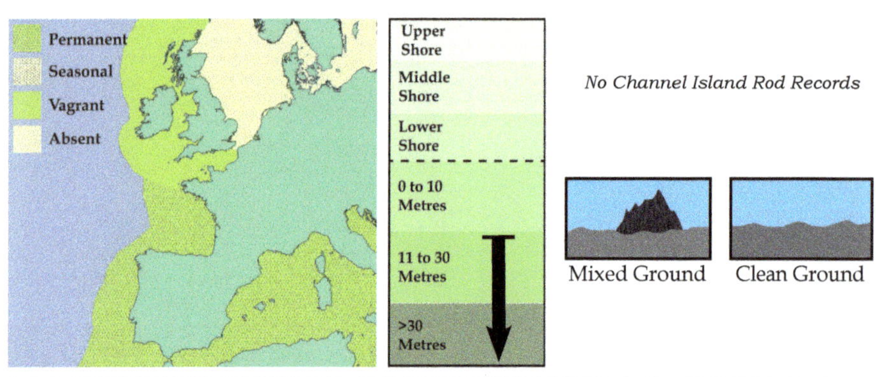

The Meagre is a large coastal fish that may weigh up to 55 kg. Its natural range just reaches the edge of the English Channel and the Meagre was said to be an irregular visitor to Guernsey and Jersey by local biologists in the nineteenth century. Several specimens were caught from the shore during the 1860s in Jersey and Guernsey including a large specimen from Bonne Nuit that was nearly two metres in length. This specimen was displayed at St Helier Fish Market as 'the monster from the deep' and then sold for one shilling per pound. Newspaper reports said the cooked flesh tasted like chicken.

There are no traceable local records since 1905 but the Meagre has been reported from western parts of the UK although specimens are said to be getting proportionately smaller with time. At present the Meagre should be considered as an historic species for the Channel Islands although as it is still being reported from other parts of the region, it probably has the potential to be caught again. Any specimens should be reported to local biological records centres.

Red Mullet

Mullus surmuletus

Rouoge Mulet

Max Length: 40 cm

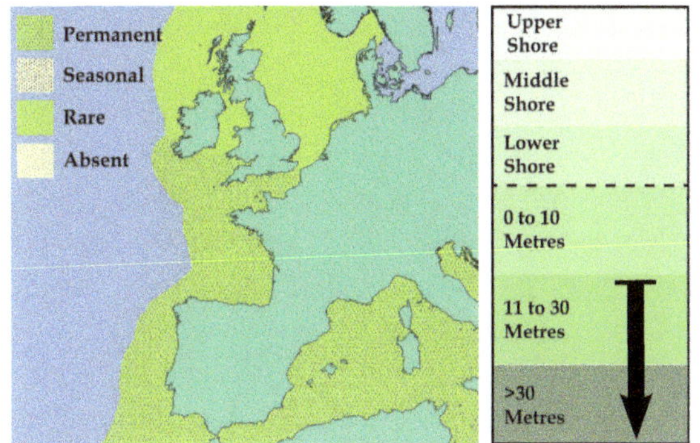

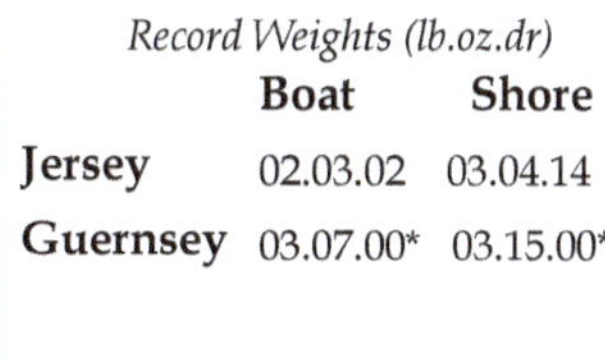

Record Weights (lb.oz.dr)

	Boat	Shore
Jersey	02.03.02	03.04.14
Guernsey	03.07.00*	03.15.00*

Mixed Ground

Clean Ground

Although it bears the name Red Mullet, this is actually a type of goatfish. It is common on sandy or mixed ground in shallow water and is easy to identify by its two chin barbels and striped dorsal fin. Red Mullet are edible and, as stocks of some other commercial species have declined, a market has developed in Europe. Local landings were for a time at several tonnes annually but are currently very low.

Historical records begin in the 1840s but, like many common species, there are remarkably few reports until the advent of local diver surveys in the late 1990s. Fast growth and maturation favour the survival of the Red Mullet and it is not considered to be under threat. It is common across the Channel Islands with British fishing records having been made in Guernsey and Alderney.

Mullet and Wrasse

The mullet family (Mugilidae) is represented by three (perhaps four) species of similar-looking fish in Channel Island waters. Mullet are large, slow-swimming fish that often congregate near to the surface, sometimes in very large numbers. Those wishing to see large mullet specimens could try visiting one of the Channel Island marinas where they will be seen swimming lazily around the pontoons. A more spectacular natural phenomenon may sometimes be witnessed at Granville on the French coast when the flooding tide concentrates dozens of mullet into small channels inside the harbour creating dense shoals of feeding fish.

With the exception of the Flathead Mullet (which has just one doubtful record), all species of mullet are common or abundant in local waters. Shallow sandy bays are particularly favoured by mullet, they can be seen following the rising tide in their hundreds or thousands, making the sea seem alive with activity. They are, however, a tricky species to catch using a rod and line although the practice of netting for them produces higher catch rates.

Getting firm identifications for mullet specimens requires care, especially underwater, and the family as a whole is under recorded despite their commonality. There are some southern European species that could stray into local waters including the Leaping Mullet (*Liza saliens*) and the as yet unconfirmed Flathead Mullet (page 183). Mullet records will be welcomed by local records centres.

Wrasse are large, often colourful, coastal fish that belong to one large family, Labridae, that is represented locally by nine species although the lone Grey Wrasse record (page 189) is probably erroneous. It would appear that Baillon's Wrasse (page 187) is a relatively recent arrival in the islands from further south, it not becoming local until the 1980s.

Wrasse are easy to spot but sometimes difficult to identify as the colours may be similar between species but very different between males and females within the same species. They are common just offshore, especially in rocky and seaweed dominated areas, and will often swim slowly enough for good identifications or photographs to be made by divers.

Dwain Clarke with the Jersey boat caught record Cuckoo Wrasse (1 lb 9 oz 4 dr).

Some wrasse have complex biologies and will change from

female to male as they grow older, often changing colour at the same time. Some males will build nests from seaweed and guard the eggs once they've been laid by the females while other species, such as the Goldsinny, simply shed their eggs into the water. The juveniles of most species will move close inshore and may even be found in deep, vegetated rock pools.

Tony Heart with the British boat caught record Ballan Wrasse (9 lb 7 oz 12 dr).

Complex reproductive strategies make some wrasee vulnerable to habitat disruption and overexploitation. There is little sign of this happening locally as catches are generally low and often through bycatch from netting and angling. Elsewhere in northern Europe adult and juvenile wrasse have been targeted to be exported live to fish farms in order to control lice infestations. In Norway, for example, wrasse landings have risen from 2 to 22 tonnes in under a decade. Reports suggest that this young fishery is already impacting coastal wrasse populations, leading to campaigns by angling and conservation organisations for better regulation. This has included calls for a minimum and maximum landing size for larger wrasse species plus a recreational bag limit.

As with many other common fish groups, there is a general lack of information about the commonality and behaviour of local wrasse species. Diver surveys coordinated by Seasearch have been the best recent source of information and with Seasearch groups now operating on all the large Channel Islands, a better picture of local wrasse is starting to emerge. More records are always welcome and can be made at a biological records centre.

Simon Gavey with the Jersey shore caught Ballan Wrasse record (8 lb 13 oz 2 dr).

Thick-lipped Mullet

IUCN: LC

CI Status: Common

Chelon labrosus

Mulet; Cornelle; Mulet Lippu

Max Length: 75 cm

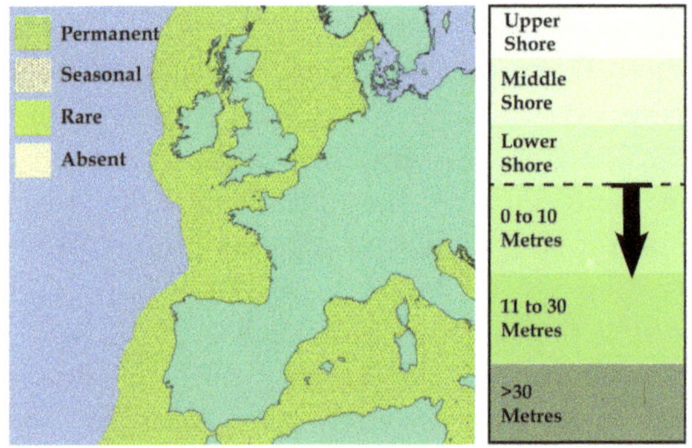

Record Weights (lb.oz.dr)

	Boat	Shore
Jersey	05.10.14	07.03.08
Guernsey	08.07.06	11.14.06

Pelagic

Thick-lipped Mullet is the most commonly reported mullet species from the Channel Islands. It prefers sheltered sandy bays and harbours where they will scrape and rake the sediment for food. They are notably common along the east coast of Jersey especially during the spring and early summer where hundreds of fish congregate just offshore. Sometimes juvenile fish will become trapped in rock pools or gullies at low water. Mullet are not heavily targeted by either commercial or recreational fishers and historical records suggest that local mullet populations have fared well since they were first recorded in the early nineteenth century.

Leigh Mullins with the 2018 Jersey shore record (7 lb 3 oz 8 drm).

Golden Grey Mullet

Chelon aurata

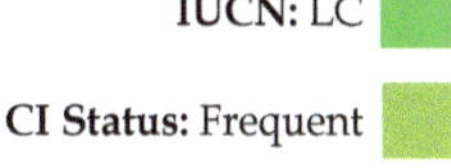

Max Length: 50 cm

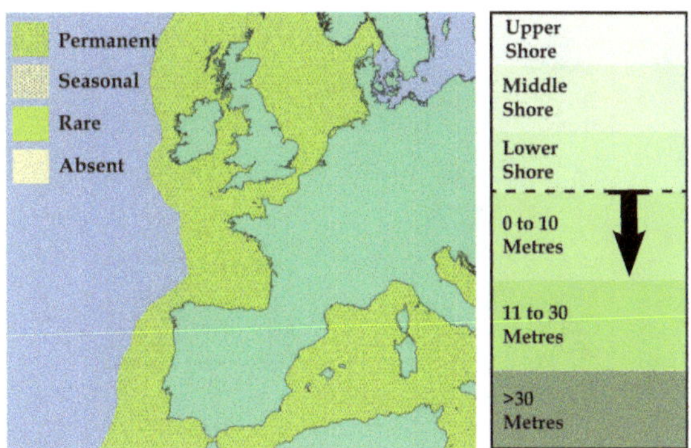

Record Weights (lb.oz.dr)

	Boat	Shore
Jersey	02.06.06	02.09.12
Guernsey	02.08.03	03.00.04

Pelagic

The Golden Grey Mullet is a smaller species than other mullets, usually growing to around half their size. It shares the same general habitat preferences as the Thick-lipped Mullet and is known from all the Channel Islands although, based on scientific surveys from the French coast, it is probably the least common of the three main mullet species found in the region. The Golden Grey Mullet has a consistent track record of reporting that goes back to the nineteenth century but may be under-recorded due to confusion with other species.

Thin-lipped Mullet

Chelon ramada

Ouothillard; Gris Mulet; Mulet Porc

Max Length: 60 cm

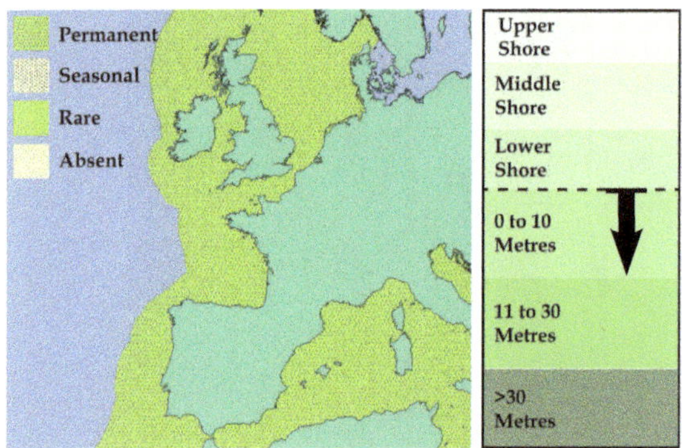

Record Weights (lb.oz.dr)

	Boat	Shore
Jersey	07.07.15	06.06.00
Guernsey	08.07.04*	08.04.01*

Pelagic

As with the other mullet species listed here, any records for the Thin-lipped Mullet, and especially historical ones, must be tempered by the difficulties associated with identifying mullet down to species level. That said, there are enough reliable records to think that the Thin-lipped Grey Mullet is common across all the islands both currently and in the past. It shares the same feeding and breeding preferences as the Thick-lipped and Golden Grey Mullet and so will be found in the same habitats. The Thin-lipped Grey Mullet may often be found feeding around sewage and hot water outfalls. The Bailiwick of Guernsey holds both the shore and boat caught British records for this species.

Daniel Ferguson with the Jersey shore record (6 lb 6 oz).

Flathead Mullet

Mugil cephalus

IUCN: LC

Max Length: 100 cm

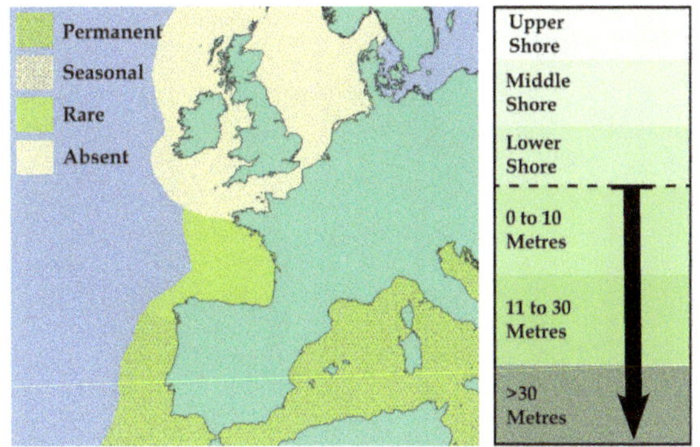

No Channel Island Rod Records

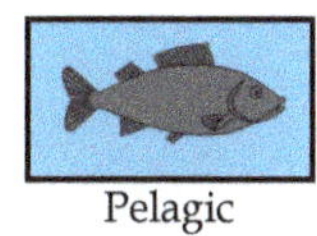

Pelagic

The Flathead Mullet is known from a single record made in the 1980s by students from Portsmouth Polytechnic who for several years made an annual field trip to Jersey. The Flathead Grey Mullet is a warm water species whose geographic range is usually said to terminate in the Bay of Biscay although there is one record from south-west England. It is not impossible that Flathead Grey Mullet have reached the Channel Islands but the absence of any independent evidence for the single Channel Islands' record, plus a lack of other local and regional records, makes it probable that the original report was a misidentification

Scale-rayed Wrasse

Acantholabrus palloni

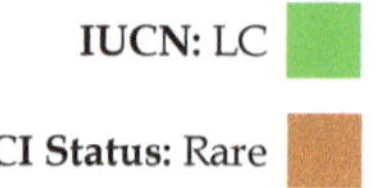

Max Length: 15 cm

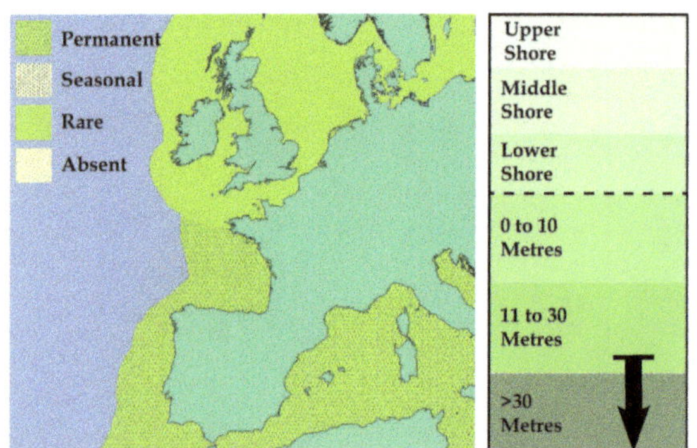

No Channel Island Rod Records

Rough Ground

The Scale-rayed Wrasse is not well-understood scientifically but it seems to prefer overhangs and caves in deeper water rocky areas that are generally out of reach of trawlers and below the range of recreational diving. It has a widespread distribution that runs from the North Sea to North Africa and the Mediterranean but has been little observed and has only rarely been seen in the UK. The lone Channel Island record comes from a scientific trawling expedition in 2012 when a specimen was taken to the north-east of Herm in about 50 metres of water, which roughly marks this species's upper depth limit. The Scale-rayed Wrasse's status in the Channel Islands is unknown but it may not be as rare as records imply although it will be restricted to the deeper, rockier regions within the islands' territorial waters.

Rock Cook

Centrolabrus exoletus

Co d'la Rocque; Co d'rotchi

Max Length: 15 cm

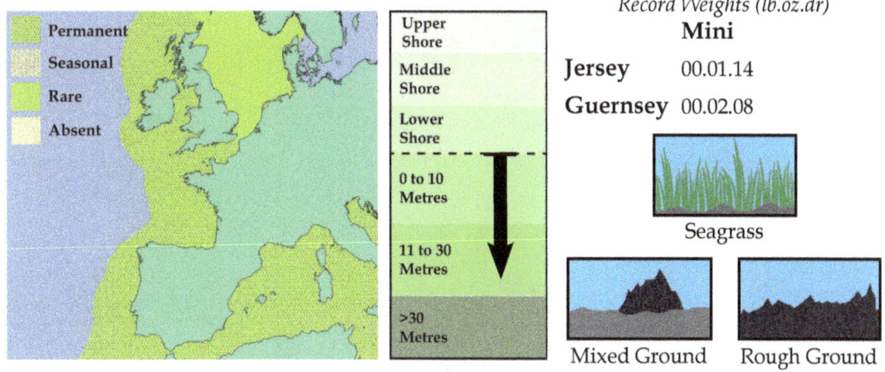

The Rock Cook is a common inshore fish around all the Channel Islands and has been recorded consistently since the 1860s. It is colourful and easy to spot on the edge of kelp patches and other dense seaweeds and is well-known to divers, from whom a majority of local records originate. This is a small wrasse species that rarely reaches weights over 80 grams and, during the spring and summer breeding season, has male fish that are more colourful than the females. This is a shallow water fish that rarely goes below 30 metres whose local population is healthy.

Comber Wrasse

IUCN: LC

CI Status: Unconfirmed

Coris julis

Rainbow Wrasse; *Verat*

Max Length: 30 cm

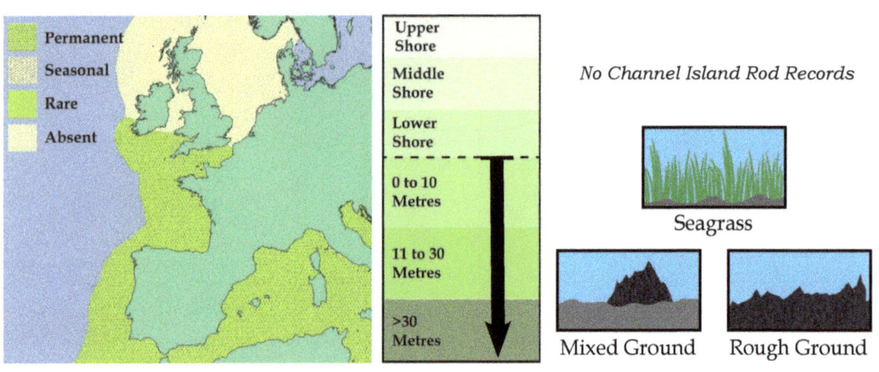

There is a single local reference to the Comber Wrasse when, in 1905, Joseph Sinel described it as being 'plentiful'. The Comber Wrasse is a southern European species that has rarely been reported from the English Channel and which has no other regional records. This makes it probable that Sinel was confusing the Comber Wrasse with another species and, indeed, he admits that there could be some confusion between the Comber and the more prevalent Cuckoo Wrasse. Without any confirmed reports this should be regarded as an unconfirmed Channel Island fish species although, with several specimens having been caught in Devon and Cornwall, there is no reason why it shouldn't occur in local waters. Recent scientific studies (which are contested by some) suggest that *Coris julis* may in fact be two seperate species with distinctive and non-overlapping ranges covering the Mediterranean Sea (*C. julis*) and Atlantic coastline (*C. festiva*).

Baillon's Wrasse

Symphodus bailloni

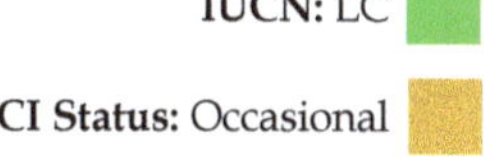

Max Length: 20 cm

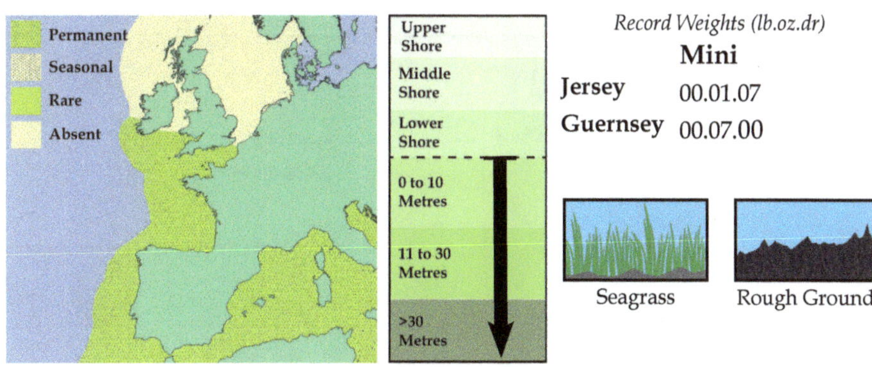

Record Weights (lb.oz.dr)

	Mini
Jersey	00.01.07
Guernsey	00.07.00

Although considered to be rare in UK waters, Baillon's Wrasse is being increasingly reported by Channel Island divers. The oldest records are from Jersey anglers during the late 1970s but by the mid-1980s it was being commonly reported both within the Channel Islands and on the adjacent French coast. More recently, males have been observed building nests off the Jersey coast, suggesting that the species is permanently resident. CEFAS trawl surveys between 2006 and 2018 have produced many specimens, mostly from shallow seabed areas around Jersey.

Baillon's Wrasse is primarily a southern European fish but, as with many other species, its range seems to have recently expanded northwards into the English Channel. This is primarily an inshore fish with a preference for seaweed cover and seagrass so it is well within the range of recreational divers. It could be confused with the larger Corkwing Wrasse and so may be under recorded. Any sightings should be reported to a local records centre.

Corkwing Wrasse

Symphodus melops

Chânaise; Trie; Pêtot

Max Length: 15 cm

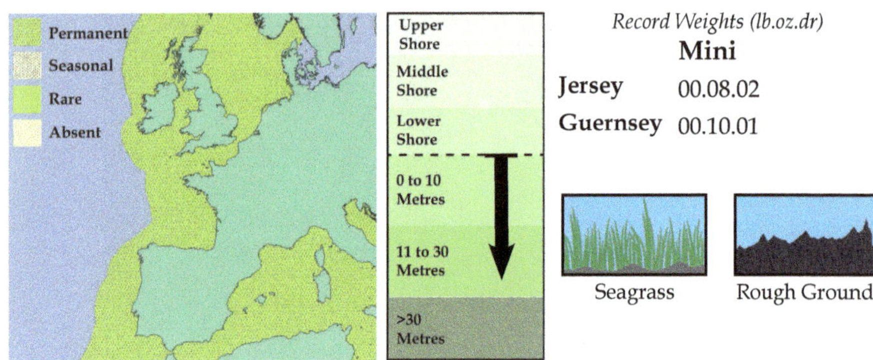

Record Weights (lb.oz.dr)

	Mini
Jersey	00.08.02
Guernsey	00.10.01

The Corkwing is a small species of wrasse that likes shallow water areas with seaweed cover. It is very frequently encountered by snorkelers and divers or, more rarely, may become trapped in rock pools at low water. The oldest local records are mid-Victorian when it was described as being 'very common' and this remains the case across the whole of the Channel Islands. This is a fish with a wide geographical distribution whose size, low key colours and abundance means it will often be ignored by divers. As with other wrasse species, the male builds and guards nests in the spring and summer. The males also have a terminal phase in which the body darkens to a reddish-brown and the face develops blue lines.

Grey Wrasse

Symphodus cinereus

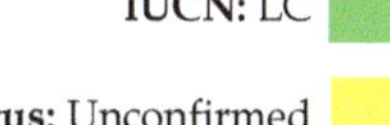

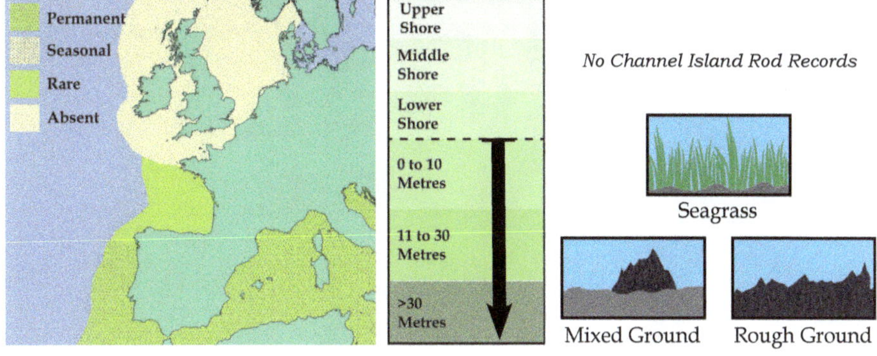

The Grey Wrasse is a Mediterranean species whose Atlantic range covers the Iberian Peninsula and the southern part of Bay of Biscay. The lone Channel Island record comes from a summary list of fish species compiled by local naturalists in 1862. There are no other regional records and it is probable that this single record represents a mistake or misidentification. The Grey Wrasse is unlikely to be found in the English Channel although, with so many other similar fish expanding their geographic ranges, it should not be ruled out for future decades.

Ballan Wrasse

IUCN: LC

CI Status: Common

Labrus bergylta

Cornelle; Pèrlé; Pielé; Êpîle; Vra; Couotheux [large]

Max Length: 66 cm

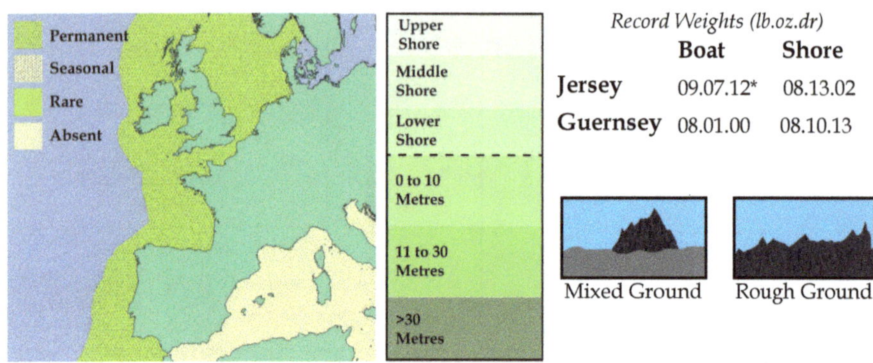

Record Weights (lb.oz.dr)

	Boat	Shore
Jersey	09.07.12*	08.13.02
Guernsey	08.01.00	08.10.13

The Ballan is the wrasse most frequently caught by anglers (sometimes as bycatch) and the one most often reported by divers. The juveniles live close inshore and may be found in rock pools while the adults will sometimes become trapped in lobster pots. Although rarely eaten, Ballan Wrasse are taken for use as bait and commercial catches have increased from virtually nothing to several tonnes a year during the past decade. There is also an emerging commercial fishery for live Ballan Wrasse as these are used by fish farms to eat the lice that often infest these facilities. In the UK this has led to a decline in local Ballan Wrasse populations and, with the species becoming scarce in some areas, there has been interest in exploiting Channel Island waters. Some angling associations advocate protecting the largest Ballan Wrasse specimens from capture/killing as they may be over 20 years old and play a disproportionately important role in the species' breeding cycle. Anglers are encouraged to return the fish live whenever possible.

Cuckoo Wrasse

IUCN: LC

CI Status: Frequent

Labrus mixtus

Green/Striped Wrasse; *Coucou; Râbi; Dèmouoûselle; Chânaise*

Max Length: 35 cm

Male

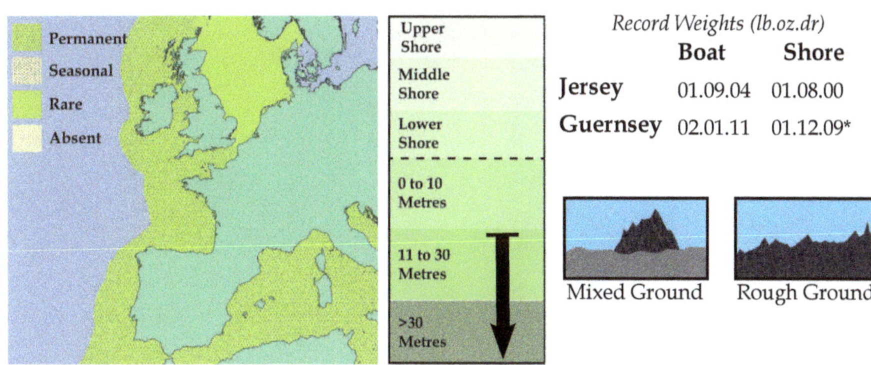

Record Weights (lb.oz.dr)

	Boat	Shore
Jersey	01.09.04	01.08.00
Guernsey	02.01.11	01.12.09*

The Cuckoo Wrasse is a colourful and distinctive medium-sized fish that is rarely seen in shallow waters but is caught by anglers, usually unintentionally. It has been consistently reported as common within the Channel Islands since the 1860s and is most frequently encountered in deeper water rocky areas where the brilliantly coloured adult males with their bright blue heads are easy to spot by divers. This is one of a handful of British fish to have a drastic colour difference between the male and female (see below). Cuckoo Wrasse are believed to be territorial and faithful to particular breeding grounds. These characteristics have made other fish species vulnerable to overfishing although there is no evidence of this for the Cuckoo Wrasse as local populations are believed to be healthy.

The female Cuckoo Wrasse.

Goldsinny Wrasse

Ctenolabrus rupestris

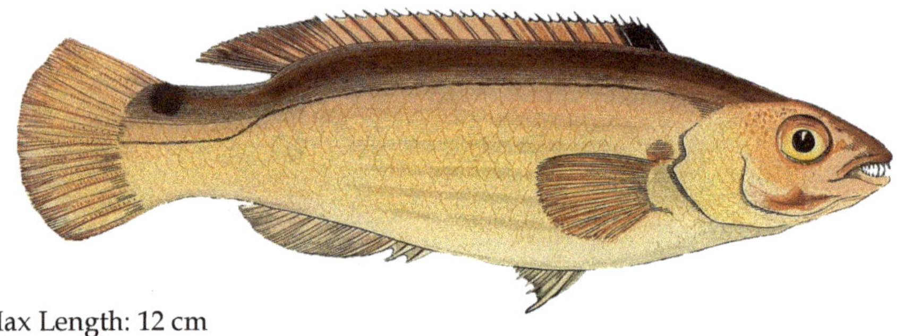

Max Length: 12 cm

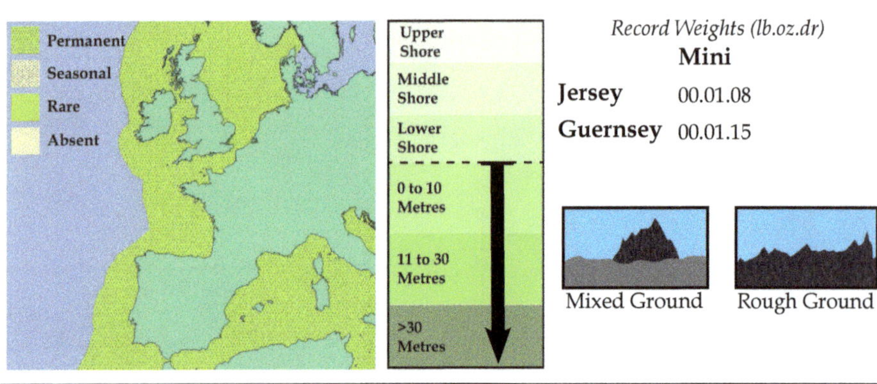

The Goldsinny is a small but distinctive species of wrasse that is common in shallow coastal areas across the Channel Islands. The diver-based biological recording scheme organised by Seasearch has provided dozens of Goldsinny reports since the 1990s, making this one of their most commonly recorded fish. However, this wrasse does not have much of an historical track record with the oldest known report being in 1897 on the adjacent French coast when it was said to be rare. The first Channel Islands' record was not until the 1970s which seems unusual and, being common around the rest of the UK, suggests that the Goldsinny may have been consistently misidentified for other wrasse species. This may explain its absence from Joseph Sinel's 1905 Channel Islands' fish list where he appears to have confused several local wrasse species, possibly because at the end of the Victorian era some wrasse species had been given multiple, similar sounding scientific names. Although its historical status may be uncertain, the Goldsinny is currently common around all the Channel Islands.

Weever Fish and Blennies

The weever fish family (Trachinidae) has just two local species, both of which are venomous. Weever fish are distinctive and will often be caught when feathering for sandeels or mackerel over sandbanks. The Greater Weever is far less often reported than the Lesser Weever as it lives in deeper water.

Blenny species belong to a single family (Blenniidae) and are probably under-recorded in the Channel Islands as they are small, difficult to identify and generally live subtidally. Blennies are rarely targeted by recreational or commercial fisheries but will be taken as bycatch, especially in nets and trawls. Some species of blenny are photogenic and will therefore attract the attention of divers, especially those with underwater cameras. An increasing amount of information is being obtained via this route including a possible first British report of the Ringneck Blenny in Jersey waters.

As with a couple of other under-reported families (such as the gobies and sandeels), the Channel Island blenny population would benefit from a systematic study to determine which species are here, how common they are and where they live. Given that most species are subtidal, this is no easy feat.

There are several species of southern European blenny whose range currently terminates in the Bay of Biscay but which could, like the Ringneck Blenny, start to be found locally. This includes the Red Blenny (*Parablennius ruber*), Tentacled Blenny (*P. tentacularis*), Diablo Blenny (*P. incognitus*) and Gurnard Blenny (*Lipophrys trigloides*). These are coastal, mostly shallow water species which will probably first be seen or photographed by scuba divers. A historical report for the Horned Blenny (*Parablennius cornutus*), a tropical species, must be erroneous.

Weever Fish Stings

Both local species of weever fish are venomous and can deliver a painful toxin through their dorsal spines. The Greater Weever does not stray into shallow water but can present a problem to anglers. The Lesser Weever is also caught by anglers but can also be found in shallow water where it will half bury itself in loose sand. It is particularly common at low tide just off exposed beaches with a strong wave and current action. The toxin is painful (one of this book's authors has experienced it) but it will chemically break down with heat so anyone treading on a weever fish should bathe the wound in warm water and, if necessary, consider seeking medical attention.

Lesser Weever

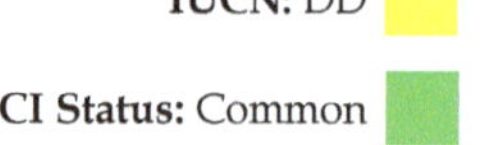

Echiichthys vipera

Vithelîn; Viselun

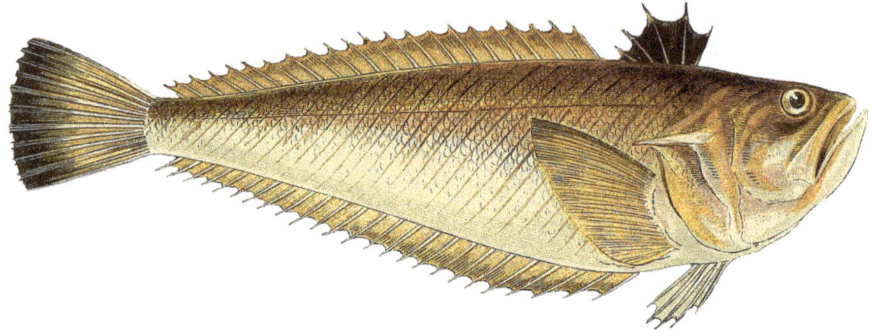

Max Length: 15 cm

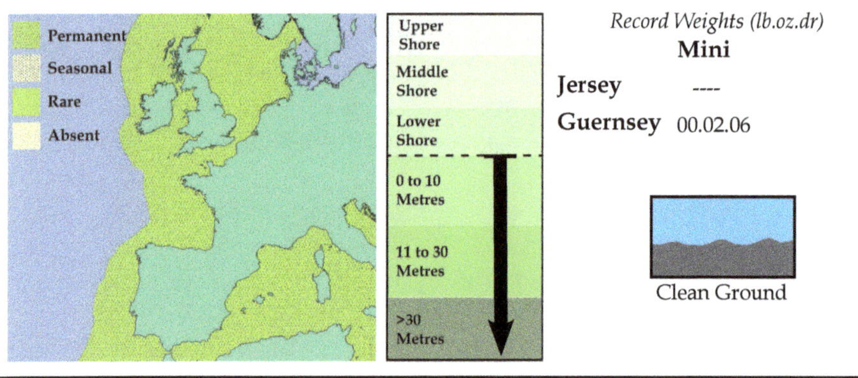

The Lesser Weever is a common species across the Channel Islands. It is most often encountered by anglers fishing for sand-eels or mackerel and, more notoriously, by unlucky bathers (see page 193). This fish is fond of coarse sand seabeds in high energy areas and may come into very shallow waters, especially during the summer months. Local records start in the 1840s and suggest that they may have been less common around the islands at this time as it was considered to only be found rare around Jersey at the turn of the twentieth century.

In 2009 a Lesser Weever was caught in Les Minquiers which had a large parasitic isopod (*Ceratothoa steindachnerii*) in its mouth. The isopod (which looks like a large woodlouse) had eaten away the fish's tongue and was sitting in its mouth, stealing its food. The isopod is southern European and had only entered the English Channel a few years previously. It would be interesting to have more reports about this isopod but great care is needed when checking inside the mouth of a weever fish.

Greater Weever

Trachinus draco

Sting Fish; Zebra Fish; *Zèbre*

Max Length: 40 cm

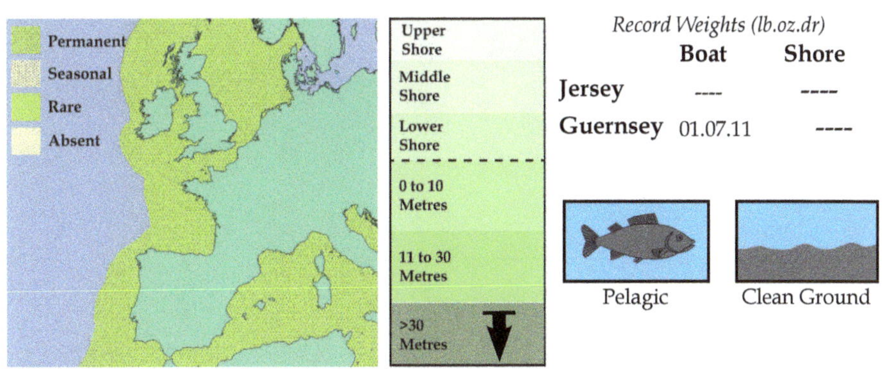

Record Weights (lb.oz.dr)

	Boat	Shore
Jersey	----	----
Guernsey	01.07.11	----

The larger and rarer of the two local species, the Greater Weever tends to be a deeper water fish that is rarely reported. The oldest records are Victorian when it was described as being uncommon across the Channel Islands and usually encountered when fishing for mackerel with feathers. There are virtually no records at all from the twentieth century and just two confirmed recent ones, both from 2007, when specimens were caught off Herm and Alderney. The paucity of records probably reflects the offshore nature of the Greater Weever and its status as a nuisance species to recreational and commercial fishers rather than its rarity in local waters. Its preferred habitats are soft sediment seabeds in offshore areas below about 30 metres. This probably makes it a species that will be more commonly found in the deeper waters to the north and west of the islands than the shallower seabed areas around Jersey.

Butterfly Blenny

Blennius ocellaris

Max Length: 20 cm

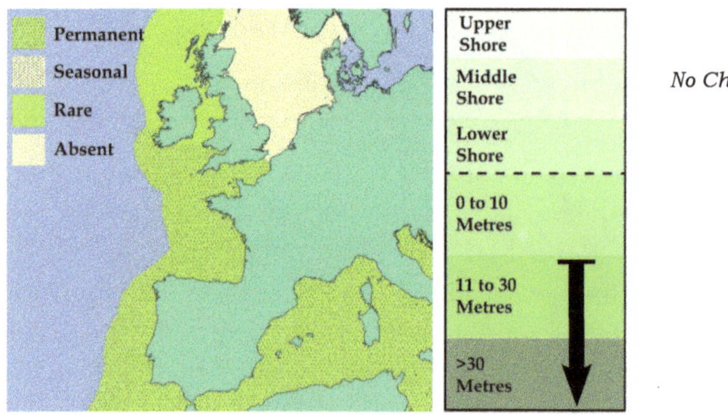

No Channel Island Rod Records

Clean Ground

The Butterfly Blenny was listed as being occasionally found off Guernsey in 1880 but records since have been sparse. The English Channel is at the northerly edge of the Butterfly Blenny's geographic range but, as an offshore, soft sediment species which is unlikely to be caught by anglers, it is probably more common locally than records suggest. This is borne out by scientific trawling studies between 2006 and 2018 which produced more than a dozen Channel Island specimens, all from deeper water areas. More local information about this species would be welcome and reports should be made to local records centres.

Montagu's Blenny

Coryphoblennius galerita

Max Length: 9 cm

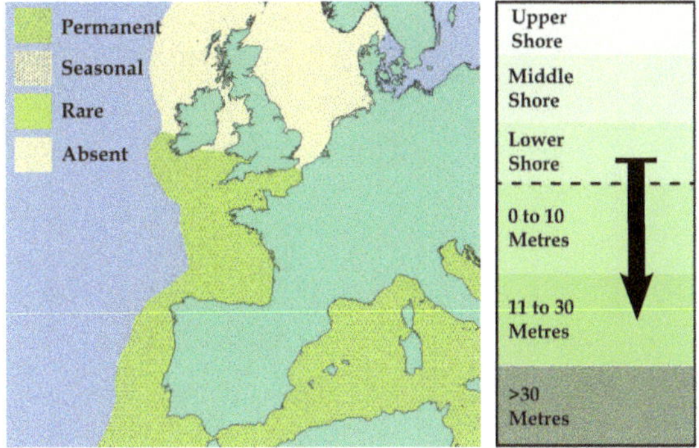

No Channel Island Rod Records

Rough Ground

Montagu's Blenny is a predominantly southern European species that lives in the shallow subtidal but which may also be found in lower shore rock pools. It has been seen in many parts of the UK but does not seem to have been widely recorded in either the Channel Islands or the adjacent coast of France. The first local record, for example, was not until 1961 in Jersey with subsequent reports being scarce. This may be because it is easy to confuse Montagu's Blenny with the Shanny both of which share the same habitat preference. Unlike the Shanny, this species has a distinctive singular tentacle of skin on its head that can be seen if you run your finger gently from the neck to the front of the fish.

Recent surveys by Seasearch and others suggest that Montagu's Blenny is probably more common than records suggest with specimens being sighted in Guernsey and off south-west Jersey. Additional reports are needed to establish its local distribution and abundance and any sightings should be made to a local records centre.

Shanny

Lipophrys pholis

Smooth Blenny; *Cabot*

Max Length: 6 cm

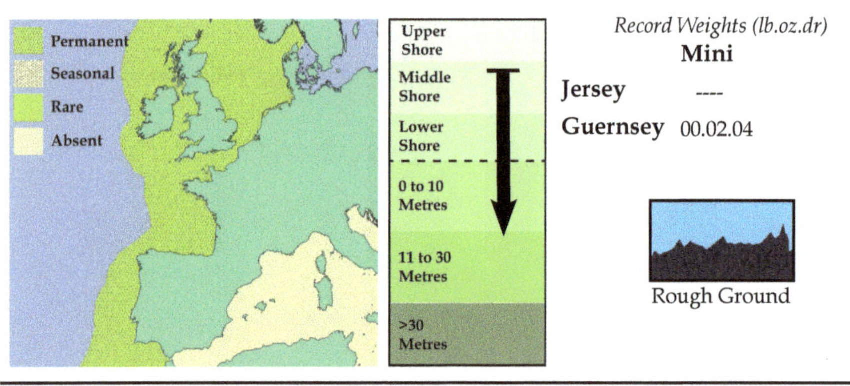

Record Weights (lb.oz.dr)

	Mini
Jersey	----
Guernsey	00.02.04

The Shanny is a distinctive fish that may be found at almost all tidal heights on rocky shores where it lives in rock pools and under stones. It is the most commonly encountered and reported seashore fish and it is not unusual for beachcombers to find two or more specimens sheltering under the same rock. During low water Shannies living on the middle and upper shore must be able to survive out of water for several hours making this one of the hardiest local fish species. Although Shannies may be seen in the shallow subtidal, the seashore seems to be where they are most often reported with records suggesting that they are abundant across all the Channel Islands. The fish is frequently picked up by adults and children but be careful if handling as they have been known to bite. The Shanny is the only European species of Blenny not to have a tentacle of skin on its head, something that helps to distinguish it from other local blenny species.

Tompot Blenny

Parablennius gattorugine

Crested Blenny; *Rouoges Cabot; Co Journieaux*

Max Length: 30 cm

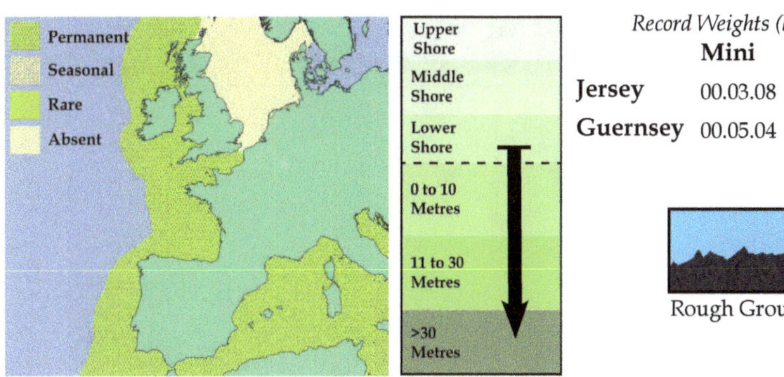

Record Weights (lb.oz.dr)

	Mini
Jersey	00.03.08
Guernsey	00.05.04

Rough Ground

The Tompot Blenny is a large and beautiful species that is popular with underwater photographers because of its habit of resting perfectly still in crevices and holes with its head protruding in a quizzical fashion. There are records from all the Channel Islands dating back to mid-Victorian times and it has been consistently described as being common or even abundant along rocky shores. Although most records are from the shallow marine, Tompot Blennies (including large adults) may sometimes be found on the extreme lower shore sheltering amongst loose rocks and boulders. Although predominantly southern European in its distribution, the Tompot Blenny's range is expanding steadily into the North and Irish Seas. Like most blennies, the Tompot is not a target species for either recreational or commercial fishers and its local population is thought to be healthy. This is one of the largest local Blenny species and it can grow up to 30 cm in length.

Ringneck Blenny

Parablennius pilicornis

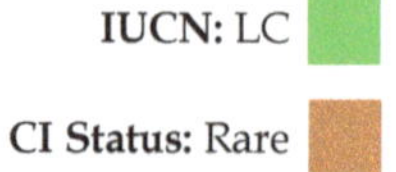

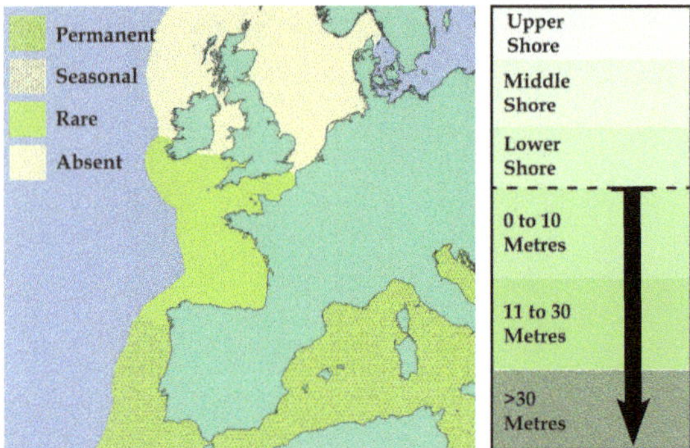

No Channel Island Rod Records

Rough Ground

The Ringneck Blenny is a warm water species whose traditional geographic range terminates in the Bay of Biscay. However, it has been moving northwards and has been on the English Channel fish watchlist for several years. In July 2017 Jersey Seasearch diver Kevin McIlwee photographed a Ringneck Blenny on a shipwreck located to the south-west of Jersey (see photo above) producing what might be the first confirmed British record for this species. The wreck sits in about 40 metres of water, which is below the species' reported maximum depth range of 25 metres. It is a distinctive, medium-sized blenny that could start to turn up in photographs taken by divers and snorkelers.

The Ringneck Blenny is probably a very recent arrival in the Channel Islands and more records are needed. Divers should also look for the Red Tompot Blenny (*Parablennius ruber*) which is expected to move north into the English Channel in the near future.

Black-faced Blenny

Tripterygion delaisi

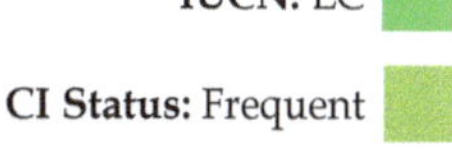

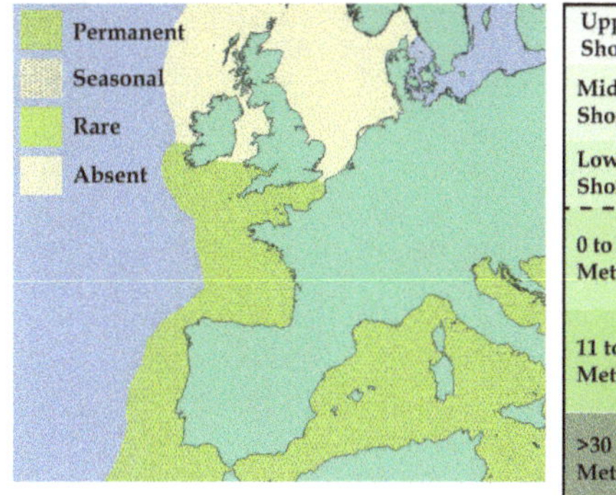

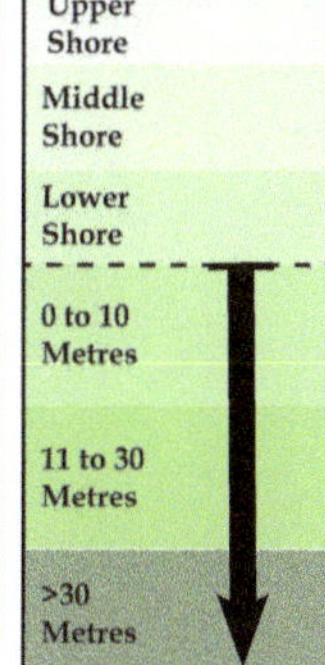

No Channel Island Rod Records

Rough Ground

It is the breeding male of the Black-faced Blenny that has a distinctive black head and bright orange (sometimes yellow) body. Females and non-breeding males are less colourful and difficult to spot but may be identified by their three dorsal fins which gives rise to their alternative name of 'triplefin'. This is a shallow marine species that likes rocky habitats and seaweed. Historical records begin in the 1960s and for a time the Channel Islands was the only British location where the Black-faced Blenny could be seen by divers. However, in the past two decades this fish has started to turn up along the south-west coast of England which suggests that it is a relatively recent arrival in the English Channel.

The Black-faced Blenny is common around the Channel Islands and has been seen in a variety of shallow marine environments between 5 and 40 metres including shipwrecks and in the marinas at St Peter Port, Guernsey. Some specimens, such as the female illustrated above, have been found in intertidal rock pools.

Red Black-faced Triplefin

Tripterygion tripteronotum

IUCN: LC

CI Status: Unconfirmed

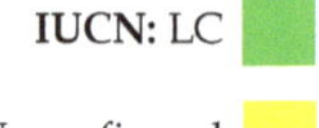

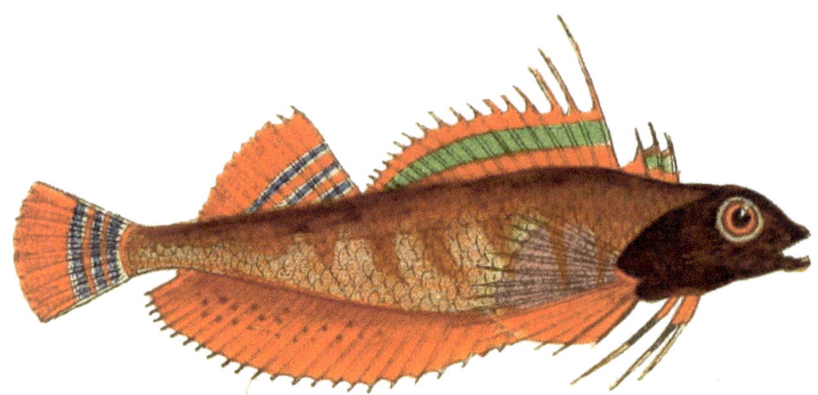

Max Length: 8 cm

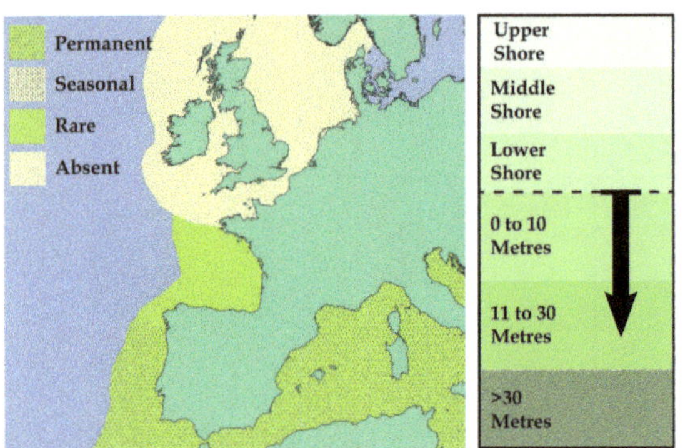

No Channel Island Rod Records

Rough Ground

The Red Black-faced Triplefin is a small southern European fish whose range normally terminates hundreds of kilometres to the south of the Channel Islands. The single local record comes from a sighting by a snorkeler off Portinfer, Guernsey, in July 1981. However, there is a strong similarity between the Red-black Triplefin and the Black-faced Blenny both of which have the distinctive three dorsal fin arrangement along their back and black-faced breeding males. This is a highly unlikely species for the region and the lone record is probably a misidentification.

Atlantic Wolf-fish

Anarhichas lupus

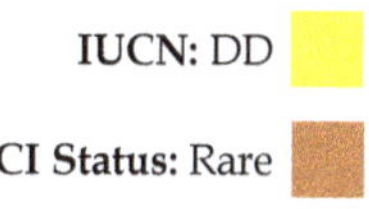

Max Length: 150 cm

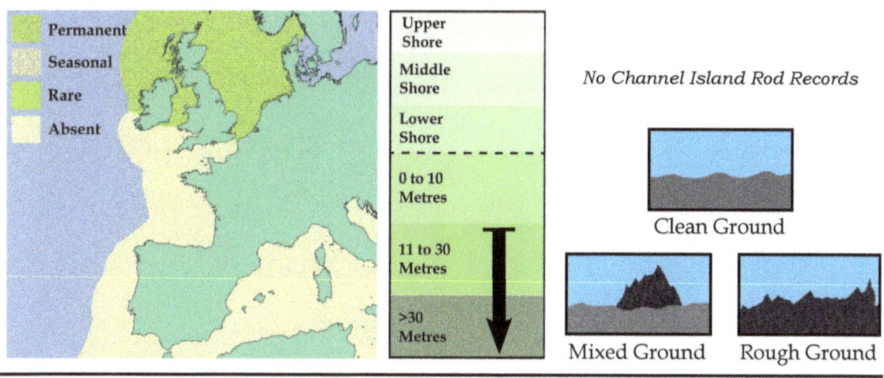

The Atlantic Wolf-fish is the largest and most spectacular looking of the northern European Blennies. It can reach a length of 1.5 metres and has an eel-like shape, powerful body and a mouth that is full of sharp teeth. Its distinctive head has featured in the photographs of many divers but, as a sub-Arctic species, the Atlantic Wolf-fish is unlikely to be seen in Channel Island waters. The lone local record comes from a specimen taken off Corbière Point, Jersey, around the turn of the twentieth century. This was examined and identified by biologist Joseph Sinel who, even then, expressed surprise at it turning up in local waters. There are Victorian reports of Wolf-fish from Cornwall, Wales and north Brittany but recent records are from more northerly locations. With colder Victorian sea temperatures, the Wolf-fish may historically have strayed into the English Channel but, if so, its range has probably since contracted considerably northwards.

Yarrell's Blenny

Chirolophis ascanii

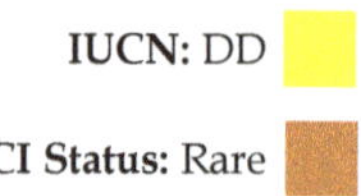

Male

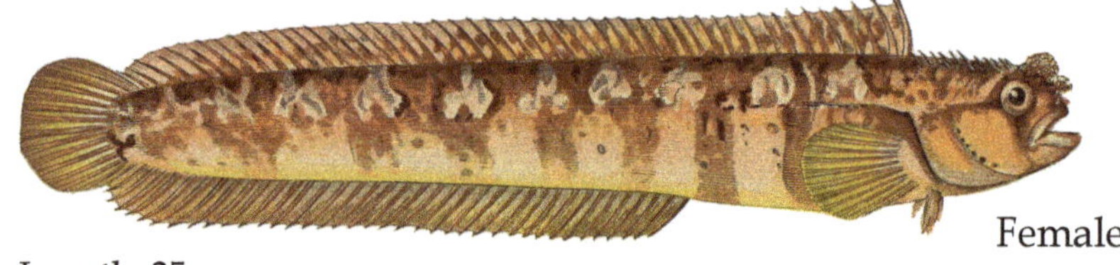
Female

Max Length: 25 cm

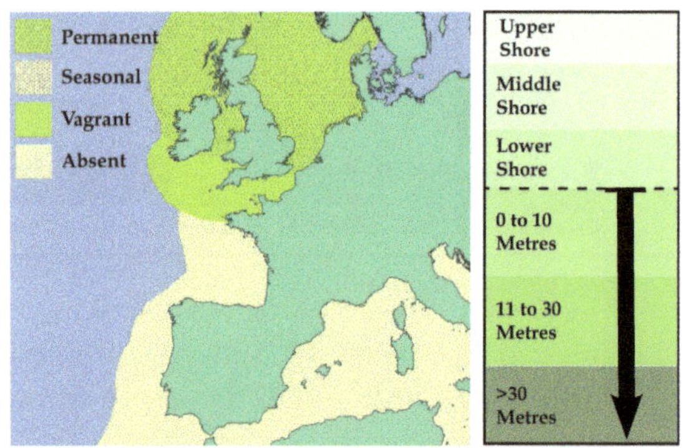

No Channel Island Rod Records

Rough Ground

This is an eel-like fish belonging to the prickleback family (Stichaeidae) that has just a handful of local records with the oldest being by Joseph Sinel who noted in his 1904 discourse on Jersey fish that 'Yarrell's Blenny is also found here'. A 2003 specimen was identified by local ichthyologist Richard Lord who was told by lobster fishers that Yarrell's Blenny is often caught in pots during the autumn months. The other reports are from scientific trawl surveys north of Alderney in 2011 and north of Guernsey in 2012.

Yarrell's Blenny is a northern species that has rarely been recorded outside of Scotland and which only seems to have been found in deep waters off Guernsey. This may explain the lack of historical records for what is probably a seasonal vagrant in Channel Island waters.

Viviparous Blenny

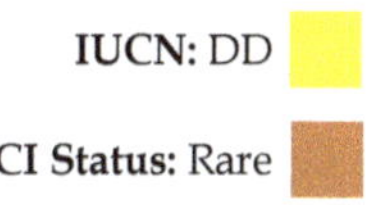

Zoarces viviparus

Viviparous Eelpout; European Eelpout

Max Length: 52 cm

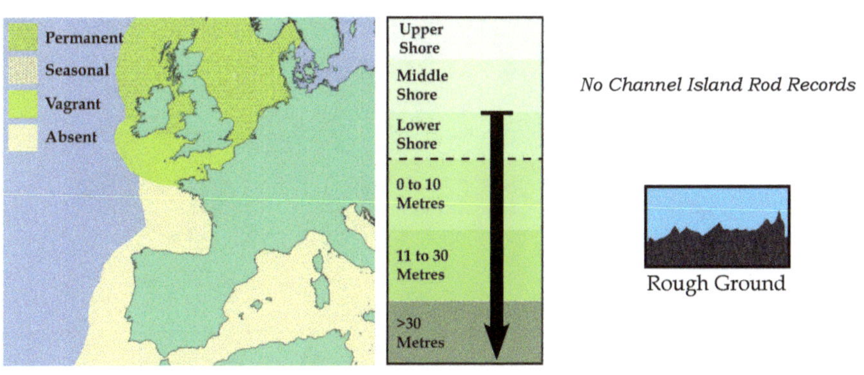

The Viviparous Blenny is a colder water species whose southerly range terminates in the western English Channel and which is large when compared to other blennies. It frequents shallow water and is notable for giving live birth to its young. The only Channel Island records come from a list of fishes made in 1862 and a 2010 scientific trawl survey made about a kilometre west of the Guernsey/France sea border (i.e. just outside Channel Islands waters). Beyond these sightings, it has not been recorded at all from the wider Bay of Granville region. The Viviparous Blenny resembles the Butterfish and could be confused with it but this is probably a rare species locally and so it is unlikely to be encountered. Any captures or sightings should be reported to a local records centre.

Butterfish

Pholis gunnellus

Gunnel; Nine-eyes; *Douoche; Tchilieuvre d'mé*

Max Length: 25 cm

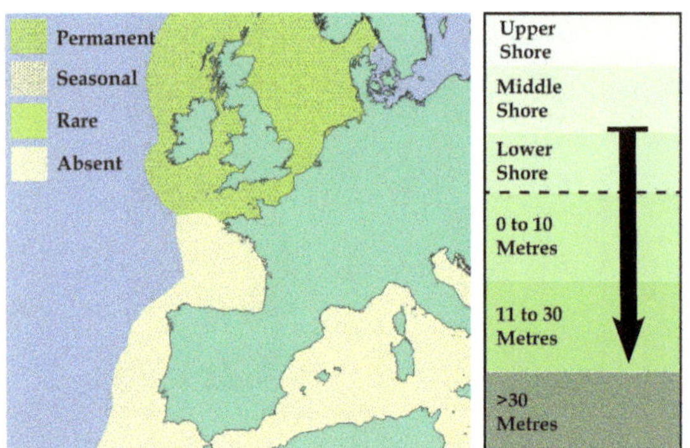

No Channel Island Rod Records

Rough Ground

Wriggly and slippery to hold (hence the common name), the Butterfish is a distinctive fish that can be identified by the black spots running down its dorsal fin. This species may be found on rocky shores and in shallow marine environments across all the Channel Islands. It was regarded as common in the nineteenth century and for most of the twentieth but survey work and anecdotal reports from the 1980s onwards suggest that its seashore population may have declined considerably. If so, then this could be a consequence of the Butterfish's preference for colder water which could mean that the population range is retracting northwards as local sea temperatures rise. Careful searching among loose stones can still produce specimens but the Butterfish may be a species that is becoming rarer and which could be used as an indicator of climate change.

Sandeels and Dragonets

The Ammodytidae (sandeels) and Callionymidae (dragonets) are two distinctive families of perciforme fish that contain similar-looking species. Both families are understudied in Channel Island waters, especially the sandeels, as some species are so similar that expertise is required to secure an identification. Given that there have been changes in sandeel populations elsewhere in Europe, a targeted research project into the taxonomy and abundance of local species would be welcome. Sandeels were once an important local food source but they are now mostly caught for use as bait although small quantities are landed commercially each year. Overfishing has reduced sandeel populations elsewhere in Europe and there is anecdotal evidence of a reduction locally. Given their importance to feeding seabirds, this is concerning.

Dragonets are easier to identify but only one species (Reticulated Dragonet) is likely to be commonly encountered by divers and snorkelers as the others prefer deeper water. Dragonets have little recreational or commercial value but will occasionally be taken as bycatch.

Mass Sandeel Strandings

Occasionally large numbers of sandeels will wash up dead on Channel Island beaches. These stranding events usually occur in the summer months and affect either juveniles or smaller species such as the Lesser Sandeel. Hundreds of specimens may be found along wide stretches of coast, a phenomenon that delights local seabirds but which often raises concerns of environmental pollution in the local media.

Several such events occurred during the summer of 2018 when large numbers of sandeels washed up along the north and east coasts of Jersey and Les Écréhous. Beyond being dead, the sandeels were found to be generally healthy and the initial cause was thought to be a lightning strike as the first event followed a thunderstorm. However, smaller strandings later in the year suggested that the sandeels may have died of heat/suffocation after becoming trapped in intertidal sandbanks during hot weather. This explains why only smaller sandeels were dying (larger ones live offshore) and why the strandings were concentrated in areas with sandy beaches/sandbanks during heatwaves.

Sandeels stranded at Les Écréhous, Jersey, June 2018.

Raitt's Sandeel

Ammodytes marinus

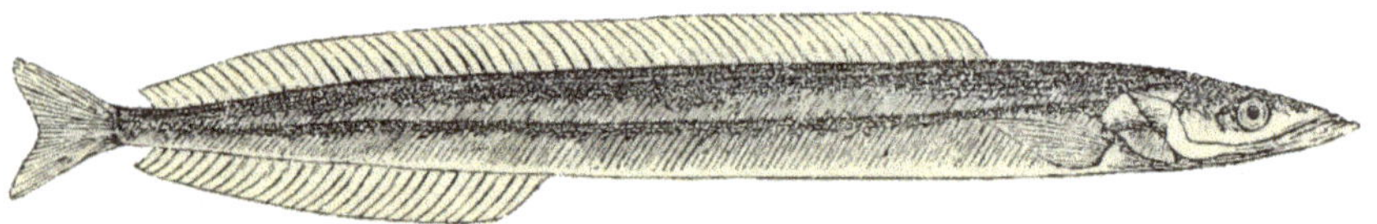

Max Length: 25 cm

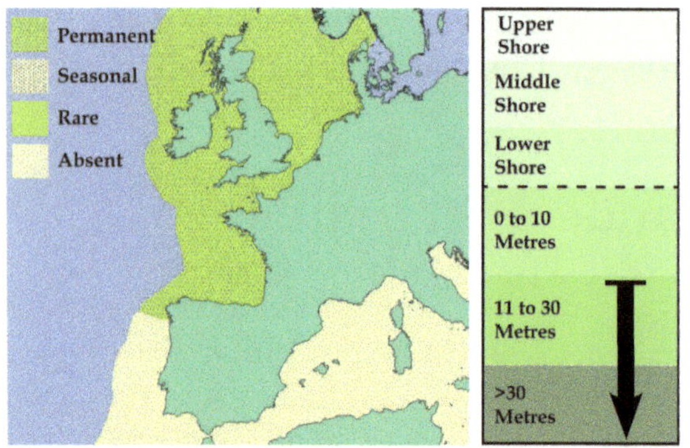

No Channel Island Rod Records

Clean Ground

Raitt's Sandeel is the least recorded of the sandeel species across the Channel Islands with only a handful of recent records. This, however, is probably not a reflection of its rarity but of the difficulties associated with obtaining a positive identification. The differences between Raitt's Sandeel and the other two smaller species comes down to the position and pattern of tail and belly scales. The easiest means of identifying Raitt's Sandeel is by looking at the tail which has no scales on it whereas that of the Lesser Sandeel will have. This requires a dead specimen, a hand lens and specialist knowledge; hence the lack of records. Raitt's Sandeel is a deeper water species that is unlikely to be seen or caught in shallow water or close to shore. All the Channel Island records are from Jersey within the last decade but it is probably not uncommon across the islands.

Lesser Sandeel

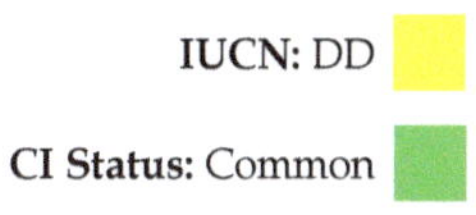

Ammodytes tobianus

Rouoge Lanchon; P'tit Lanchon

Max Length: 20 cm

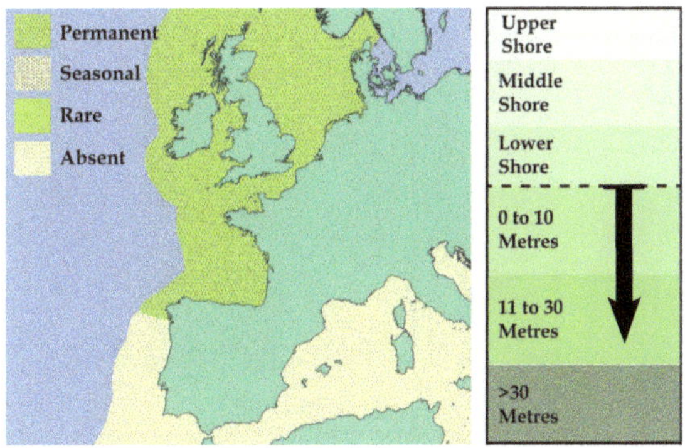

No Channel Island Rod Records

Most small sandeels are recorded as *Ammodytes tobianus* although a firm identification actually requires close examination with a hand lens or microscope (see page 208). Nonetheless, reports of the Lesser Sandeel dominate the biological records back into the early nineteenth century and it is this species that was said to form the abundant shoals found on sandbanks and reefs across the Bay of Granville. Densities of 32 fish per square metre were recorded in the 1980s and for many years there was a healthy commercial sandeel fishery based around the St Malo and Mont St Michel areas.

The Lesser Sandeel has been heavily exploited across Europe through midwater and beam trawling and, although this has been less of an issue in Channel Island waters, the local status of this (and other smaller) sandeel species is not fully understood. However, anecdotal information suggests that historically prime coastal sandeel fishing areas now have fewer fish in them. Intertidal sandbanks around Jersey (such as the appropriately named La Laconnière near La Rocque) were once regularly raked by low water fishers for sandeels but the practice has been all but abandoned in recent decades with a lack of fish being the most commonly cited reason.

Smooth Sandeel

Gymnammodytes semisquamatus

IUCN: LC 

CI Status: Common 

Max Length: 28 cm 

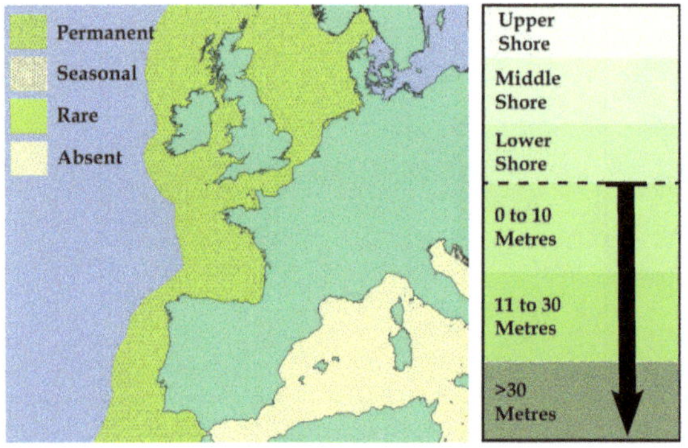

No Channel Island Rod Records

Clean Ground

The Smooth Sandeel is possibly synonymous with the *Touche* of the nineteenth century which, according to local naturalists, was 'a third species of sandeel' that local anglers could distinguish from the Lesser and Greater species. To modern ichthyologists the distinguishing characteristic is a lack of scales on the rear part of the body and an undulating dorsal fin. This fine distinction means that the only regional records have come from targeted scientific studies. Indeed, there are just three Channel Island reports all of which are from Jersey in the 1940s and 50s when the amateur marine biologist Ronald le Sueur was actively surveying inshore fish species. Studies from the adjacent French coast, and especially the Bay of Mont St Michel, suggest that this is a regionally common species and that, contrary to its sparse track record, the Smooth Sandeel is probably not uncommon across all the Channel Islands.

Corbin's Sandeel

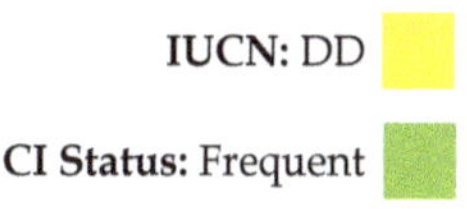

Hyperoplus immaculatus

Rouoge Lanchon; P'tit Lanchon

Max Length: 35 cm

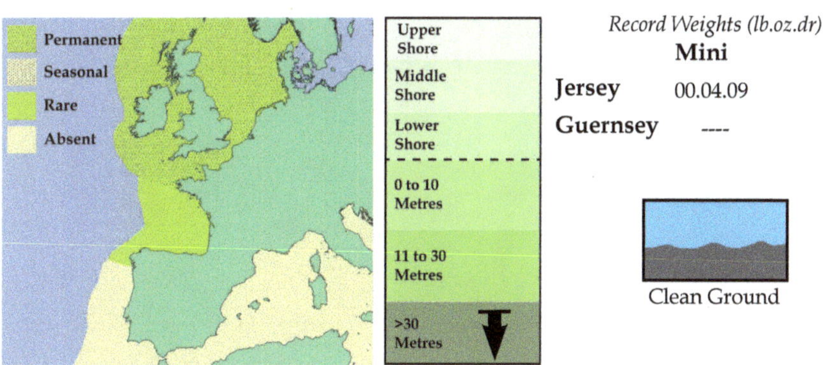

Corbin's Sandeel and the Greater Sandeel are nearly identical in size and may only be distinguished from one another by the length of their pectoral fins (Corbin's is longer) and the presence of a dark patch on the snout of the Greater Sandeel. The difference between the species was only discovered in 1950 and so regional records are rare but a specimen was caught north-west of Jersey in 1978 and several records are known from the Bay of Mont St Michel. Although sometimes listed as an offshore deeper water species, the Jersey and French records were all from relatively shallow coastal waters. Corbin's Sandeel is almost certainly under recorded and is probably widespread across the Channel Islands.

Greater Sandeel

Hyperoplus lanceolatus

Launce; *Vèrt Lanchon*

Max Length: 35 cm

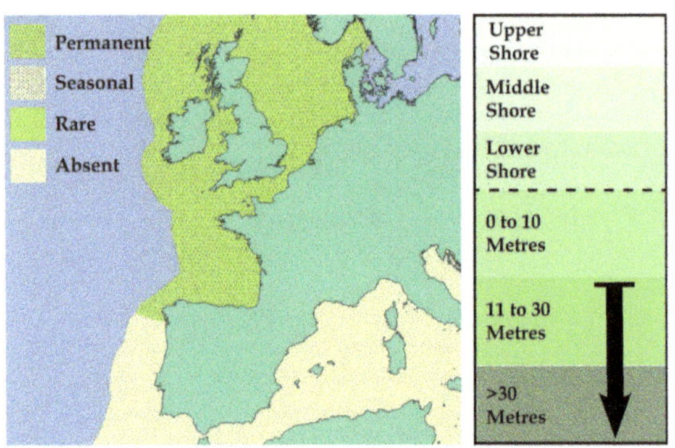

Record Weights (lb.oz.dr)

	Mini
Jersey	00.07.14
Guernsey	00.08.07

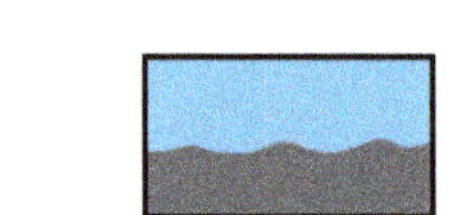

Clean Ground

Better known to most anglers as the Launce, the Greater Sandeel was historically widely eaten across the Channel Islands and is one of the few fish species to have been mentioned in local medieval records. Easily distinguished from smaller sandeel species by its size, the Greater Sandeel is nonetheless difficult to tell apart from Corbin's Sandeel (*q.v.*). Often seen by divers and snorkelers over coarse sand and gravel, Greater Sandeels can be found around all the islands and may be particularly common across offshore sandbanks and reefs. It was described as abundant in the nineteenth and twentieth centuries but may have declined locally since, as have populations elsewhere in Europe. It is, however, still commonly seen and, as with other sandeel species, is an important food source for birds and larger predatory fish such as Bass and Pollack.

Common Dragonet

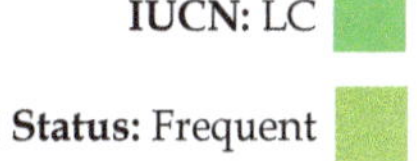

Callionymus lyra

Yellow Sculpin; *Cabot Volant*

Max Length: 30 cm

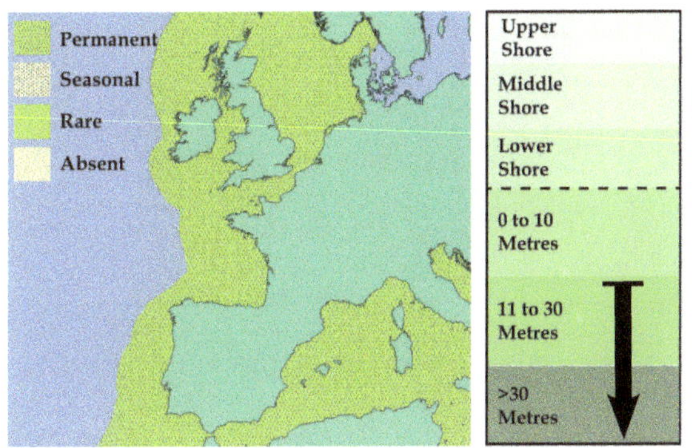

Record Weights (lb.oz.dr)

	Mini
Jersey	00.03.10
Guernsey	00.04.02

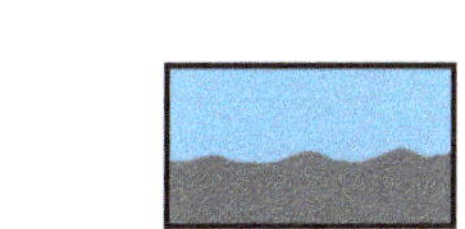

Clean Ground

Distinguishable from other dragonet species by its tall dorsal fin (which can be very tall in males), the Common Dragonet is the second least reported of the three species known from the Channel Islands. Local sightings come from Jersey, Guernsey, Alderney and Sark, usually by divers in seagrass, sand or maerl habitats. Historically it was said to be rare locally but by the late twentieth century it was being listed as common and scientific trawling between 2006 and 2018 produced a number of specimens from across the islands. This suggests it may be inhabiting deeper waters beyond the range of most divers. Whether the increase in recent reports represents an expanding population is not known but the Common Dragonet is said to be abundant off some parts of Brittany and is probably common around the Channel Islands.

Reticulated Dragonet

Callionymus reticulatus

IUCN: LC

CI Status: Common

Max Length: 11 cm

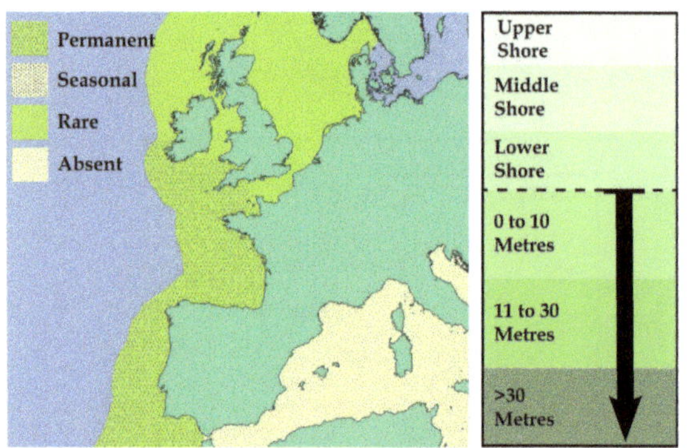

No Channel Island Rod Records

Clean Ground

Observing Reticulated Dragonets skip slowly across the seabed is a treat for many divers. They are common on muddy or gravelly sediments where their distinctive camouflage pattern allows them to blend into the seabed. Despite being common and readily observable there are almost no regional records prior to the 1970s and reports have only become regular during the past 20 years. The Reticulated Dragonet does not feature in the classic Channel Island and regional French fish lists of the nineteenth and mid-twentieth centuries. This suggests that it may be a recent arrival in the region, something that is supported by it being a predominantly southern European species that, while common in the Channel Islands, becomes increasingly rare further north. This is an attractive fish that often remains still enough to permit good photographs to be taken.

Spotted Dragonet

Callionymus maculatus

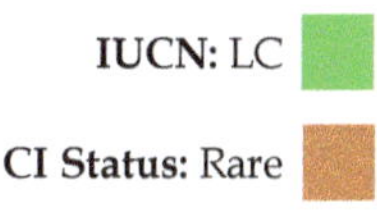

Max Length: 16 cm

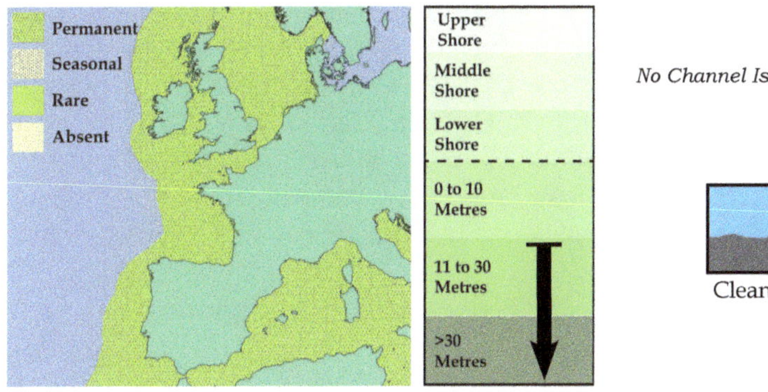

No Channel Island Rod Records

Clean Ground

The Spotted Dragonet is generally a deeper water dweller than other dragonets, preferring soft sediments below about 40 metres depth. Based on its distribution elsewhere in the English Channel this species was long suspected to be present in Channel Island waters but the first confirmed report was only in March 2018 when a specimen was taken in a trawl off the west coast of Jersey. The Spotted Dragonet is small and distinctive but, as a deeper water fish which is unlikely to be caught by anglers, it has probably escaped the attention of naturalists and biologists until now. It is perhaps more common than records suggest in the deeper water areas to the west of the Channel Islands.

Gobies

The fish family Gobidae (gobies) is the most diverse in the Channel Islands with 16 reported species although one of these is almost certainly an identification error (the Broad-finned Goby). Most goby species are common and may be found intertidally or in shallow marine areas making them amongst the most common and abundant of local fish. However, smaller species (which is most gobies) can be exceptionally difficult to identify and will normally require a specimen or clear photograph. For this reason, many species are known from only a handful of records, even though they may be common locally.

Gobies have no commercial or recreational value (other than small fisheries for some pelagic species that are used for whitebait) and they will only ever be caught as bycatch. Local populations have probably not changed historically beyond the probable arrival of the Giant Goby and Leopard-spotted Goby, neither of which have records before the 1950s, despite being large and easy to identify. These may be species whose range expanded north from the Bay of Biscay to include the Channel Islands and then afterwards the UK. The Giant Goby was, for example, unknown in the UK prior to 1903 when specimens were found in Cornwall. This may help to date its arrival to the late nineteenth or early twentieth centuries as the Giant Goby does not feature in Joseph Sinel's thoroughly researched list of local fish species which he compiled at exactly this time.

The Channel Islands would benefit from a systematic study of its goby species in order to find out which species live here and how abundant they are. Some excellent work has been achieved recently by underwater photographers whose clear photographs has permitted identification to species level. Reports of gobies are of definite scientific interest and a local or regional study would make a good citizen science project.

Transparent Goby
Aphia minuta

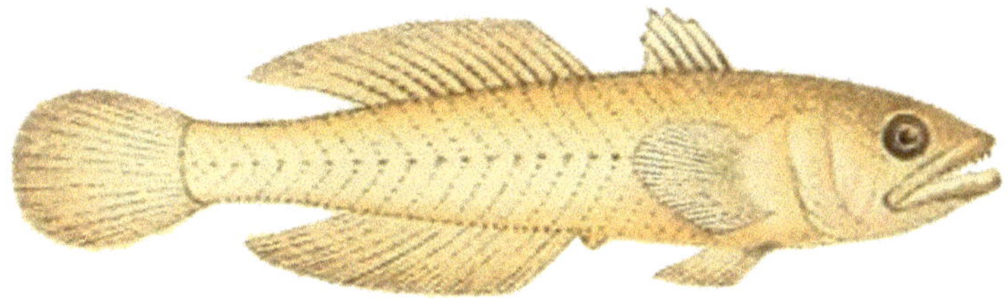

Max Length: 3 cm

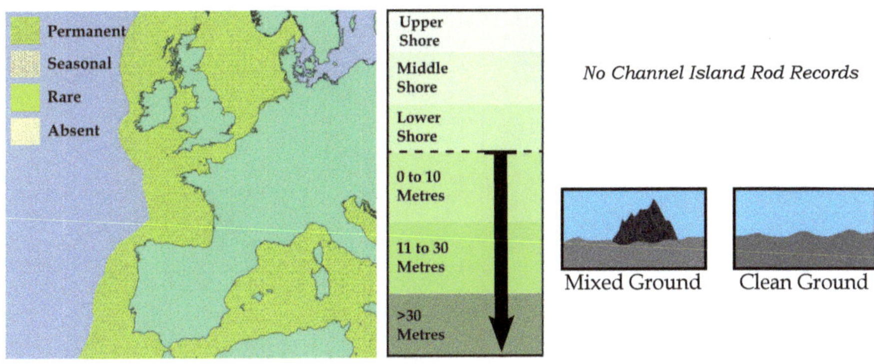

There are no reports of Transparent Gobies in the Channel Islands but this minute fish has been recorded many times along the adjacent Normandy and Brittany coasts. As such, it is probably an unreported local species but being small, difficult to identify and often pelagic, the Transparent Goby is usually only recorded as part of scientific surveys. As the name implies, this fish is almost transparent and it may be easily confused with other small fish, especially the Crytsal Goby. It has a lifespan of a year and is common in shallow coastal waters and estuaries. If the Transparent Goby does occur locally then it is most likely to be found swimming in areas of soft sediment with weed or seagrass but may be found close to the seabed in deeper waters too.

Jeffrey's Goby

Buenia jeffreysii

IUCN: LC

CI Status: Occasional

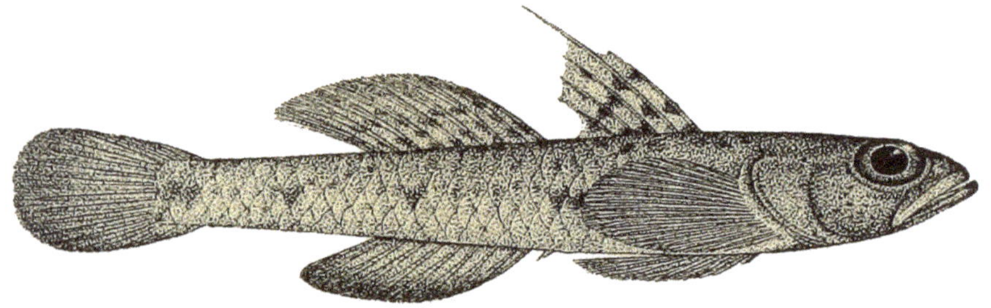

Max Length: 6 cm

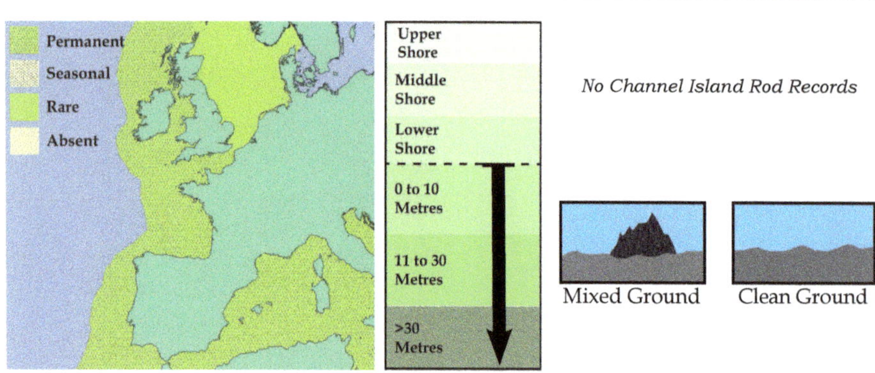

No Channel Island Rod Records

Although easier to identify than some related species (it has an elongated second ray in its dorsal fin), there are only a handful of Channel Island records for Jeffreys's Goby, almost all of which come from CEFAS beam trawl surveys. These produced nine records between 2006 and 2018 from around the Islands but especially from just south of the Schole Bank, Guernsey. The only other regional record comes from a 1970s seabed survey made south of Les Minquiers by French scientists. Outside the Channel Islands Jeffreys's Goby has relatively few records across its geographic range but this is thought to be due to under-recording rather than general rarity. Searching in shallow marine coarse sediments (particularly maerl beds) ought to produce specimens but firm identification often requires a clear photograph or an actual specimen.

Crystal Goby

Crystallogobius linearis

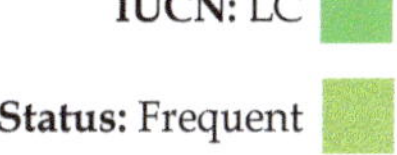

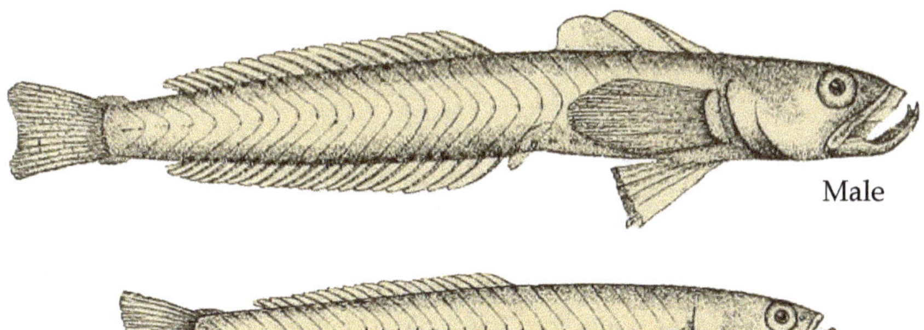

Female

Max Length: 5 cm

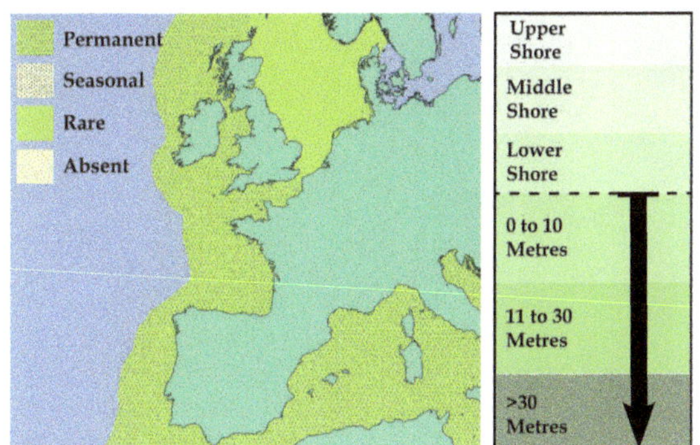

No Channel Island Rod Records

Named because of its semi-transparent body, the Crystal Goby has individual records from Guernsey and Jersey in 2006 and 2012 respectively. Otherwise it is regionally known from a handful of sightings in other parts of the Bay of Granville, especially towards Mont St Michel. The Crystal Goby is small and easy to confuse with other species including the Transparent Goby which occurs in similar habitats and will swim in small shoals above the seabed. This could be a common but under recorded species within the Channel Islands, as it is on UK coasts and additional reports would be welcome. For identification purposes it is worth noting that female Crystal Gobies do not have pelvic and first dorsal fins whereas the males do.

Broad-finned Goby

IUCN: LC

Psammogobius biocellatus

CI Status: Unconfirmed

Sleepy Goby

Max Length: 12 cm

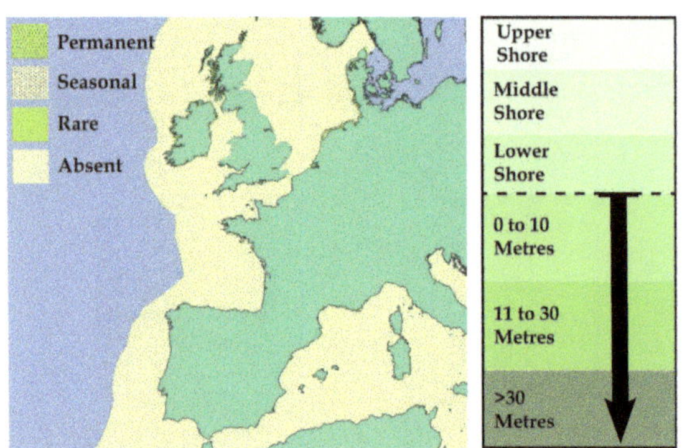

No Channel Island Rod Records

Clean Ground

In 1905 the naturalist Joseph Sinel claimed that several preserved specimens of the Broad-finned Goby that were on display in the Jesuits' Museum, Jersey, had been captured locally in St Clement's Bay. Given that the natural range of this species is the Indo-Pacific Ocean, this seems highly unlikely and suggests that the museum specimens had been either misidentified or mislabeled. Mix-ups such as this were a common occurrence during Victorian times, especially for specimens that had been supplied by unwitting or unscrupilous commercial dealers. In more regularly traded animal groups, such as seashells, this was a common cause of many tropical species being erroneously included on Channel Island, British and other European faunal lists.

Giant Goby

Gobius cobitis

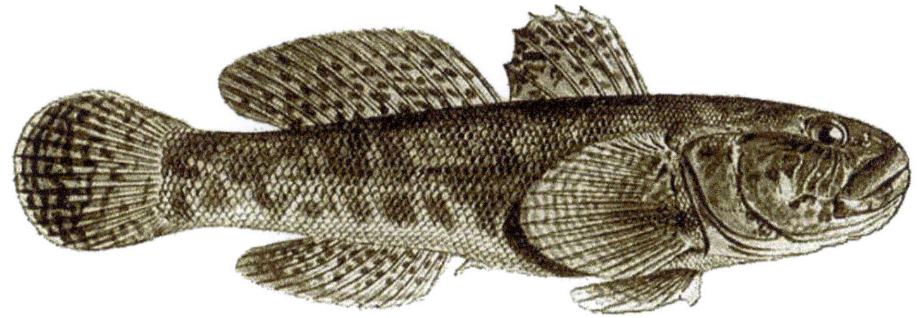

Max Length: 25 cm

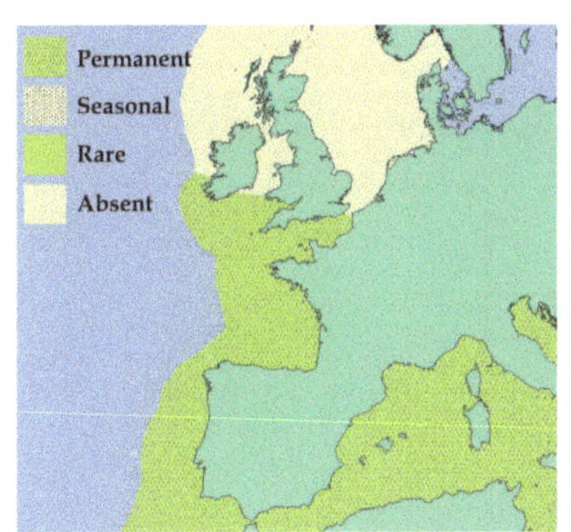

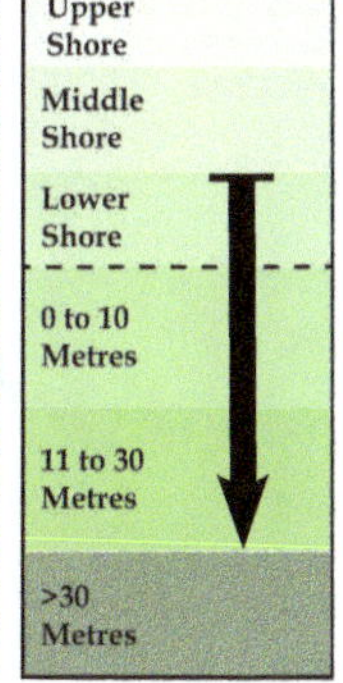

Record Weights (lb.oz.dr)

	Mini
Jersey	00.05.07
Guernsey	00.09.04

Rough Ground

The Giant Goby is the largest of the European Goby species and is unmistakable when encountered in rock pools. Aside from its length and stout stature, this fish will often remain still, especially when guarding eggs. This fish may have been a relatively recent arrival to the region for, despite its size and distinctiveness, the oldest records are only from the 1950s although it doesn't seem to have become common until the 1980s. In the UK the Giant Goby remains rare and is legally protected but local reports suggest that it is common within the Channel Islands. Specimens are sometimes accidentally caught by anglers but they should always be returned alive. Any specimens on the seashore should not be handled or disturbed as they may be protecting eggs under nearby stones.

A Giant Goby at L'Étacq, Jersey.

Steven's Goby

Gobius gasteveni

Max Length: 12 cm

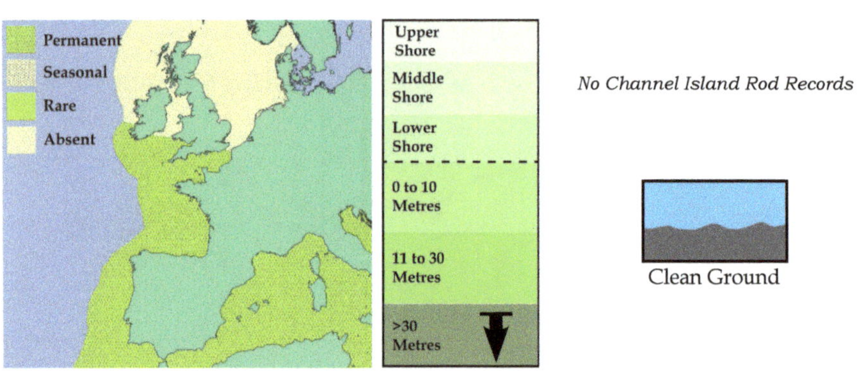

There are a handful of local records relating to Steven's Goby, the oldest being from a 2000 seagrass survey at Fliquet, Jersey. Other records come from beam trawl surveys off Guernsey, Alderney and Les Minquiers between 2006 and 2018. It is not surprising that the only records of Steven's Goby come from scientific surveys due to this species preferring subtidal habitats. It is also visually similar to several other goby species which means specimens are only likely to be identified by experienced naturalists and biologists. The Channel Islands are located near to the northern edge of its geographic range and the current data suggest that it is probably frequent in water deeper than 25 metres.

Black Goby

Gobius niger

Nièr Cabot; Célérîn; Manchouette

Max Length: 17 cm

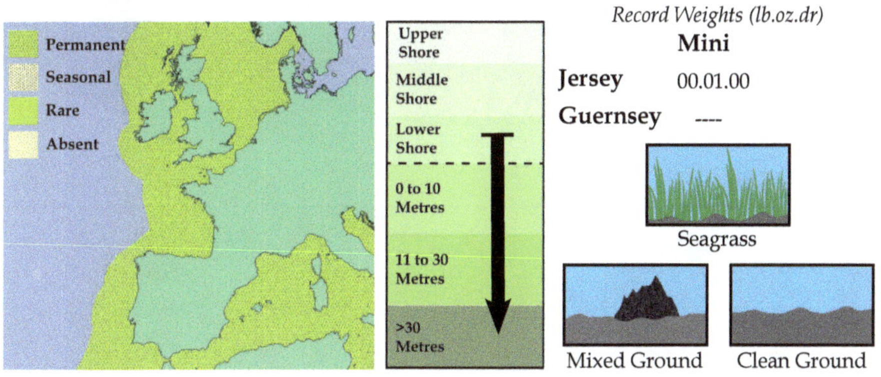

The Black Goby is common around all the Channel Islands and has a good historical record back to the early nineteenth century. It is frequently found in sandy bays, among seagrass or in large sediment-floored rock pools and may be common in some areas. Medium-sized and attractive, this fish could be confused with the Rock Goby although the two have different habitat preferences. Anglers are unlikely to catch specimens but people going prawning or using draw nets at low water in sandy areas may encounter them. Its current population status is probably unchanged from when it was first recorded in the 1860s.

Rock Goby

Gobius paganellus

Gris Cabot

IUCN: LC

CI Status: Common

Max Length: 13 cm

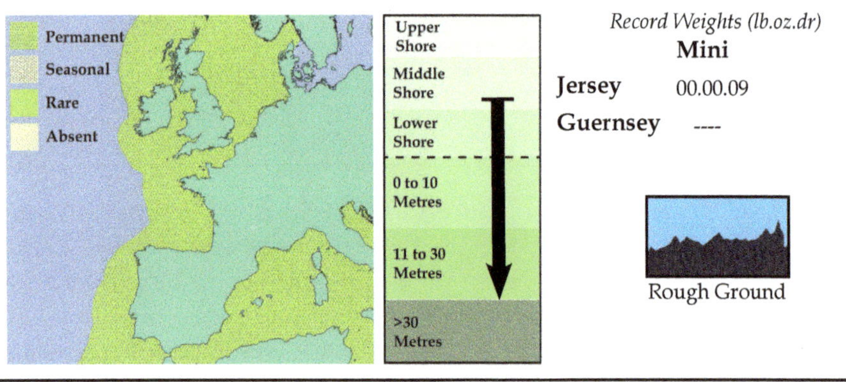

Record Weights (lb.oz.dr)

	Mini
Jersey	00.00.09
Guernsey	----

If searching among stones in rock pools at low water then you are likely to encounter the Rock Goby. It is a robust, moderately-sized fish that is distinctively mottled with dark colours and, unlike the Giant Goby, which may be found in similar habitats, the Rock Goby will swim or wriggle away quickly. The Rock Goby may have been more common in the late nineteenth and early twentieth centuries than today but it is still regularly encountered on rocky shores across all the Channel Islands. Fish specimens should not be handled or moved from their rock pools as they may be guarding eggs. The Rock Goby is variable in colour as the above illustration shows.

Two-spotted Goby

Gobiusculus flavescens

Max Length: 6 cm

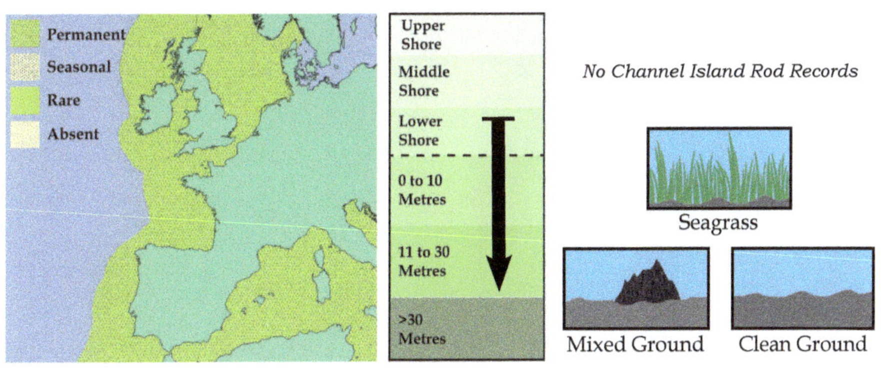

The Two-spotted Goby is an easily identifiable small species found in rock pools and areas of seaweed or seagrass in the shallow marine. It is common and there are a large number of reports from all the Channel Islands. It is most often seen by snorkelers and divers, usually just offshore and in kelp forests. The Two-spotted Goby tends to be found in small to medium-sized shoals close to the seabed or seaweed and males may be distinguished from other similar species by the presence of a spot at the base of the tail and a second one behind the pectoral fin. Unlike most gobies, this species will swim well above the seabed.

A Two-spotted Goby from St Ouen's Bay, Jersey.

Guilleti's Goby

Lebetus guilleti

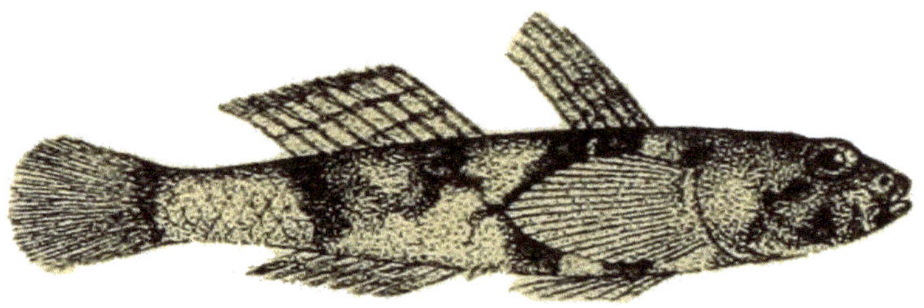

Max Length: 3 cm

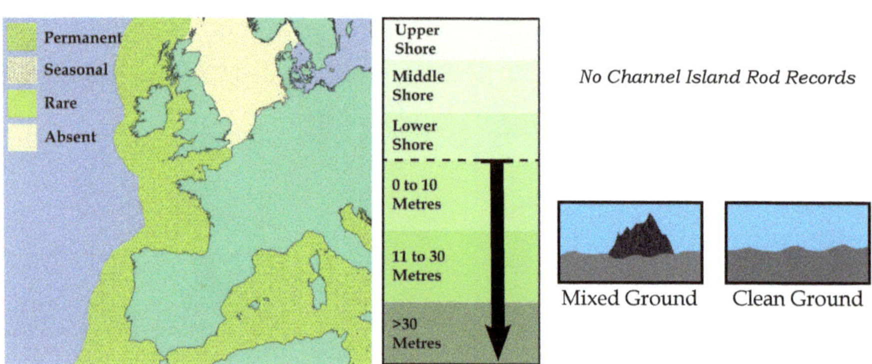

Guilleti's Goby is a recent addition to the Channel Islands' fish list after specimens were recorded at St Catherine's Bay, Jersey, and Les Écréhous in 2013 and 2014 respectively. This is one the smallest local fish and it is difficult to see and identify especially as it generally frequents coarse sediment seabeds from just offshore to deep water.

Guilleti's Goby is easily confused with the Diminutive Goby (*L. scorpioides*), a species which currently has no Channel Island records although it is probably present despite being near the southern edge of its range. With very small goby species such as these, obtaining specimens or clear photographs is the only reliable method of identification, as records made by sight alone may be unreliable.

Fries's Goby

Lesueurigobius friesii

Slender Goby

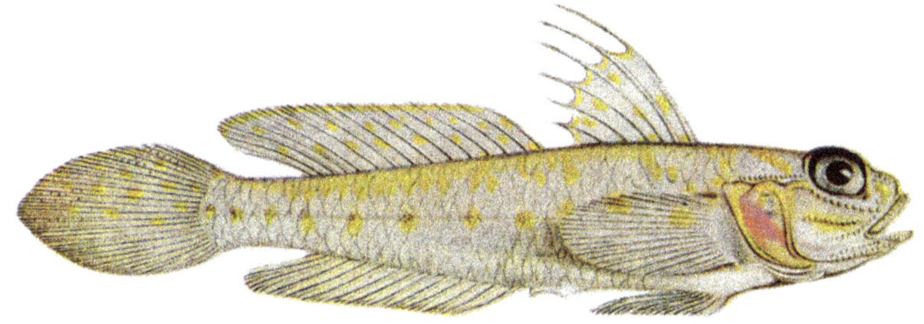

Max Length: 13 cm

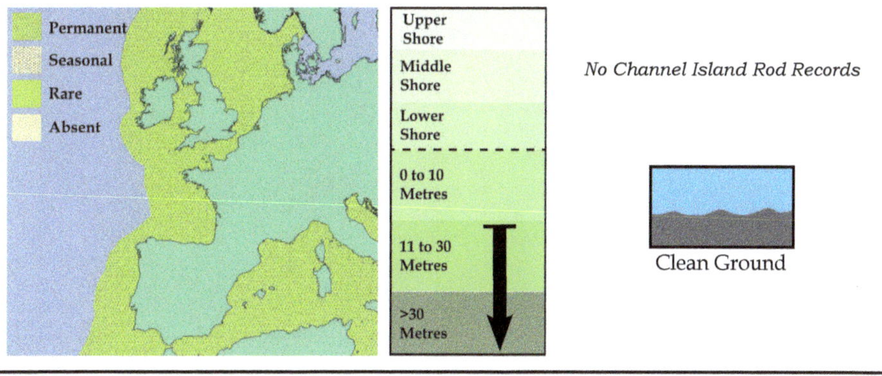

There are very few Channel Island records for Fries's Goby. The oldest is from Joseph Sinel's 1905 summary of fish species in which he claimed that it was 'not common' and could be found in seagrass beds and sandy shores. The only other regional records are from a beam trawl survey west of Guernsey in 2009 and, regionally, from off St Brieuc, Brittany, in 2018.

Fries's Goby is an offshore species that generally lives below 20 metres which suggests that Sinel's marginal marine records are probably a misidentification. The lack of records is probably because the usual limit of recreational diving (30 metres) is at the shallow end of this species depth range. Although this is certainly a local fish, its status is not known and can probably only be resolved through a concerted study of all Channel Island goby species.

Lozanoi's Goby

Pomatoschistus lozanoi

IUCN: LC

CI Status: Occasional

Max Length: 8 cm

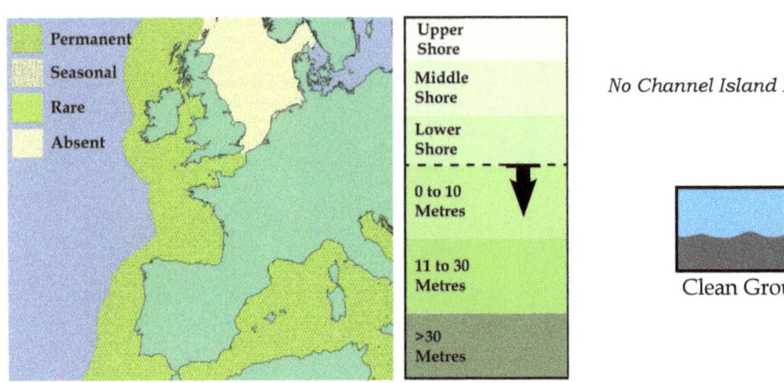

No Channel Island Rod Records

Clean Ground

Lozanoi's Goby is a small species that is exceptionally difficult to tell apart from the Sand Goby. The species was only scientifically discovered and named in 1923, initially as a subspecies of Sandy Goby but later work raised its status to that of a full species. There is just one unattributed historical record from the Channel Islands but scientific surveys in the Bay of Mont St Michel in the 1990s, 2003 and 2005 produced many specimens. Lozanoi's Goby is probably present in the Channel Islands, living in shallow water on sandy sediments. Further records would be helpful to confirm it as a local species.

Common Goby

Pomatoschistus microps

IUCN: LC

CI Status: Common

Max Length: 7 cm

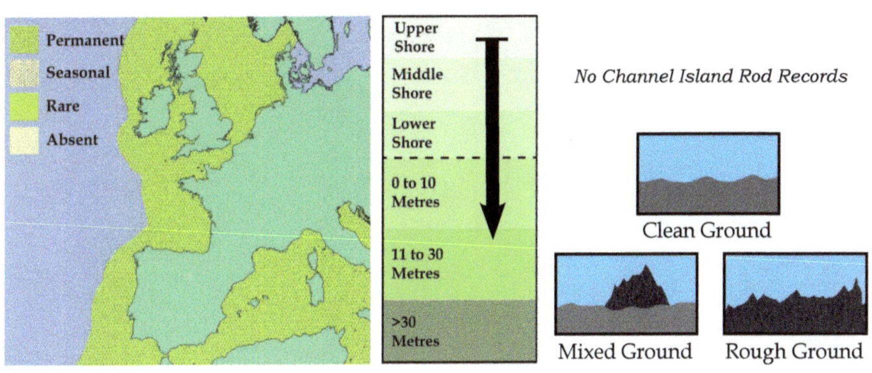

The Common Goby was not recorded at all in the Channel Islands until 2003 and only rarely since then. The 2003 records all came from a study of fish species in seagrass meadows around Jersey with other records since coming from divers undertaking Seasearch surveys. It has been a common feature of scientific surveys in the Bay of Mont St Michel and the Rance estuary which may tie in with its ability to live in brackish water and intertidal pools. Just how abundant the Common Goby is locally cannot be determined without survey work but it is possible that some of the Channel Island records are misidentifications, especially those made from deeper waters. This species prefers estuarine environments with juveniles temporarily migrating into fresh water. A lack of estuarine environments in the Channel Islands may explain why it has rarely been sighted.

Sand Goby

IUCN: LC

CI Status: Common

Pomatoschistus minutus

Little Goby

Max Length: 10 cm

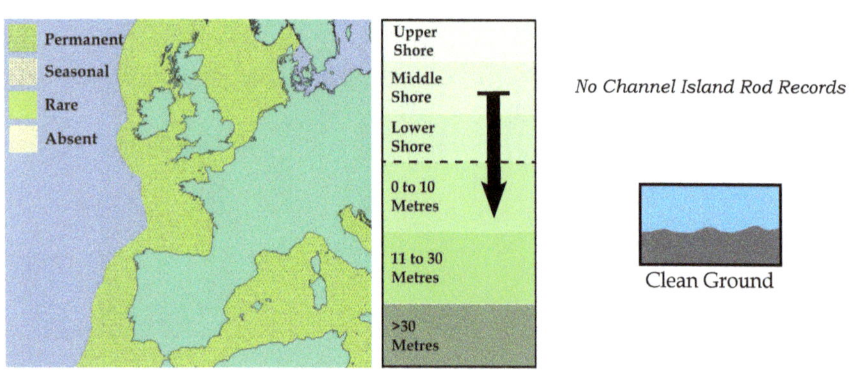

No Channel Island Rod Records

Clean Ground

The Sand Goby is probably one of the commonest fish species in the Channel Islands and yet it has only a handful of records, most dating from the 1990s onwards. As with other *Pomatoschistus* spp. this almost certainly reflects a lack of study rather than rarity. With densities of over 10,000 fish per hectare on the French coast, the Sand Goby will be common across all the Channel Islands where it will frequent shallow water sandy seabeds. It is probably the main species constituent of the many gobies that skip away from bathers and snorkellers but is easily confused with both Lozano's and the Common Goby although it is larger than the latter. Specimens or photographs are needed to secure a firm identification.

Painted Goby

Pomatoschistus pictus

IUCN: LC

CI Status: Common

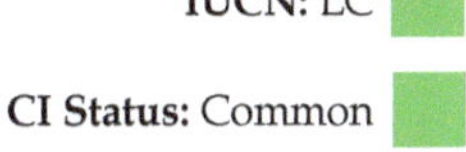

Max Length: 6 cm

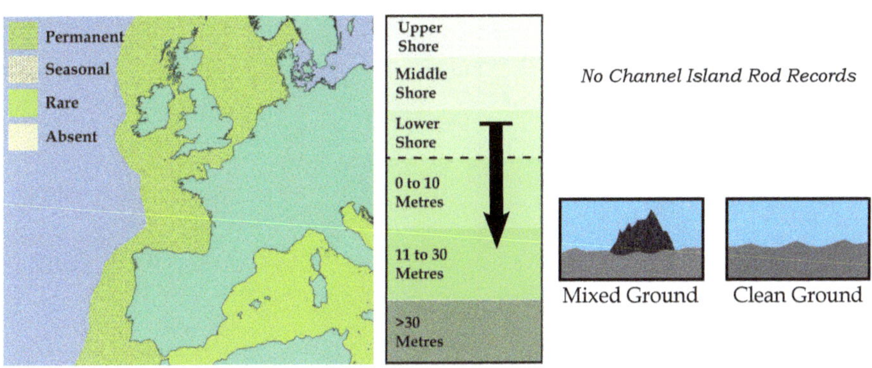

This species is similar to the Common and Sand Gobies with the exception of the breeding males which sport a distinctive blue-black dorsal fin which provides both the common and scientific name (*pictus* = painted). There are no local records at all prior to 1967 but afterwards it was regularly reported in Jersey but not the other islands. This probably does not represent the Painted Goby's local distribution or abundance but is due to simple under-recording in other islands. It has virtually no records at all in the Bay of Granville, perhaps because it favours coarser shallow marine sands and gravel whereas most French surveys have been in sheltered sandy bays. Painted Gobies are reportedly common in large, gravel-floored rock pools but, as with all local goby species, further recording work is needed.

Leopard-spotted Goby

Thorogobius ephippiatus

IUCN: LC

CI Status: Frequent

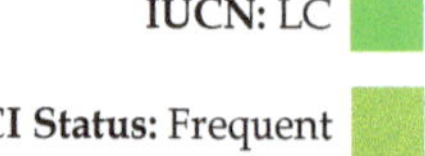

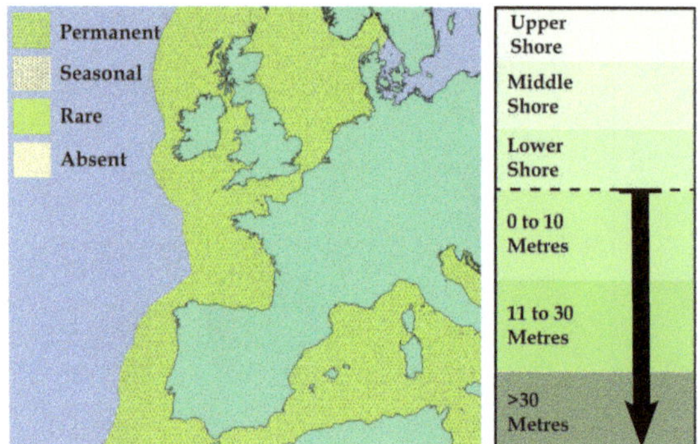

No Channel Island Rod Records

Mixed Ground

Rough Ground

It is the dark, patchy spots that give the Leopard-spotted Goby its common name and make it identifiable by sight alone. The oldest known record is from 1955 when a member of the Plymouth Marine Biological Laboratory observed a specimen while diving in St Aubin's Bay. This was said to be the first British record and there were no more local reports until the 1990s when an increase in diving and underwater photography led to many sightings around all the islands.

Although distinctive, the Leopard-spotted Goby is hard to observe as it will normally hide amongst rocks and boulders in the shallow subtidal. There have, however, been rare sightings of specimens in lower shore rock pools (the above photograph is one such example). This fish may be a recent arrival to the Channel Islands and is probably reasonably common across all the Channel Islands. Additional reports should be made to a local records centre.

Mackerel and Tuna

The Scombridae family are agile, pelagic fish such as mackerel, tuna and bonito, which normally live in open waters but will seasonally migrate into coastal areas. Most members of the family are large and active predators that offer great sport for recreational anglers. Once a shoal is located they can be easy to capture which, paired with them being edible and commerically expensive, has led to overfishing. Offshore commerical techniques, such as pair trawling, has been particularly disasterous for Scombridae stocks with a reported 70 percent decrease in worldwide stocks between 1970 and 2010. This has resulted in species such as mackerel and tuna being some of the most heavily regulated fisheries around the world's oceans.

Species such as tuna are ranked highly as sports fish by recreational anglers. However, persistent industrial scale overfishing means that within northern Europe most tuna species may only be landed as commerical bycatch and may usually only be taken by anglers under a scientific licence. The migratory patterns of tuna are changing and in recent years they have been sighted in areas where they have not been recorded for decades, if at all. This has created tension between fisheries managers, who are obliged to protect tuna under EU regulations, and local commerical and recreational fishers who wish to fish for a valuable commercial species that may rarely be seen locally.

In September 2018 an influx of Northern Bluefin Tuna created one such problem in Jersey where, despite the island being on a zero catch quota for the species, a legal misalignment still allowed recreational anglers to land specimens. The Jersey regulations were swiftly changed but not before a large specimen was landed at St Helier. The incident generated protests from the recreational and commerical fishing communities, who wished to fish for tuna, and from local and UK conservation organsiations who were concerned that Jersey had facilitated the capture of an endangered species. Although unusual locally, situations such as this often occur in other parts of the world where authorities' need to conserve overfished species conflicts with anglers' perceived right to catch them.

The controversial landing of a Bluefin Tuna at St Helier in 2018.

Silver Scabbardfish

Lepidopus caudatus

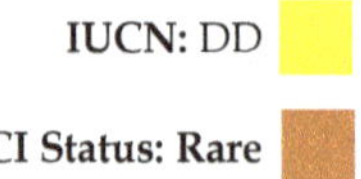

Max Length: 210 cm

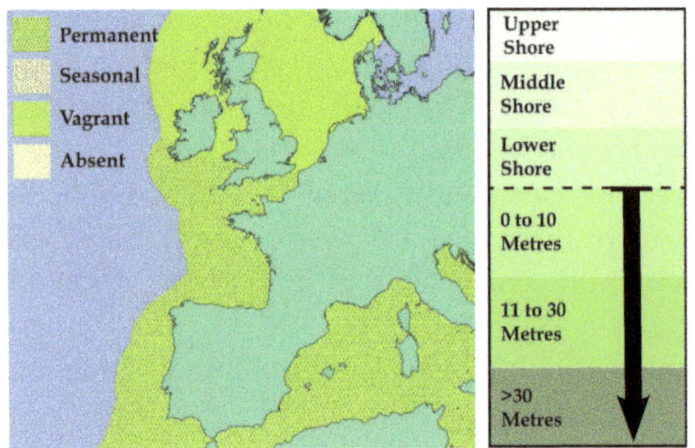

No Channel Island Rod Records

Pelagic

The Silver Scabbardfish is a distinctive, slim fish that can grow to over two metres in length. It is a southern European species that has very few British records and just two Channel Island ones, from 1818 and 1840 when individual specimens were caught off Guernsey. It is generally a deep water dweller but will occasionally migrate into shallower waters. With no records for over 150 years, the Silver Scabbardfish can be classified as one of those fish that was a rare historical visitor to the Channel Islands.

Bullet Mackerel

IUCN: LC

CI Status: Unconfirmed

Auxis rochei

Bullet Tuna

Max Length: 50 cm

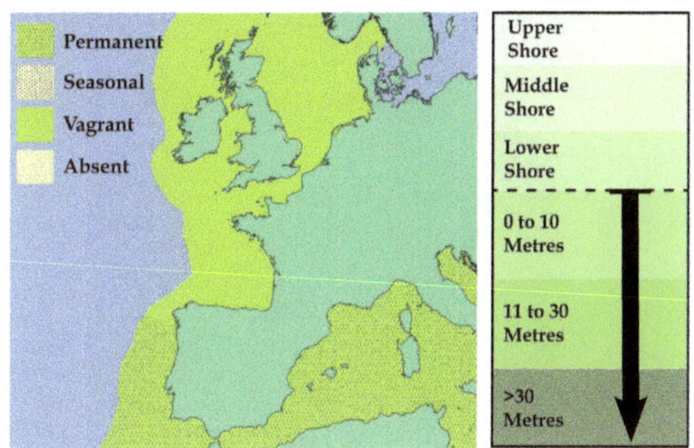

No Channel Island Rod Records

Pelagic

A very rare visitor to the English Channel, the Bullet Mackerel is a large predatory fish that forms shoals in surface waters. There are just two Channel Island records, one made in a list of Guernsey species published by naturalist Edgar MacCulloch in 1882 and the second of a specimen caught off Guernsey in January 1889. The Bullet Mackerel was captured infrequently in British waters during Victorian times but, beyond the two Guernsey records, there are no other reports for the Normano-Breton Gulf area. The Bullet Mackerel is currently rarely seen north of Gibraltar and the Victorian specimens probably represent fish that strayed into local waters perhaps at a time when tuna species were more plentiful and wide-ranging than at present.

Skipjack Tuna

Katsuwonus pelamis

Max Length: 110 cm

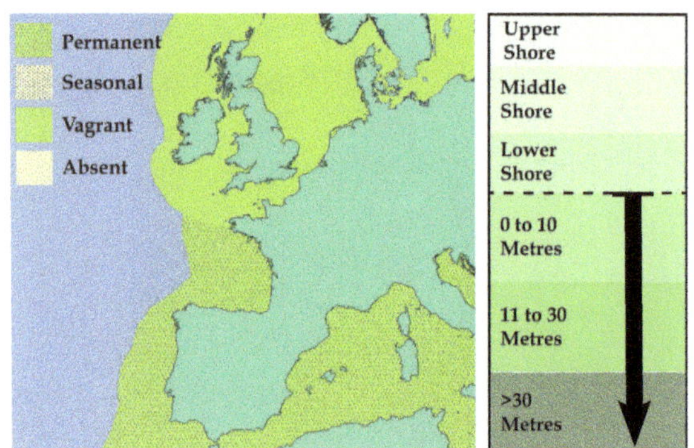

No Channel Island Rod Records

Pelagic

The Skipjack Tuna is normally an offshore species but there are confirmed records from Jersey in 1956 and 1958. The 1956 specimen was taken by a Polish tourist who managed to capture a 50 cm specimen at Green Island, using his hands. It was later identified by the local naturalist Ronald le Sueur.

Victorian records note that the Skipjack Tuna was an occasional visitor to Guernsey waters although there are no confirmed reports from this time. It is a shoal species that is commercially fished although, unlike most other large tuna species, its population is listed by the IUCN as being of least concern. It may be attracted to floating objects, such as boats and weedlines, and is capable of straying into Channel Island waters in the summer months. The absence of any reports since the 1950s suggests that any forays into the Normano-Breton Gulf are rare.

Atlantic Bonito

Sarda sarda

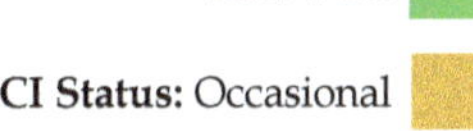

Max Length: 90 cm

Permanent
Seasonal
Rare
Absent

Upper Shore
Middle Shore
Lower Shore
0 to 10 Metres
11 to 30 Metres
>30 Metres

Record Weights (lb.oz.dr)

	Boat	Shore
Jersey	05.02.05	----
Guernsey	05.15.00	----

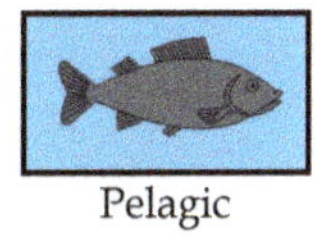

Pelagic

The Atlantic Bonito could be mistaken for a mackerel were it not for the large body size and striking banding on the upper part of the body. Prior to World War II only a handful of Bonito records were known from British waters. Specimens started to be caught locally about 15 years ago and within a decade this fish was being taken every summer. The Bonito is considered to be a vagrant to British waters but for the Channel Islands it is a regular summer visitor. The Bonito is a species that will increase in abundance and size as the sea temperatures rise. Local catches currently average around 1.8 kg but this is increasing and elsewhere Bonito have been known to reach 8 kg. This is a good sport fish when using light tackle and will eagerly hit almost any small lure. Reports of specimens are still useful scientifically and any captures should be reported to a local records centre.

Paul Ogier with the Guernsey equal record Bonito (5 lb 15 oz).

Atlantic Mackerel

Scomber scombrus

Maqu'sé; Maqu'thé

Max Length: 60 cm

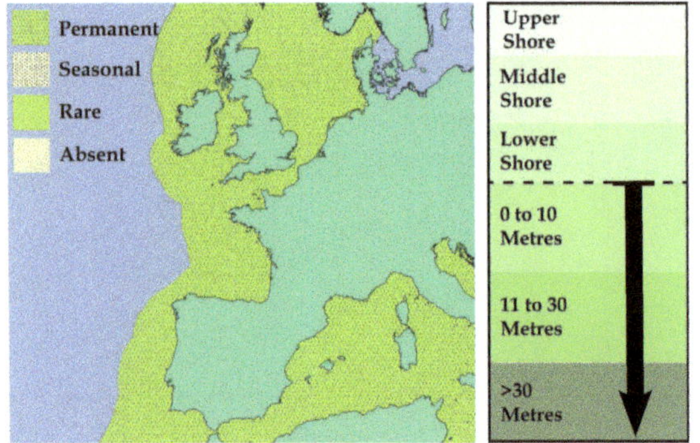

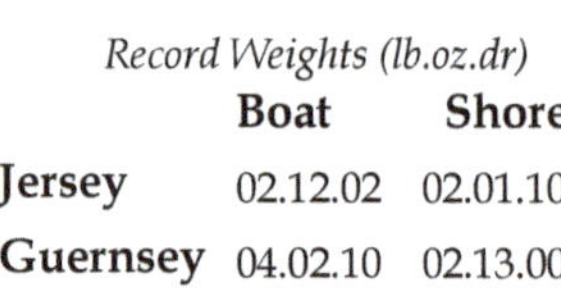

Record Weights (lb.oz.dr)

	Boat	Shore
Jersey	02.12.02	02.01.10
Guernsey	04.02.10	02.13.00

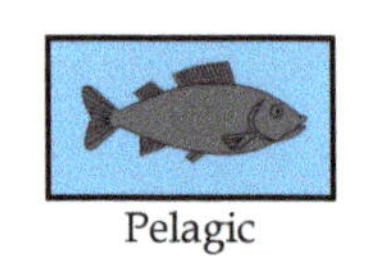

Pelagic

The Atlantic Mackerel is the most frequently caught fish by Channel Island recreational anglers with a 2015 survey estimating that 22,000 individuals (around 11 tonnes) are taken annually in Jersey alone. This is probably a rare instance where the recreational landing weight of a fish is higher than that of the commercial fishing sector whose recent catches are only a few tonnes annually (although they have been over 20 tonnes in some years).

The reason for the Atlantic Mackerel's popularity is its taste and because it is a pelagic fish that can form huge shoals offshore which then migrate into coastal waters during the spring and summer to feed and spawn. This is when they are most often caught both from the shore and boats usually by jigging with feathers. The average weight is around 500 grams and it is one of the easiest fish species to catch with it being possible to have up to six on a line at one time. It is jigging for Mackerel that tempts many beginners into recreational fishing. Sometimes a shoal will come close inshore in pursuit of bait fish causing the fish to bubble up on the water surface. When this occurs it is not uncommon for anglers to catch dozens of fish in a short time. In the winter months the fish move offshore into deeper water before returning into the English Channel around March or April.

Atlantic Mackerel are the most frequently caught fish in the Channel Islands and are sometimes landed in large numbers.

Perhaps unsurprisingly for such a popular fish, there is a good historical record for the Atlantic Mackerel with one of the earliest references to the fish being in a 1348 document concerning the importation of Channel Islands fish into England. In the nineteenth and twentieth centuries it was consistently described as abundant around the Islands and it remains a common summer migrant.

Mackerel stocks are heavily exploited across Europe and there are signs (such as reduced average fish length and erratic occurence) that the species is being overfished. There are anecdotal tales locally about Mackerel being currently scarcer than in past years but, being a highly mobile migratory fish, any conservation measures will need to operate across the whole of its range to be effective. Atlantic Mackerel do not like being handled and can die easily, even if released. It is therefore important to only fish for your requirements and to stop fishing when no more are needed.

Capture Technique: When in large shoals, Atlantic Mackerel will eat almost anything that moves. They can be caught using small metal lures and float fishing but the main way to catch Mackerel is with the use of feathers, although this method requires minimal skill and can quickly result in catching too many. Extremely light tackle can be used to offer great sport with small lures but when using feathers, slightly heavier gear should be used. When the summer shoals arrive they can be caught almost anywhere including off beaches, the end of piers and from boats where they are chasing baitfish. If float fishing, different depths should be experimented with and fishing can be greatly improved with the use of shirvy around harbour areas.

Atlantic Chub Mackerel

IUCN: LC

Scomber colias

CI Status: Occasional

Max Length: 40 cm

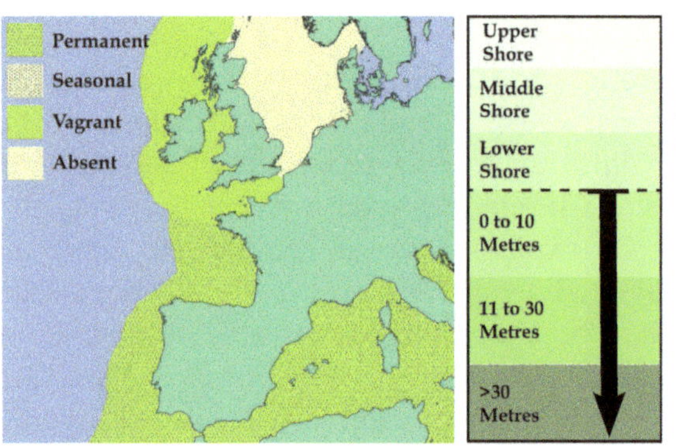

Record Weights (lb.oz.dr)

	Boat	Shore
Jersey	-----	01.09.04
Guernsey	01.15.00*	01.02.15

Pelagic

There has been historical confusion between two individual species, *Scomber colias* (Atlantic Chub Mackerel) and *S. japonicus* (Pacific Chub Mackerel), both of which have historically been called the Spanish Mackerel but which have very different geographic ranges. It is presumed that all Channel Island records refer to *S. colias*, which is known from British waters even though some of the local records give *S. japonicus* which is an Indo-Pacific species.

The Atlantic Chub Mackerel is a warm water species that is rare north of the Bay of Biscay. There is a lone Victorian record for the Channel Islands from the 1860s and then nothing further until 2001 when a specimen was caught off Alderney. Since then there have been several other fish caught off Guernsey and Jersey, the latest being in 2018. This suggests that the Atlantic Chub Mackerel is an uncommon but regular visitor to local waters. As with some other temperate migratory species, this fish could become more common in the islands as the sea temperature rises. It will often be found mixed in with shoals of Atlantic Mackerel (*S. scombrus*) and any captures should be reported to a local records centre.

Albacore

IUCN: LC

CI Status: Unconfirmed

Thunnus alalunga

Longfin Tuna

Max Length: 100 cm

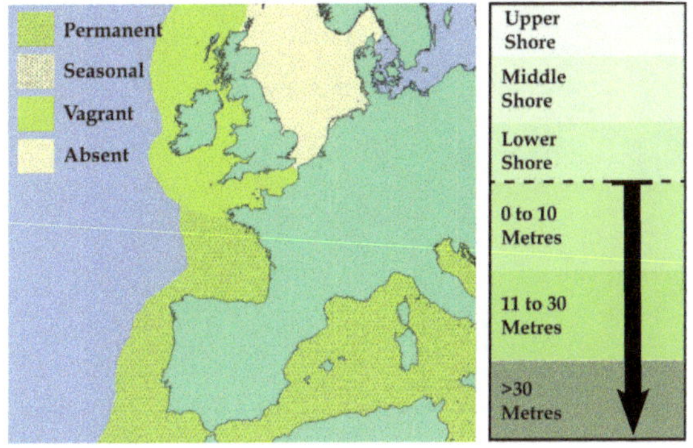

No Channel Island Rod Records

Pelagic

Although common in the Bay of Biscay and further south, the Albacore is a rare summer visitor to the English Channel. There is one unconfirmed capture of an Albacore in July 1861 when a Guernsey angler trapped a 27 kg specimen in nets he had set for mackerel. The newspaper article describing this event refers to the fish as being 'another fine specimen of the Albacore' which suggests that others may have been caught around that time. The Albacore has the potential to occur in local waters but, based on a lack of modern records, must do so exceptionally rarely. The Albacore averages 4 to 24 kg and is easy to identify as it has noticeably long pectoral fins for its size and a white trailing edge on the caudal fin. As with the Northern Bluefin Tuna, the Channel Islands are on a zero catch quota for the Albacore so this species should not be targeted or landed.

Northern Bluefin Tuna

Thunnus thynnus

Thon

IUCN: EN

CI Status: Rare

Max Length: 455 cm

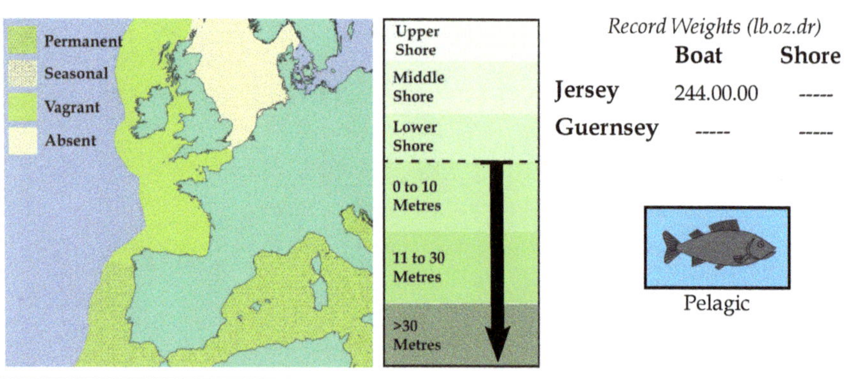

Record Weights (lb.oz.dr)

	Boat	Shore
Jersey	244.00.00	-----
Guernsey	-----	-----

Anecdotal stories from Brittany suggest that the largest of the tuna species, the Northern Bluefin Tuna, was once a regular visitor to the Normano-Breton Gulf and in Victorian times was targeted by offshore fishers each summer. This is partially confirmed by local records which, in the 1860s, list Bluefin Tuna as being seen occasionally off Guernsey with several confirmed captures being made in 1861. There are sighting records from Jersey waters in 1949 and 1953 and north of Alderney in 1962. In 2017 shoals were seen west of Jersey and Guernsey and in August 2018 French pair trawlers accidentally took several tonnes of Bluefin Tuna very close to Jersey waters. This was followed by the controversial landing of a Bluefin Tuna at St Helier by recreational anglers (see page 233). Although perhaps once a more regular summer visitor to the islands, the global population of Bluefin Tuna has been fished to near extinction. This fish is prized around the world but especially in Japan where other species of Bluefin have fetched exceptionally high prices. This is a zero catch quota species in the Channel Islands and it should not be targeted or landed.

Luvar

Luvarus imperialis

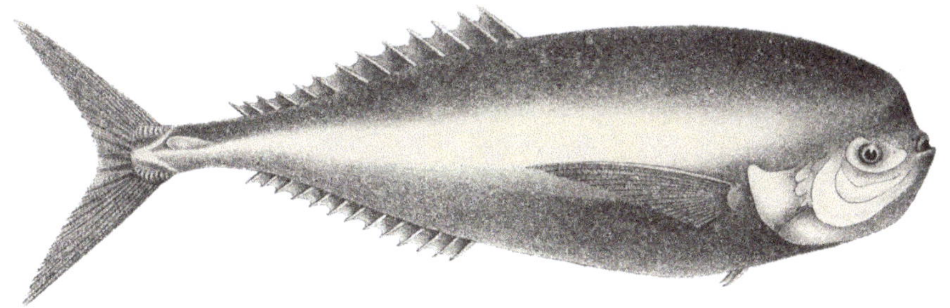

Max Length: 200 cm

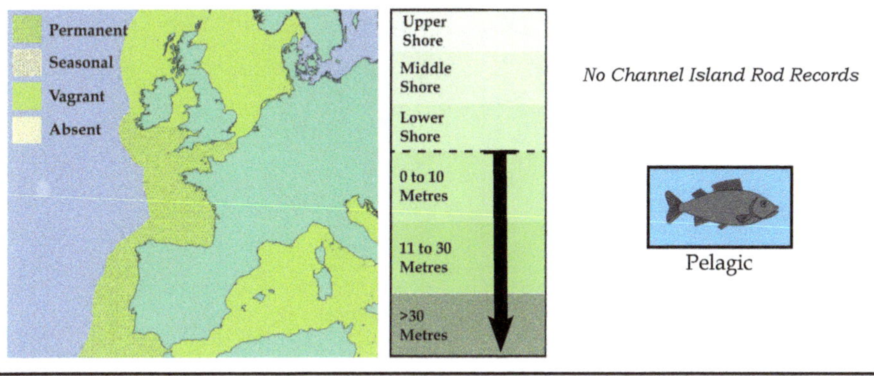

No Channel Island Rod Records

Pelagic

The Luvar (or Louvar) is a large, distinctive fish that is more commonly found in the open ocean than coastal waters. The lone regional record comes from a specimen, some 1.5 metres long, that was caught in June 1902 off St Martin's Point, Guernsey. The catch was so unusual that the specimen was sent to the Natural History Museum in London, where it remains to this day. No other records are known from the Normano-Breton Gulf which suggests that the Luvar should be considered a rare vagrant.

Swordfish

Xiphias gladius

Max Length: 455 cm

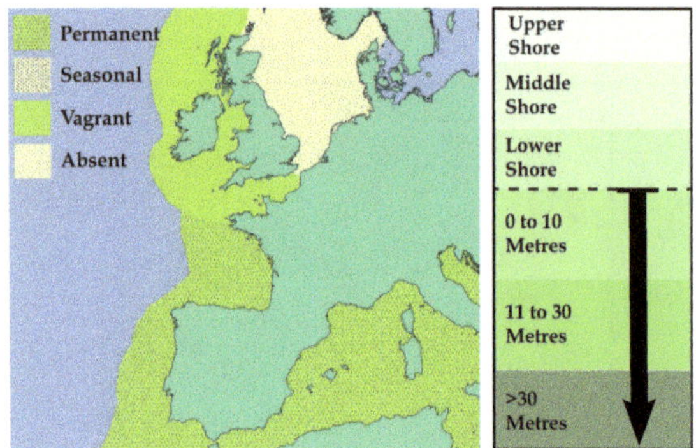

No Channel Island Rod Records

Pelagic

The Swordfish is a fast swimming apex predator that can reach over four metres in length. Although more commonly associated with warmer waters, the Swordfish is a highly migratory oceanic species that is irregularly sighted or caught within the Channel Islands.

Reports are scarce and usually come from trawlers working offshore in the summer months. However, recreational records include a 2.5 metre specimen was caught in July 1861 using a net inside a Guernsey Bay. Even more bizarre was the three metre Swordfish caught by hand in St Ouen's Bay in October 1968 after the animal had been observed in the surf. In the 1990s there are reports of Swordfish leaping clear of the water just offshore. Although prized as a game fish, there are concerns about Swordfish stocks and the species is on the zero quota list for the Channel Islands which means it should not be targeted or landed. Any accidental captures should be released at once and a report submitted to a local records centre. There is a 1993 boat sighting that was said to be an Atlantic Sailfish (*Istiophorus albicans*) although it is more likely to have been a Swordfish.

Blackfish

Centrolophus niger

Rudderfish

Max Length: 150 cm

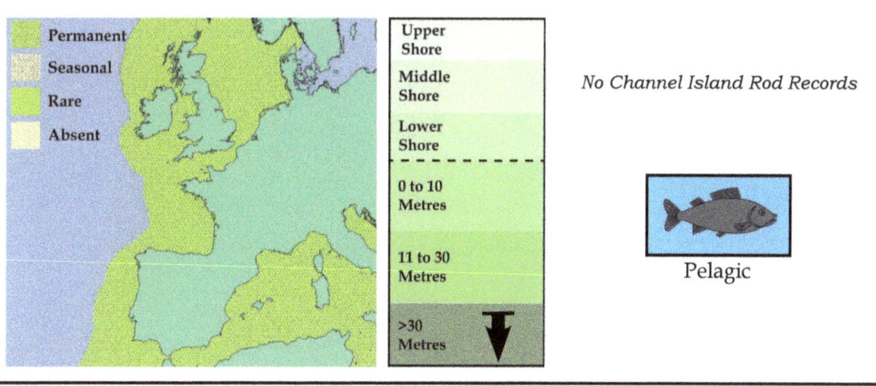

The Blackfish is a large offshore species that generally lives deeper than 100 metres although specimens have been found in surface waters and may sometimes be associated with floating objects such as logs and seaweed rafts. There is just one Channel Island record from June 1988 when a live specimen was found in a rock pool at L'Étacq, Jersey. The fish was 72 cm long, weighted 3.2 kg and was handed in to a fish merchant who passed it on to a local naturalist. Eventually the Blackfish specimen was dontaed to the Société Jersiaise who made a cast of it that still survives in their archives. The Blackfish is an unexpected fish for Channel Island waters but stray specimens have turned up across Europe. It is a rare vagrant to local waters.

Cornish Blackfish

Schedophilus medusophagus

IUCN: DD

CI Status: Rare

Max Length: 50 cm

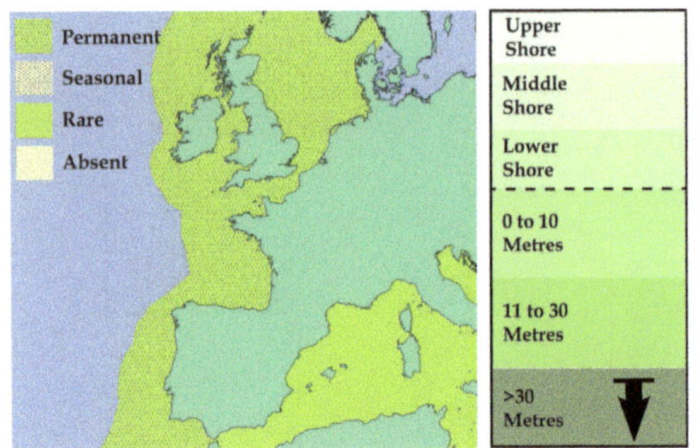

No Channel Island Rod Records

Pelagic

There is just one regional record for the Cornish Blackfish when a recreational angler took a specimen south of Guernsey in 2010. The identification was confirmed by a local ichthyologist. This is normally a deep water, pelagic species although younger fish can be found closer to surface waters, often in association with jellyfish. The presence of a Cornish Blackfish in local waters is unusual and the individual concerned was probably a vagrant from the Atlantic Ocean. This is unlikely to be a resident species within the Channel Islands.

Flatfish

Flatfish are a diverse and distinctive group of fish within the Order Pleuronectiformes. They have a fossil record that goes back at least 50 million years and are sometimes cited as a classic example of adaptive evolution because of the way that both eyes are found on the same side of the body. Within the Channel Islands flatfish species belong to one of four families: Scophthalmidae (topknots, brill, turbot, etc.); Bothidae (scaldfish); Pleuronectidae (plaice, flounder, etc.); and Solidae (sole).

Once a flatfish reaches the end of its larval stage, one of the eyes will migrate across the fish's head so that both eyes lie on the same side. Depending on the species, the eyes will either be on the right or the left side of the body, when viewing the fish from the front. In general terms species within families Scophthalmidae and Bothidae are left-eyed fish while the others are right-eyed.

Being able to lie on the seabed offers many advantages in terms of camouflage and feeding. For this reason, many flatfish prefer sandy seabeds where they can blend into the background although other species will hide amongst rocks or even swim pelagically. Flatfish are either benthic or demersal dwellers and are a popular target for recreational and commercial fishers. Most can camouflage themselves on the ocean floor to avoid predation and to hunt smaller fish.

The flatfish family includes many important commercial species such as turbot, brill and plaice. They are particularly susceptible to benthic and pelagic trawling and many of the most popular species have been heavily overfished. Indeed, it was drastic declines in flatfish species such as plaice and halibut that first alerted scientists to the possibility that individual fish stocks can be fished to the point of collapse. Prior to this it was assumed that fish stocks could not be harmed by prolonged and intensive fishing.

The identification of flatfish is sometimes reliant on slight differences in body shape and colouration between similar-looking species. A further complication can be the occurence of hybrid specimens from genetically similar species such as flounder and plaice. Care is needed when identifying flatfish, especially with the smaller species.

At the time of writing Channel Island commercial landings of flatfish are low and total just a few tonnes a year although this was considerably higher in the 1990s. However, French trawlers operating in local waters are probably more active in this area with ICES figures suggesting that they may be landing large quantities of sole and other species.

Norwegian Topknot

Phrynorhombus norvegicus

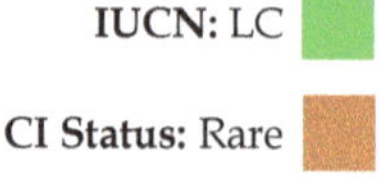

Max Length: 14 cm

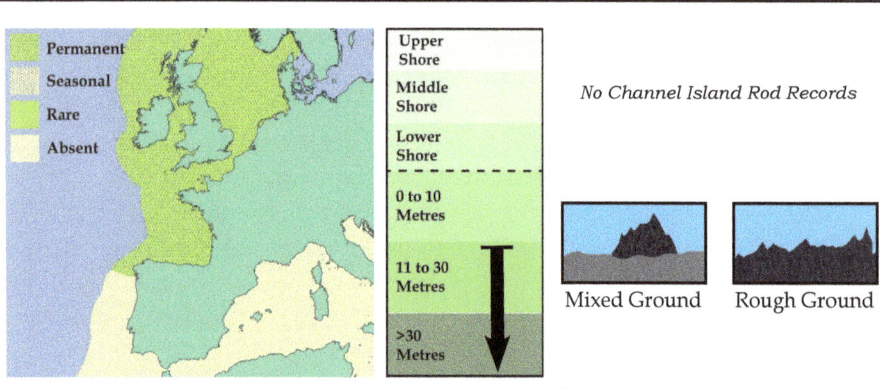

The Norwegian Topknot is a flatfish that prefers hard or rocky substrates. The Channel Islands lie close to the southern limit of its range and it has no historical records. However, CEFAS beam trawl surveys between 2006 and 2018 have produced specimens from across the Channel Island waters for most years. This suggests that it has been under-recorded locally, perhaps because of a close similarity to other members of the topknot family or because of its small size. It can live in shallow to moderate depths. Anglers are unlikely to catch this species but it is possible that divers might observe the Norwegian Topknot. The CEFAS surveys suggest it is not uncommon on the harder seabeds to the west of Jersey and Guernsey and north of Alderney.

Eckström's Topknot

Zeugopterus regius

IUCN: DD

CI Status: Rare

Max Length: 23 cm

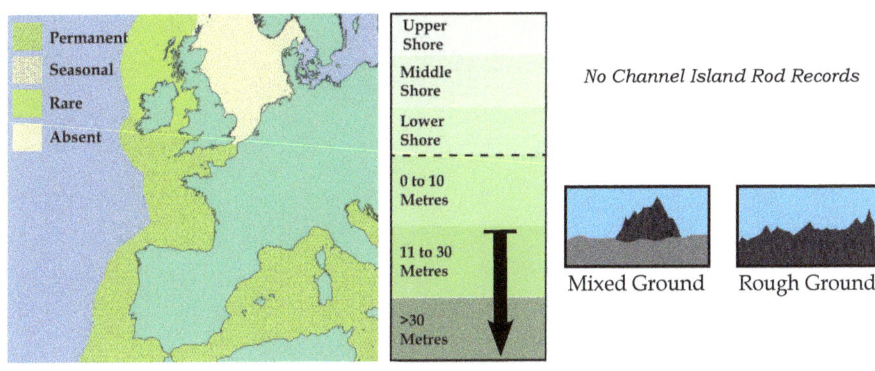

No Channel Island Rod Records

This predominantly southerly species has occasionally been reported after becoming trapped in lobster pots around Guernsey. It is very difficult to distinguish from the Common Topknot with the main difference being in the shape of the head and, in live specimens, a dark 'V' pattern that may be present across the middle of the body. The handful of specimens taken during recent CEFAS trawl surveys suggest that this is probably an under-reported species across most of its range. Eckstrom's Topknot may prefer deeper water than the Common Topknot and so is unlikely to be found on the seashore although a specimen was photographed intertidally at La Coupe, Jersey, in 2018. Any specimens encountered in Channel Island waters should be reported to a biological records centre.

Turbot

Scophthalmus maximus

Teurbot

Max Length: 100 cm

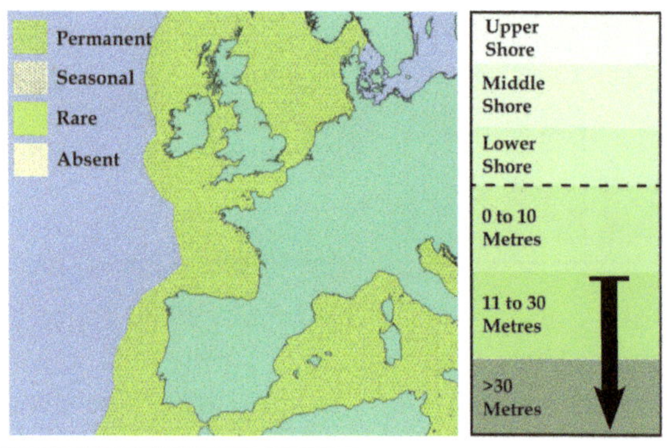

Record Weights (lb.oz.dr)

	Boat	Shore
Jersey	23.08.00	14.09.08
Guernsey	30.04.00	22.03.00

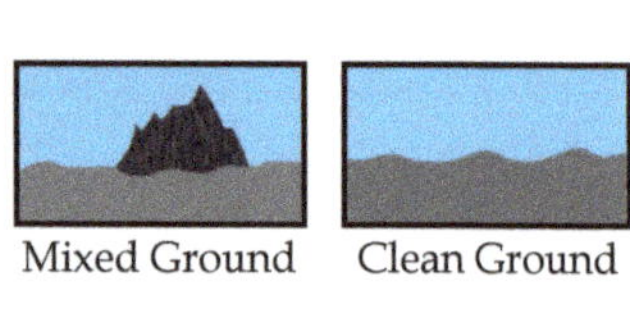

A popular fish with recreational boat anglers, the Turbot is widespread around the islands and is particularly common across offshore banks that have large sand ripples. Highly prized as an edible fish, the Turbot is an important commercial species and is generally caught by benthic trawling although it is also reared through aquaculture, including within the Channel Islands. The Channel Islands are known for their excellent Turbot fishing during the spring and summer months with many charter boats heading south from the UK to target them. Recent commercial catches have varied between almost nothing to more than ten tonnes annually with much of this being landed in Guernsey by trawlers.

Turbot live in deeper water during the winter months but will move into shallow, inshore areas in spring time. This is when they are often caught by anglers, usually from a boat, although shore captures do occur. The shore angler may come across juveniles over sandy substrate in the summer. The species is believed to return annually to the same spawning ground which, in some parts of Europe, has made the Turbot vulnerable to commercial trawling when known spawning sites are heavily fished year after year.

Local historical records start in the 1860s but reports are sporadic perhaps because adult Turbot generally live below 10 metres depth and are experts at camouflage. However, smaller specimens of 30 cm or so were being caught in rock pools in the nineteenth century with one observer remarking that Channel Island Turbot will only grow to around a third of the length of those caught in the English Channel. The Turbot's offshore preference means it is mostly seen by anglers rather than by naturalists and divers although, as borne out by historical reports, juvenile Turbot may be found in very shallow water (but are difficult to identify). The local status of the Turbot population is not known but as an important offshore species that can be targeted by trawlers, it is susceptible to overexploitation and is listed as vulnerable by the IUCN.

Capture Technique: Turbot and Brill are mostly caught by boat anglers drifting over sandbanks in water exceeding 80 feet in depth but wrecks have been known to often produce large specimens. Long flowing traces around 5 feet or more in length are common using 25 lb test or higher hook lengths. A running ledger rig is a great option for Turbot and Brill paired with a long boom to avoid tangles whilst drifting. Attractive beads and spoons are often used above the bait. Turbot and Brill have large mouths making hooks in the range of 5/0 a common choice. Using braided mainline is best as the angler is able to feel when the bait is drifting on the seabed. Fishing close to the seabed is vital when Turbot/Brill fishing.

Bait Preference: Live sandeel is a common choice by anglers although dead ones can be just as effective. Mackerel and sandeel strips are the most common bait used and are a well proven option.

Brill

IUCN: LC 

CI Status: Frequent

Scophthalmus rhombus

Brille

Max Length: 75 cm

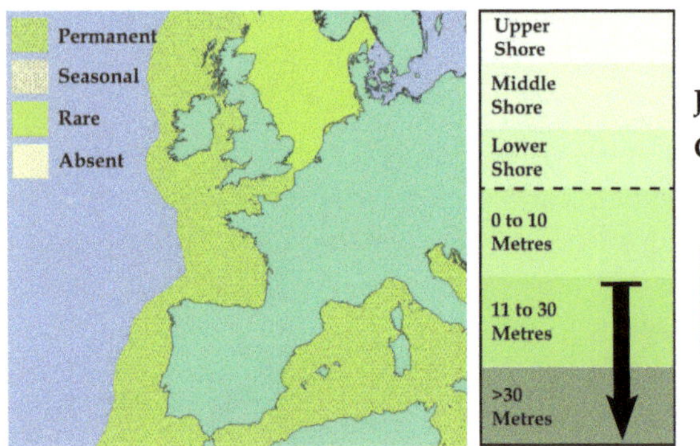

Record Weights (lb.oz.dr)

	Boat	Shore
Jersey	09.15.06	04.00.08
Guernsey	13.09.00	04.13.08

Mixed Ground

Clean Ground

Brill are morphologically similar to Turbot (but are smaller and more elongated) and equally as popular with boat anglers. They are often caught on offshore sand and gravel banks and overwinter in deeper water, coming into shallower areas during the spring and summer. It is said to be coming inshore steadily earlier in the year around the Channel Islands which is perhaps a consequence of warmer seas.

The Brill is an important commercial species and annual landings have reached over 20 tonnes although they have decreased in recent years. It is mainly caught through trawling and rod and line fishing over sandbanks. Historical records go back two hundred years but are patchy and almost non-existent after the 1960s. Nonetheless anecdotal information suggests that the Brill remains a common species across the

Channel Islands although it is possibly more abundant in Guernsey waters than around Jersey. The Brill prefers soft sediments against which it is superbly camouflaged, making it difficult to be seen by divers. Although heavily fished in Europe, the population is not believed to be under threat. For fishing technique and bait preference, see the entry for the Turbot.

There is a single 1904 reference to the Windowpane Flounder (*Scophthalmus aquosus*) occuring in Jersey waters. This is a tropical species closely related to the Brill and Turbot but the report must be erroneous as this species could not have been found in Channel Island waters.

Megrim

Lepidorhombus whiffiagonis

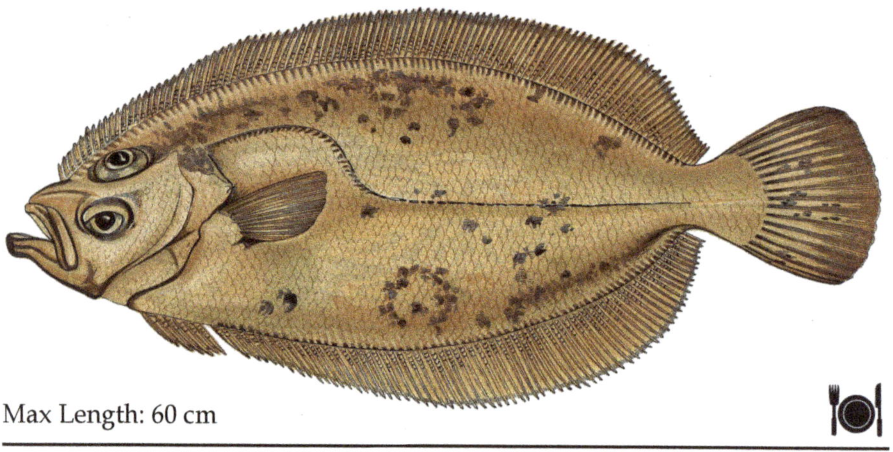

Max Length: 60 cm

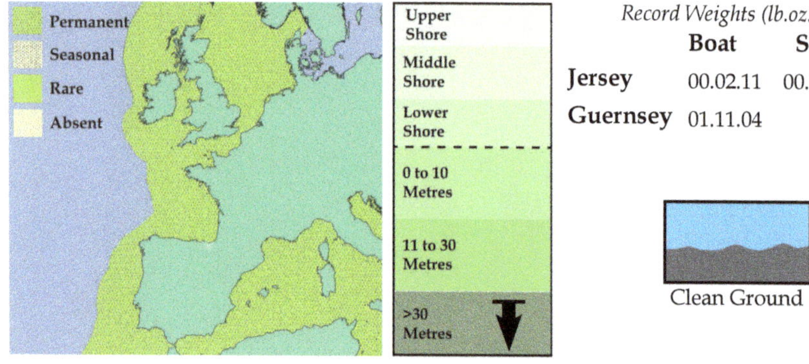

Record Weights (lb.oz.dr)

	Boat	Shore
Jersey	00.02.11	00.02.11
Guernsey	01.11.04	----

The Megrim is a deep water flatfish with a wide distribution. It had only historical records from the Channel Islands until the late 1990s when small quantities were landed at St Helier by Jersey commercial fishing boats. The last such landing was in 2002 and the origin of these Megrim catches is not known but it is possible that they were caught outside of the Channel Islands region. With no other records beyond this, the presence of the Megrim in Channel Island waters requires confirmation.

Topknot

Zeugopterus punctatus

Sole dé Rotchi

IUCN: DD

CI Status: Frequent

Max Length: 25 cm

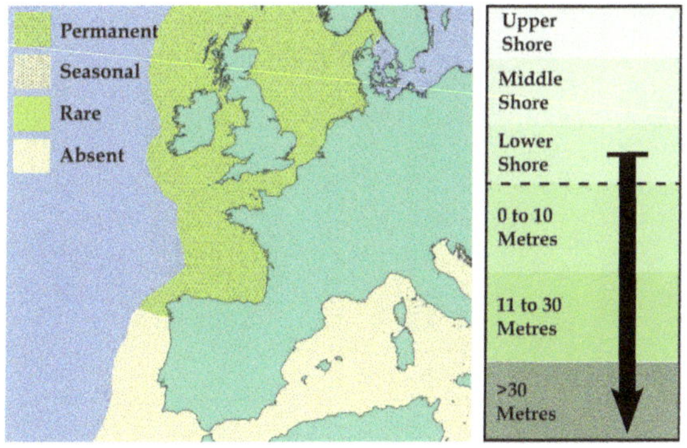

Record Weights (lb.oz.dr)

	Mini
Jersey	00.11.08
Guernsey	00.13.08

Mixed Ground

Rough Ground

The Topknot is one of the few flatfish that can be regularly seen in the intertidal area, especially on big spring tides where they can sometimes be found clinging to the faces of boulders and under overhangs. Although it shares a common name with other flatfish species called 'topknot', this fish is actually a type of turbot. Topknots can be found by divers and snorkelers on rocky ground and by rock poolers with careful searching. It is not targeted by recreational anglers ('It has never been fished for,' according to a 1904 newspaper article) and has little commercial value, as such most historical records come from naturalists. It regularly turns up in scientific trawling surveys and if anecdotal reports from the seashore and anglers are correct, the population has remained steady since the late nineteenth century.

Scaldfish

Arnoglossus laterna

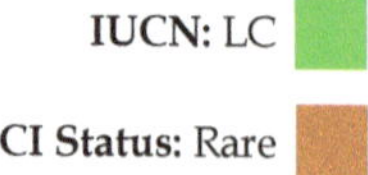

Max Length: 15 cm

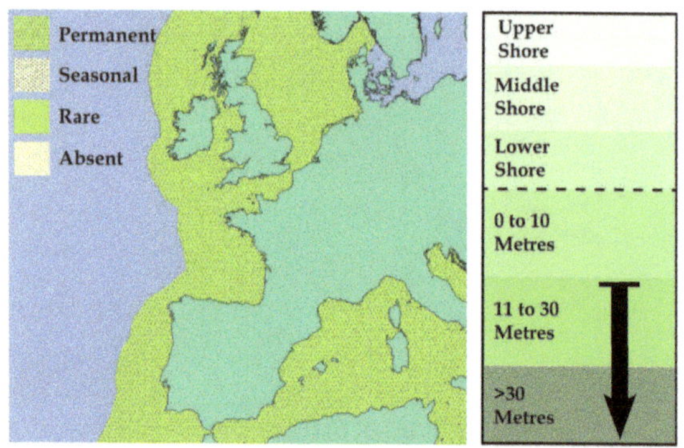

No Channel Island Rod Records

Clean Ground

Although sometimes encountered in the Bay of Mont St Michel, the Scaldfish has just two Channel Island records; one in a summary list of 1865 and the second from a 2018 beam trawl survey west of Guernsey. This small fish is difficult to identify and is rarely reported by naturalists; most records come from commercial or scientific surveys of benthic fish stocks. Experience in the UK suggests that the species is routinely overlooked by both anglers and divers and so may be more common than records suggest. Although present in Channel Island waters, the Scaldfish is probably rare and more information about the local presence of this species is desirable. Any sightings should be reported to a biological records centre.

Thor's Scaldfish

Arnoglossus thori

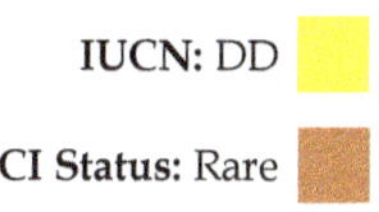

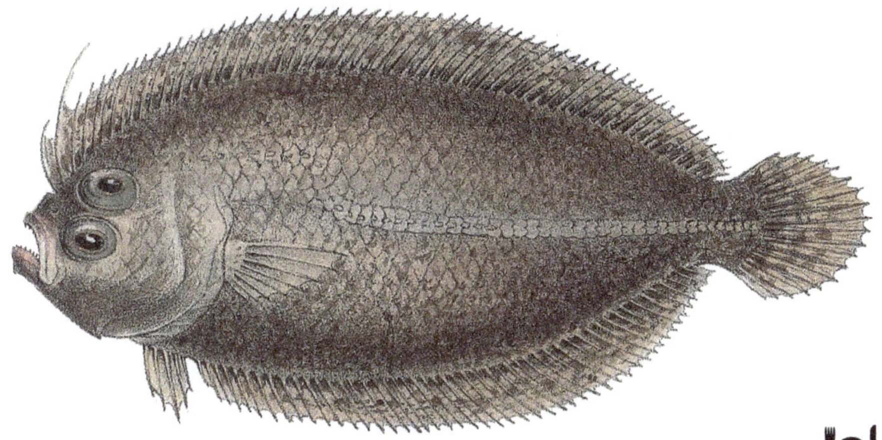

Max Length: 18 cm

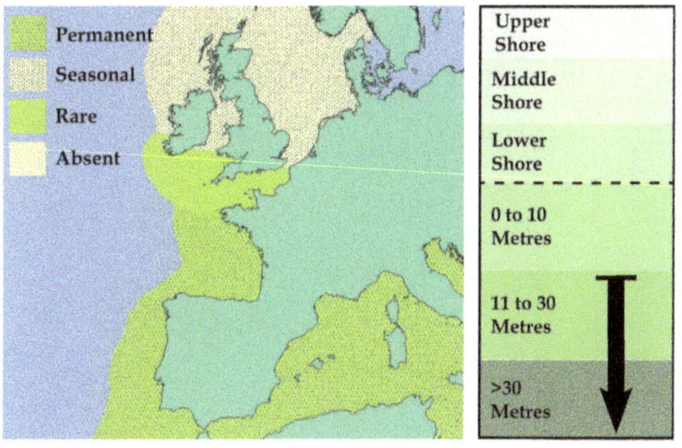

No Channel Island Rod Records

Clean Ground

Thor's Scaldfish is distinguishable from the Scaldfish by elongated rays at the front end of the dorsal fin. There are no Channel Island reports for this species but it was recorded in several scientific surveys in the Bay of Mont St Michel in the 1970s and may be present locally. Thor's Scaldfish is predominantly a southern European species but specimens have occasionally been found in the English Channel and it could be a species whose range is expanding northwards. As with the Scaldfish, its small size and lack of commercial value could cause it to be under-recorded regionally. This is a species of interest and any, if encountered, should be reported to a Channel Island biological records centre.

Witch Flounder

Glyptocephalus cynoglossus

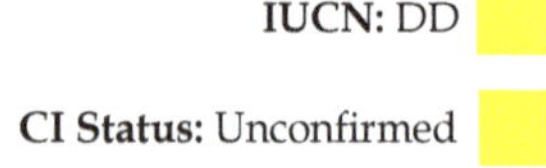

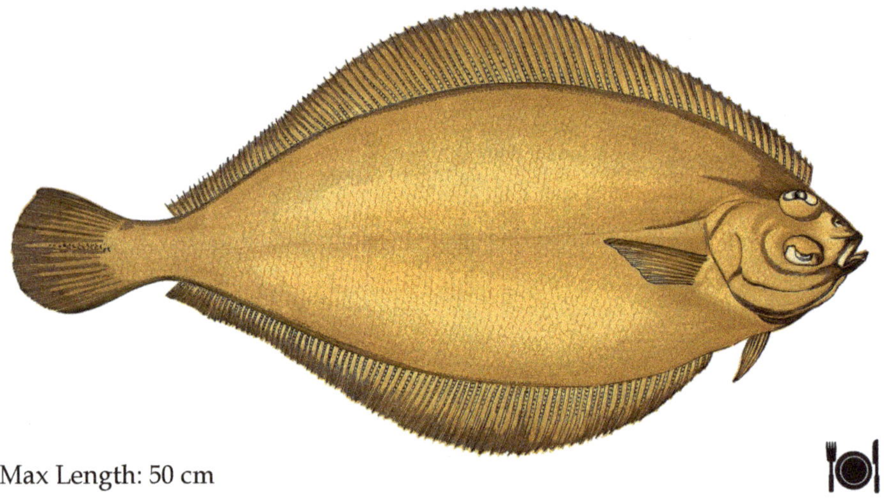

Max Length: 50 cm

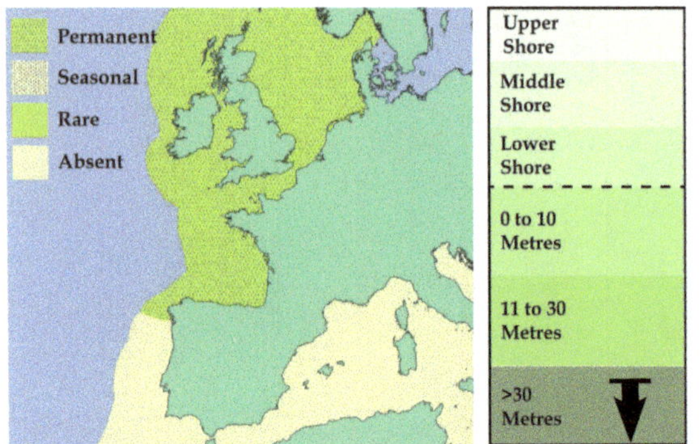

No Channel Island Rod Records

This is an unlikely fish species for the Channel Islands as the Witch Flounder prefers waters that are generally deeper than are found locally. There were, however, small but consistent commercial fishing landings of Witch Flounder in Guernsey between 1981 and 1986. Whether these specimens came from local waters or from boats returning from further afield is hard to say but, beyond these landings, there are no other local records. The Witch Flounder is found in the English Channel but at present is not a confirmed Channel Island fish species. Any catch records would be of scientific interest and should be made to a local records centre.

Long Rough Dab

Hippoglossoides platessoides

IUCN: DD

CI Status: Unconfirmed

Max Length: 80 cm

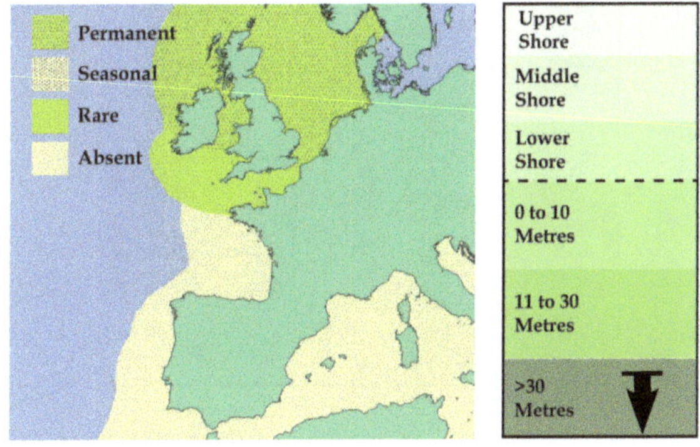

No Channel Island Rod Records

Clean Ground

As with the Witch Flounder and Halibut, the Long Rough Dab is only known from a small quantity of commercial landings made in Guernsey during 1985. Although the Long Rough Dab is known from the English Channel, it is rare and prefers colder, deeper waters and is most commonly fished to the north of the British Isles. Without further proof this should be considered a doubtful record for the Channel Islands. However, should any specimens be caught in the Channel Islands then these should be reported to a local records centre.

Atlantic Halibut

Hippoglossus hippoglossus

Max Length: 300 cm

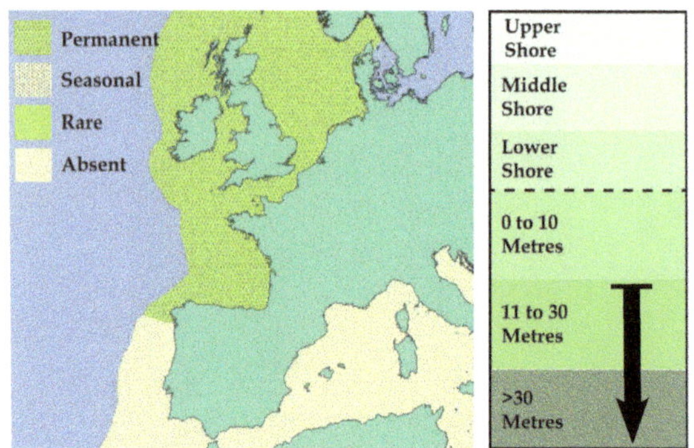

No Channel Island Rod Records

The Halibut is a legendary fish both for its size (up to three metres) and for being one of the first North Sea fish populations to be brought to the edge of collapse through overfishing. This is because maturity is reached late in the Halibut's life, at around eight years for males and eleven for females. Slow growing species are susceptible to overfishing and the Halibut remains endangered.

The Halibut is a cold and deep water species not known from the English Channel and is highly unlikely to be resident (or even a vagrant) in Channel Island waters. The species is only included in this book because of a 1981 commercial catch landing made in Guernsey. Whether this was a misidentification or from fish that were captured elsewhere in Europe and landed in Guernsey is not known. The Halibut is probably not a local species.

Dab

Limanda limanda

IUCN: LC 

CI Status: Occasional 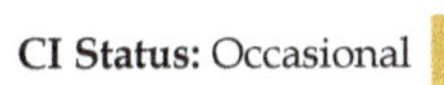

Max Length: 40 cm

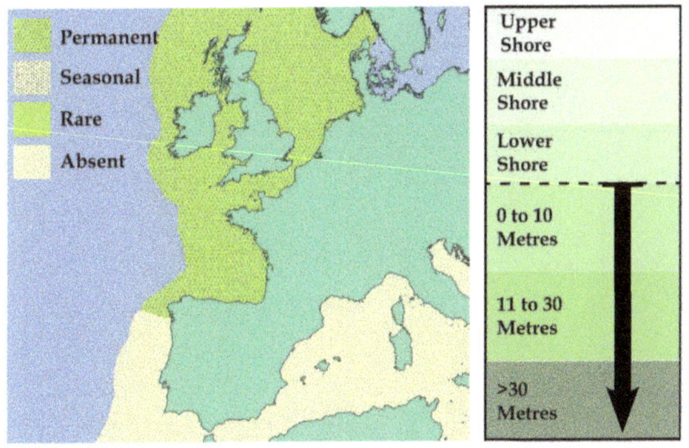

Record Weights (lb.oz.dr)

	Boat	Shore
Jersey	01.03.02	01.01.02
Guernsey	01.11.01	01.09.01

Reported to be abundant locally in the nineteenth century and not uncommon in the 1960s, by the twenty-first century the Dab was considered to be a rare catch by recreational boat anglers. Commercial catches are mostly taken as bycatch in trawls but annual landings have been low since the late 1980s. The Dab is a summer migrant with a preference for sandy sediments, moving into shallower waters to spawn in the spring months; recreational reports suggest that it is being caught increasingly earlier in the year. Historical records suggest that the local population has markedly decreased over the past century but this may not be the case elsewhere in its range and in some areas its population is believed to be increasing. As with many shallow marine species, it may be under reported.

European Flounder

Platichthys flesus

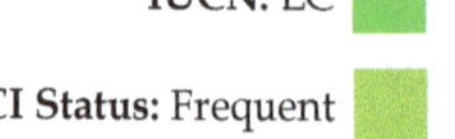

Max Length: 60 cm

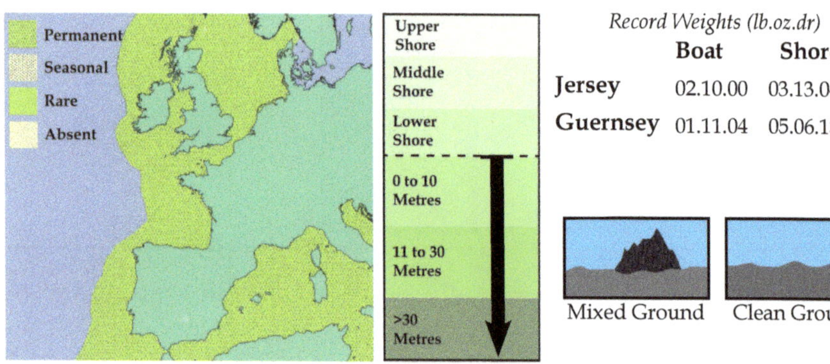

Record Weights (lb.oz.dr)

	Boat	Shore
Jersey	02.10.00	03.13.04
Guernsey	01.11.04	05.06.13

The Flounder is a medium-sized flatfish that lives in deeper water during the winter months and comes inshore during the spring and summer. It is related to the European Plaice and can be confused with it although the Flounder is generally smaller and less patterned. A genetic similarity to the Plaice means that the two species will sometimes produce hybrid specimens. Historical records for the Flounder are poor for the Channel Islands but it seems to be common in the Bay of Mont St Michel, perhaps because of its preference for sand and muddy substrates especially in association with estuaries. (Flounder can migrate into freshwater environments and are associated with estuaries in Europe.)

Local records and commercial catches (which are low annually) suggest that the Flounder is not common across the Channel Islands and that it is most prevalent during the spring months. It is occasionally caught by recreational anglers but is otherwise rarely reported. Elsewhere in Europe it is an important commercial species with thousands of tonnes a year being landed. The Flounder is certainly more abundant around UK shores than in the Channel Islands with it being heavily used as lobster and crab pot bait. The European population is believed to be decreasing but is not yet considered to be endangered.

Jack Gavey with his 2018 Jersey shore record Flounder (3 lb 13 oz 4 dr).

European Plaice

Pleuronectes platessa

Pliaie

Max Length: 100 cm

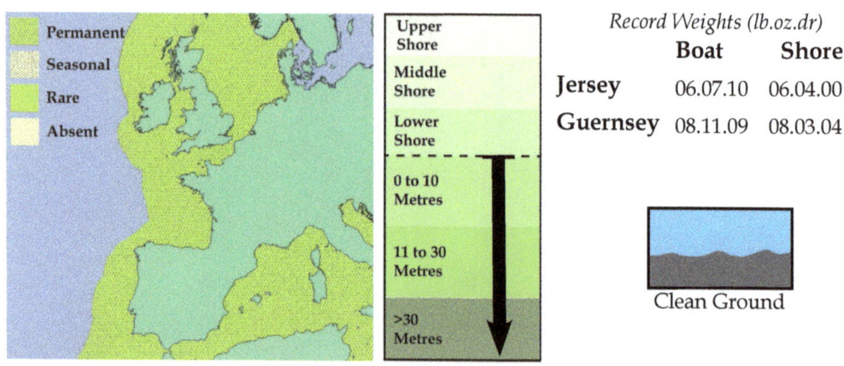

Record Weights (lb.oz.dr)

	Boat	Shore
Jersey	06.07.10	06.04.00
Guernsey	08.11.09	08.03.04

The Plaice was described as being abundant across the Channel Islands in the early nineteenth century but by the turn of the twentieth century it was listed as having been overfished around Jersey by biologist James Hornell. His naturalist father-in-law, Joseph Sinel, concurred, commenting that by 1905 few specimens reached a length of more than 30 cm and that southerly winds would drive juveniles into Jersey's sandy bays while northerly winds would keep them offshore. The abundance of Plaice seems to have varied considerably in the century that followed but the general trend appears to have been towards decline. In 2008 the expert Guernsey angler Len le Page noted that the Plaice 'has declined dramatically in recent years to the point where it's almost a rare catch'.

The Plaice is often confused with the Flounder but can be distinguished by a series of hard protruding areas across the back of the head as well as bright orange spots on most specimens. It is an important commercial species across Europe and has been heavily fished in many areas with annual landings running into the hundreds of tonnes. Channel Island commercial catches peaked at around 20 tonnes annually in the late 1990s but have been just a few tonnes in recent years. The local scarcity may well be a consequence of overfishing in the English Channel where stocks have been heavily targeted by trawlers.

Adult fish live on soft seabeds just offshore while juveniles may come close inshore and can sometimes be seen swimming rapidly along the low water mark or in intertidal puddles on sandy beaches. Traditional Channel Island methods for catching Plaice included 'spiking' in which a person would wade chest-deep at low water with two pronged poles (often broom handles with nails at the end). The person would walk forwards constantly spearing the seabed ahead of them in order to spike flatfish. Naturalist Ronald Le Sueur recounted the tale of a spiker who, when using a metal pole, speared an electric ray with predictable consequences. Spiking was widely practiced on Jersey, particularly along the east and south coast, but is now rarely used as a fishing method. While still not uncommon locally, the Plaice modern population is probably a fraction of what it was in early Victorian times.

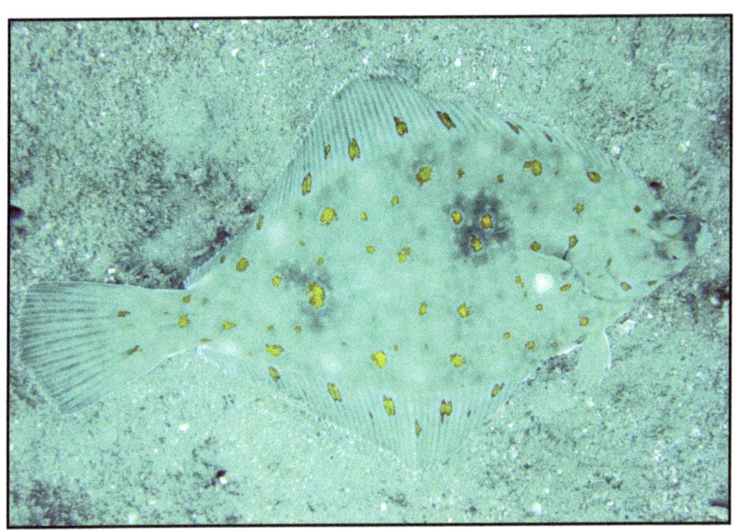

A Plaice (with distinctive orange spots) on the seabed off St Brélade's Bay, Jersey.

Lemon Sole

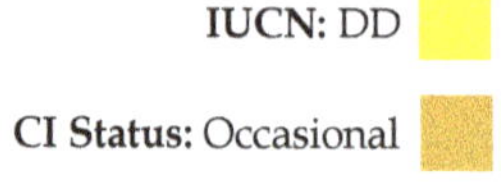

Microstomus kitt

Lînmon Sole

Max Length: 60 cm

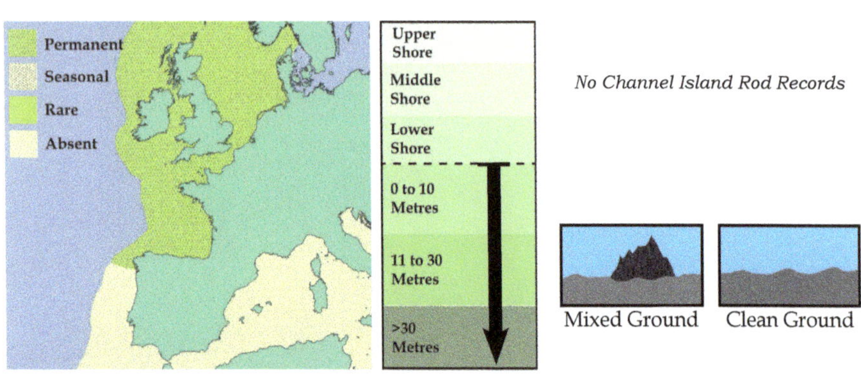

Rarely recorded by naturalists and anglers but landed in small numbers by local commercial fishers, the Lemon Sole is a shallow water species that can tolerate a variety of seabed types. It is a colder water species whose southerly range only just reaches the Bay of Biscay. Like many flatfish, the Lemon Sole moves offshore during the winter months, returning to the shallows in the spring. Since mid-Victorian times there has been just a handful of independent records and recent commercial catches have declined from several hundred kilos annually to practically zero. This may reflect fewer Channel Island trawlers, a lack of devolved EU catch quota to the islands or a contraction of its range with warming seas. Even so, it has occasionally featured in recent diver surveys and is probably not uncommon across the islands.

Solenette

Buglossidium luteum

Yellow Sole; Little Sole

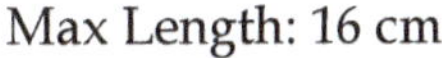

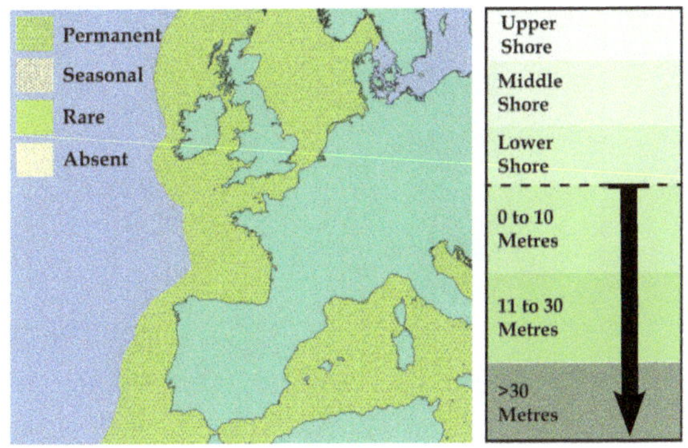

No Channel Island Rod Records

The Solenette is a small fish whose size, ability to hide in the sand and lack of commercial and recreational value means that it has been rarely recorded from the Channel Islands. It does, however, turn up frequently in regional scientific surveys, including a specimen south of Sark in 2012, which suggests it is probably one of those fish species that has been overlooked by naturalists and anglers. It is a shallow water, sandy seabed fish which is probably not uncommon across all the islands. Any captures would be of interest and should be reported to a local records centre.

Thickback Sole

Microchirus variegatus

Max Length: 35 cm

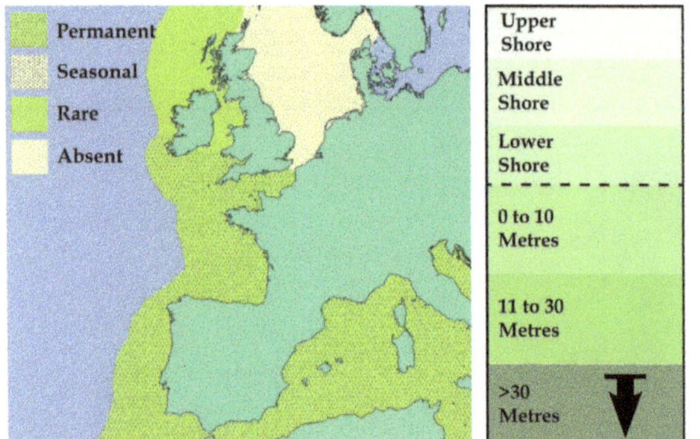

No Channel Island Rod Records

Clean Ground

The Thickback Sole is a southerly species whose range extends to the British Isles but is not commonly reported, perhaps because it can be confused with other sole species. The oldest local record is from 1904 when the Thickback Sole is described as being 'not very numerous' around Jersey in comparison to the Dover Sole. All other known records are from CEFAS scientific surveys operating off Jersey and Guernsey in 2006, 2010, 2011 and 2018 where it turned up infrequently in trawls. As with other local flatfish species, the Thickback Sole seems to have been regionally under-reported possibly because it generally lives below 30 metres in depth which places it out of the range of most naturalists. This is a species of interest and any, if encountered, should be reported to the relevant Channel Island records centre.

Sand Sole

Pegusa lascaris

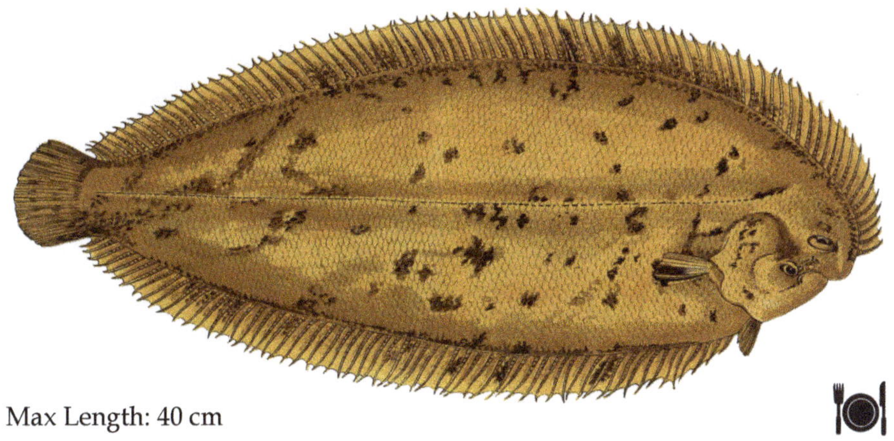

Max Length: 40 cm

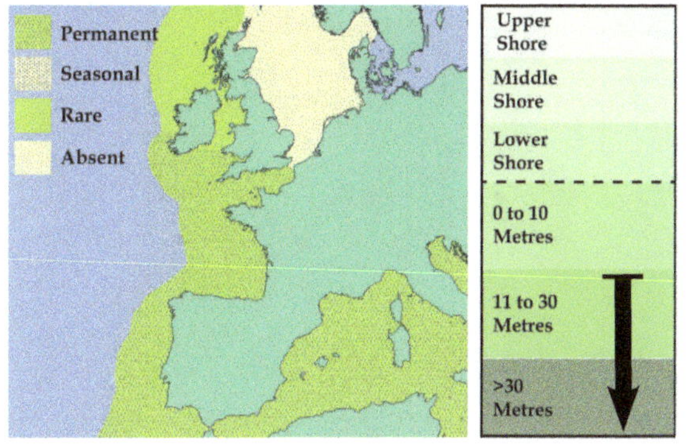

No Channel Island Rod Records

Clean Ground

The Sand Sole is a southern European species that is not uncommon in the western English Channel but which becomes increasingly rare further north. There are just two historical records for the Sand Sole for the Channel Islands, the first in 1862 and the second in 1904. There are no angling records which is unusual given it is a medium-sized shallow water species. There are, however, regular scientific records and commercial landings from the 1970s onwards and reports from CEFAS trawl surveys from 2006 to 2018. This suggests that the Sand Sole is not uncommon within the Islands and that its distribution is primarily to the north of Guernsey and Herm with almost no specimens at all coming from Jersey waters. The Sand Sole is easily confused with other sole species which may also explain its apparent under-reporting. A key identification characteristic to look for is a rosette-shaped nostril underneath the body.

Dover Sole

Solea solea

Sole

IUCN: DD

CI Status: Frequent

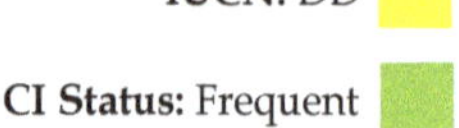

Max Length: 70 cm

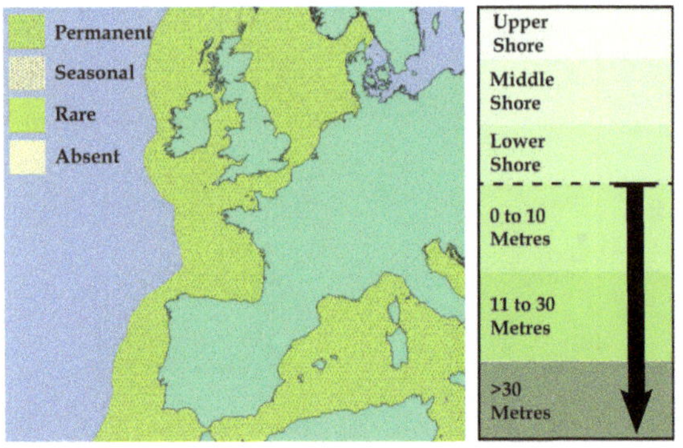

Record Weights (lb.oz.dr)

	Boat	Shore
Jersey	02.12.11	04.07.14
Guernsey	04.01.12	06.08.10*

The Dover Sole is a relatively common fish that comes into shallow water in the spring and summer months where it is popular with recreational shore anglers although, as a largely nocturnal feeder, the majority are caught at night. The Dover Sole is an important commercial species and annual landings have been over 20 tonnes at times although complications with EU quotas within the Channel Islands have largely curtailed local catches in recent years. Elsewhere in Europe the Dover Sole is heavily fished but most populations are believed to be stable. Historical records for the Dover Sole begin in the nineteenth century when it was described as being abundant. Most reports since then suggest that it is common across the islands, something that is backed up by commercial catches from netters and trawlers. Divers and snorkelers may see the Dover Sole half buried on sandy seabeds and the juveniles are often seen in the summer months at low water swimming fleetingly along the edge of the tide line.

Triggerfish, Pufferfish and Sunfish

The last section in this book contains a handful of unusual species from the Tetraodontiformes order of fish, each of which is the sole local representative for their biological family. This includes the Grey Triggerfish (Balistidae), Oceanic Pufferfish (Tetraodontidae) and Sunfish (Molidae). Also covered in this section is the Crucian Carp which is from the Cypriniformes order of fish. Cypriniformes are predominantly freshwater but the Crucian Carp has two reliable local marine records and so, while normally out of place in a book on sea fish, it has been included for the sake of completeness.

Of these species it is the Sunfish that is most likely to be encountered, as it is a large surface swimmer that will occasionally be seen by boaters during the summer months. The pufferfish is a vagrant known from just one specimen and the triggerfish, while probably common, is subtidal although it is occasionally seen by divers or gets caught in lobster pots. Sometimes almost intact triggerfish specimens will be washed up following cold weather or storms.

The Crucian Carp is unlikely to be seen in the marine environment although evidently it must occasionally stray, or is perhaps washed by storms, into saltwater areas.

All these species are of scientific interest and additional records would be welcome. Triggerfish are a climate change indicator, having apparently only been present in the English Channel since World War II. Sunfish sightings are collected by natural historians as part of studies into large pelagic animals such as dolphins and sharks. Sightings may be submitted to local biological records centres.

Jack Gavey with the Jersey shore record Grey Triggerfish (3 lb 12 oz 1 dr).

Grey Triggerfish

IUCN: VU 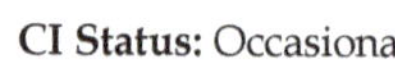

CI Status: Occasional

Balistes capriscus

Leather-jacket

Max Length: 60 cm

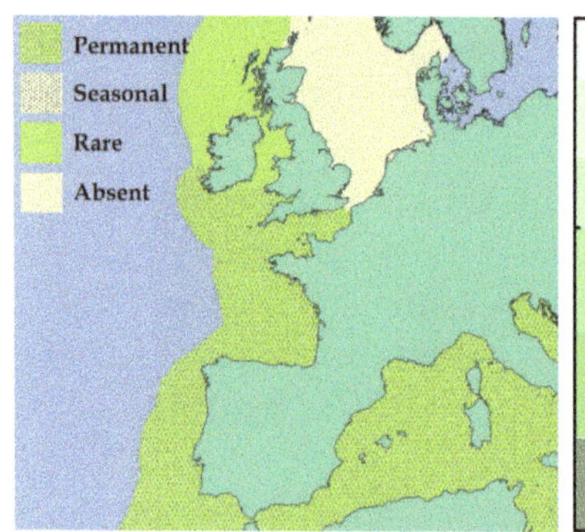

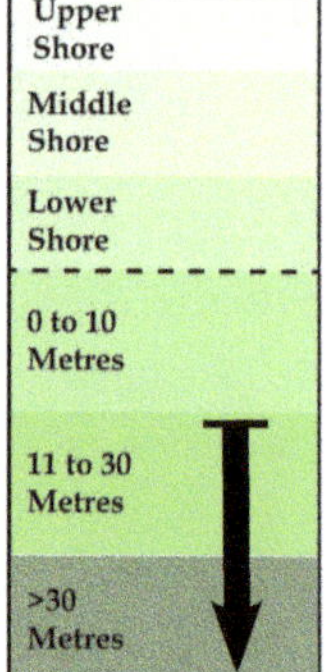

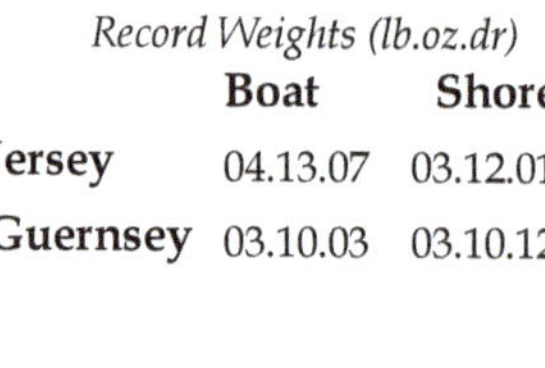

Record Weights (lb.oz.dr)

	Boat	Shore
Jersey	04.13.07	03.12.01
Guernsey	03.10.03	03.10.12

Mixed Ground

Rough Ground

The Grey Triggerfish is large, distinctive and a relatively recent arrival in Channel Islands waters. Although there are occasional Victorian records from England, the first local record was in 1930 from Guernsey. By the 1950s Jersey anglers started to report that Triggerfish were becoming trapped in lobster pots and from this point on they seem to become more common locally. This seems to be a southerly species whose permanent range expanded north during the early twentieth century to include the Normano-Breton Gulf and the southern United Kingdom. Specimens are sometimes caught and sold commercially and it is possible that they do not tolerate the cold as dead specimens have been observed to wash up more frequently during severe winters. The Oceanic Triggerfish (*Canthidermis maculata*) has been reported as a rare visitor to southern England but not yet to our region.

Oceanic Pufferfish

IUCN: LC

Lagocephalus lagocephalus

CI Status: Rare

Globe Fish

Max Length: 61 cm

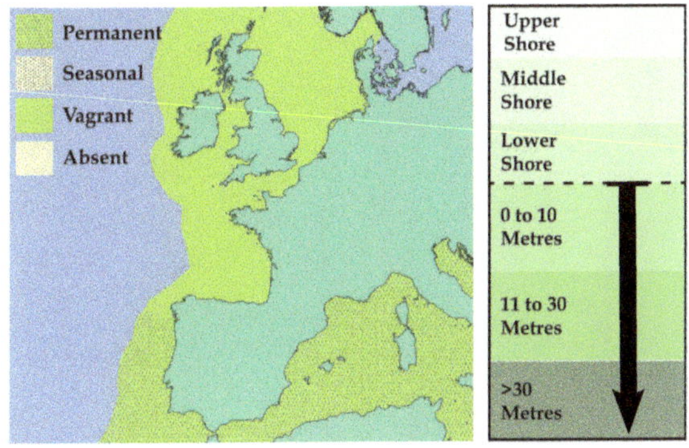

No Channel Island Rod Records

Pelagic

The Oceanic Pufferfish is so named because it can inflate its chest when threatened, almost doubling its size. Common in the world's tropical and subtropical seas, the Oceanic Pufferfish will sometimes stray into temperate waters with specimens having been caught off Scotland and even in the North Sea.

The only regional record comes from a specimen caught off L'Étacq, Jersey, in September 1907, the identification of which was confirmed by local biologist Joseph Sinel. With no other records known, this should be considered a very rare visitor to the Normano-Breton Gulf. The flesh of the Oceanic Pufferfish is potentially poisonous and should not be eaten.

Sunfish

Mola mola

Solé

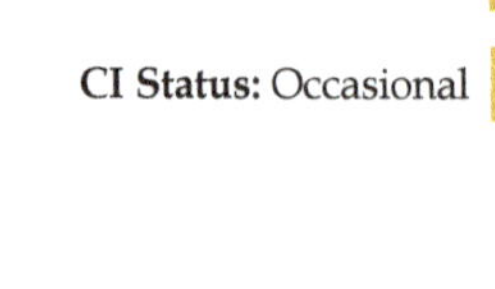

Max Length: 250 cm

Permanent
Seasonal
Rare
Absent

Upper Shore
Middle Shore
Lower Shore
0 to 10 Metres
11 to 30 Metres
>30 Metres

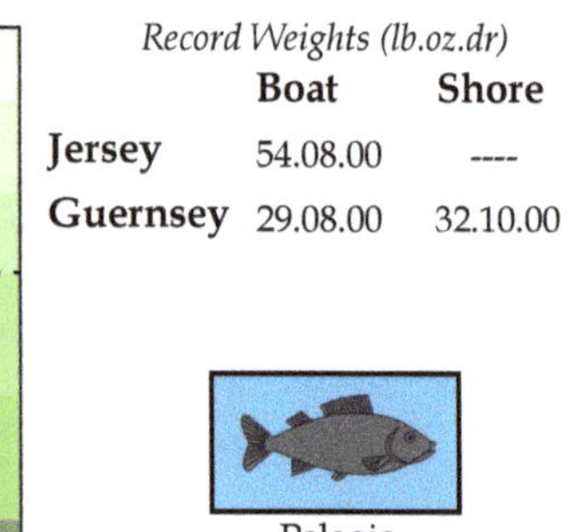

Record Weights (lb.oz.dr)

	Boat	Shore
Jersey	54.08.00	----
Guernsey	29.08.00	32.10.00

The bizarrely-shaped Sunfish is, after dolphins and seals, the most commonly reported large marine animal by Channel Island leisure boaters. The sight of its tall dorsal fin protruding above the water makes the Sunfish easy to spot from a distance and the fish will often remain swimming at the surface for a short while before diving into the depths. Despite its size and apparent awkwardness, the Sunfish will sometimes jump clear of the water, especially if startled.

An adult Sunfish may reach three metres in length and over a tonne in weight making it the heaviest bony fish in the world. It mostly feeds on jellyfish and seems to follow the swarms of Barrel Jellyfish (*Rhizostoma pulmo*) that drift into local waters from the Atlantic Ocean every summer. Local reports of Sunfish go back to the 1840s and have been constant ever since with the first sightings normally being around June or July. There is some evidence that sightings are more numerous in some years than others which may be a reflection of jellyfish abundance or other factors such as prevailing winds. The Sunfish has only minor commercial interest but, being pelagic, it is often caught as bycatch in drift nets and this does seem to have had a negative impact on the European population. The Sunfish is classed as vulnerable by the IUCN and, while capture is unlikely, any Sunfish sighted at sea should be approached slowly and at a reasonable distance.

This juvenile Sunfish became trapped in St Peter Port marina in July 2010. It swam about frantically for several hours until it was able to find its way out at high tide.

Crucian Carp

Carassius carassius

Max Length: 35 cm

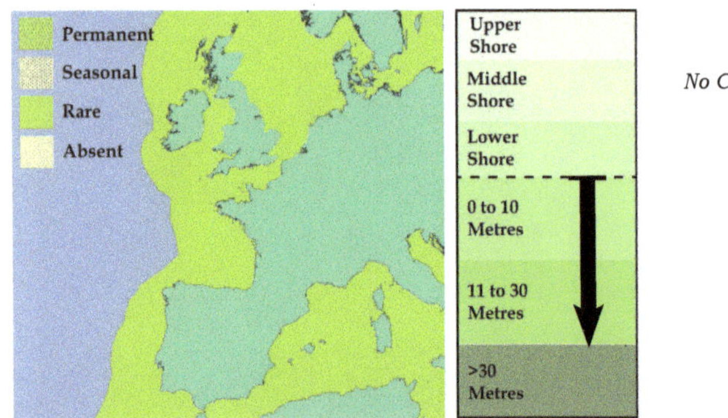

No Channel Island Rod Records

Pelagic

The Crucian Carp is a predominantly freshwater species that, while tolerant of brackish water, would not be expected to occur in fully marine areas such as the Channel Islands. The single local report comes from Jersey naturalist Joseph Sinel who identified a specimen caught by an angler from one of the island's pierheads in the early twentieth century. Even Sinel was bemused by its occurrence describing the specimen as an 'oversized goldfish' that had 'lost its way'. Although identified by a competent naturalist, this record of a predominantly freshwater species was initially viewed as a doubtful inclusion for this book until the discovery of a second regional specimen taken south of Chausey in the CEFAS beam trawl survey of 2009. The Crucian Carp is probably a very rare and unusual visitor to Channel Island waters.

How to Report Fish Records

One of the surprising discoveries that came from researching this book was the lack of available information about many local fish species. Even those fish that we think of as being common, such as mackerel, bass and flatfish, have relatively few official records. We are currently in a period when many local fish species are arriving, leaving, increasing or declining in the region, primarily due to changes in climate and fishing patterns. Never before has reliable evidence about fish species been so important.

This lack of information is probably because most people (including many naturalists and scientists) do not think to make and submit records of species that are regarded as common. Also, it is only relatively recently that the Channel Islands have had biological records centres that are devoted to collecting and storing wildlife sightings for wider public access.

More information is needed for all local fish species and if you have any records, whether of common or unusual fish species, then please send them (ideally with photographs and accurate location information) to one of the following biological recording centres:

Jersey Biodiversity Centre
jerseybiodiversitycentre.org.je

Guernsey Biological Records Centre
www.biologicalrecordscentre.gov.gg

Alderney Wildlife Trust
www.alderneywildlife.org

Société Sercquaise
www.socsercq.sark.gg

Additionally, the authors of this book would be grateful to learn of any Channel Island captures or sightings of fish species that either do not feature in this book or are unusual or rare. We may be contacted via the Marine Biology Section of the Société Jersiaise (*www.societe-jersiaise.org*).

Changes in Local Fish Populations

Making pronouncements about the status of individual fish populations is fraught with difficulty and separating anecdotal-based theories from independently obtained evidence is a hurdle that faces most modern fisheries. In this book we have attempted to look for evidence of increases or decreases in abundance in order to estimate the population status of key species since Victorian times. The casual nature of biological recording prior to the 1980s means that this is not an exact science but we think that there is enough available information for many species to deduce trends through time. A summary of our conclusions is given below.

Expirated Species

Local fish records suggest that there are at least five fish species which were once regularly seen in the Channel Islands but have since completely gone (i.e. expirated) from the area. These are: the Spurdog; Monkfish; White Skate; Common Skate; and Long-nosed Skate.

It is no coincidence that these are all cartilaginous sharks or rays (i.e. elasmobranchs) as these are generally long-lived but slow to mature and breed. Slow growth and late maturation makes fish species vulnerable to overexploitation as intensive regular fishing (often in combination with incorrect or absent minimum landing sizes) will remove or kill individuals before they can breed to replace themselves. In such situations a population will steadily decrease and, in the worst cases, collapse often with remarkable speed. This phenomenon does not just affect sharks and rays but also other late maturing (often predatory) species such as seabass, some flatfish and bream.

The five expirated species listed above are currently subject to protection or heavy fishing restrictions within the EU fisheries framework but all animal populations will have critical thresholds below which it is difficult for them to recover. The absence of these five species from the Channel Islands follows a pattern of decline seen elsewhere in the wider region and current trends suggest that a full recovery may take years to occur, if ever.

Decreasing Fish Populations

As noted earlier, judging historical abundance is never easy, especially as there are no evidence-based studies for the region prior to the 1980s. Even commercial landing data can be difficult to interpret especially in the Channel Islands where the fishing fleet is small and subject to short-term trends depending on local and international regulations. The addition or removal of one or two large and active vessels from a fleet can lead to dramatic falls or rises in landings that are related to a drop in fishing effort, not a species' abundance.

There are, however, a few species whose populations are probably much smaller now than they were pre-World War Two. These include the Porbeagle Shark; Common Eel; Conger Eel; Red Bream; Black Bream; European Seabass; Atlantic Mackerel; Bluefin Tuna; Dab; Turbot and Plaice. These are all species that have been heavily fished on a local, regional and international scale and any population decline is probably due to overfishing. Most of these species' populations have the ability to recover if suitable management measures are adopted.

Changing Geographic Ranges

During the past century local sea temperatures have warmed by around one degree centigrade probably as a consequence of human-induced climatic warming. This rise affects the local winter seasonal sea temperature more than the summer one, which possibly permits southern European fish to migrate northwards earlier in the year towards Channel Island waters. Conversely, the lack of a colder water seasonal period may be forcing some colder water fish species to contract their ranges northward towards the Irish and North Seas.

The absolute geographic range for any marine species is rarely clear cut but there are a handful of fish within the Channel Islands that are probably at their southern edge of their natural range. This list includes: Northern Rockling; Norway Bullhead; Pogge; sea-snail species and Lemon Sole. Although still present in the region, they could become

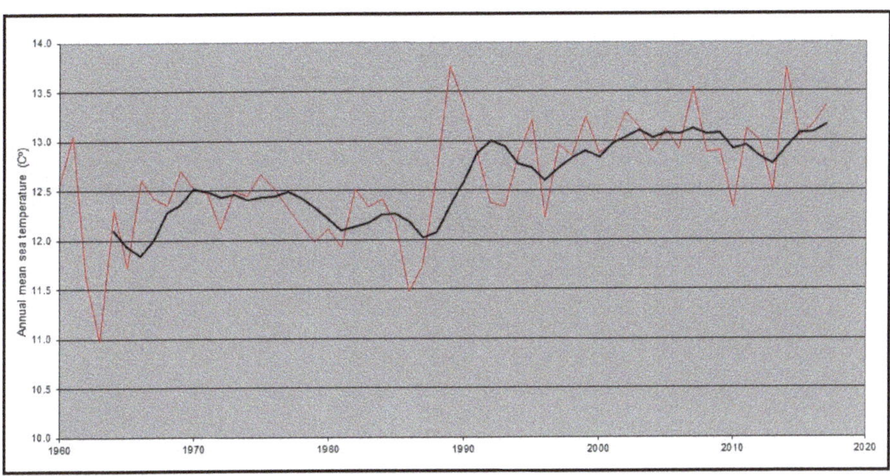

Average annual sea temperatures (with a five-year moving average imposed) at St Helier between 1960 and 2017 indicating a rise of around 1°C. (Source: Jersey Met)

scarcer with time. There are other cold water species, such as the Wolf-fish and Torsk which have patchy historical records but which might have been more common in the past.

A clearer picture is presented by fish species from southern Europe which, since World War II have started to move into the Normano-Breton Gulf from the Bay of Biscay. This wave of migrant species was pioneered by the Triggerfish, Couch's Bream, Black-faced Blenny, Leopard-spotted Goby, Reticulated Dragonet and Giant Goby, none of which have a Victorian presence but which were resident and common by the 1970s. Other possible species in this group include Ballion's Wrasse and Long-snouted Seahorse neither of which has a historical track record going back more than a few decades.

Since the 1990s a new wave of southern fish species has started to be recorded regularly in the islands. These are mostly mobile migrants whose seasonal range seems to be expanding with warming seas. This list of species is long and includes several species of jack and bream (e.g. amberjacks, Bogue, *Diplodus* spp., Pandora, etc.), Atlantic Saury, Spotted Sea-bass and Bonito all of which are now regularly caught by anglers in the summer months.

Additional to this are several southern fish species that have just one or two records but which have the potential to become more common in the near future. This list includes: the Blue Jack Mackerel; Silver Dory; Blue Mouth; Scorpion Fish; Dusky Perch; Comber and Ringneck Blenny.

Future Arrivals

Finally, there are fish species in the Bay of Biscay that have not yet been recorded from our region but whose range is expanding towards the Channel Islands. Some already have English Channel records and are potentially fish species that will be seen in the near future. The list includes: Black Scorpionfish (*Scorpaena porcus*); Longfin Gurnard (*Chelidonichthys obscurus*); Red-mouthed Goby (*Gobius cruentatus*); Red Tompot Blenny (*Parablennius ruber*); Shi Drum (*Umbrina cirrosa*); Striped Seabream (*Lithognathus mormyrus*); Pompano (*Trachinotus ovatus*); Plain Bonito (*Orcynopsis unicolor*) and Little Tunny (*Euthynnus alletteratus*). Captures or sightings of any of these species should be reported (ideally with photographs) to a local records centre (see page 277).

Sustainability

When it comes to fishing sustainably, humans have an appalling track record that goes back several centuries. The pattern of overfishing, waste and habitat destruction that we are familiar with today was not, as many believe, pioneered in modern seas but instead in European rivers, ponds and lakes. Even by late medieval times, overexploitation, pollution and dam building had collapsed many major freshwater fish species' populations and, in the absence of wild fishing, many communities resorted to freshwater aquaculture, creating ponds for trout and other species. St Ouen's Pond in Jersey may be an example of this and, once stocked with fish, the rights to fish in such ponds were jealously guarded by the manors that owned them.

Marine fishing is a difficult and dangerous occupation so it was only after the rivers and lakes had been exhausted of their fish that people started to make regular offshore boat journeys in search of new supplies. The invention of the trawl and, more particularly the advent of motor-powered vessels, had a profound effect on fishing effort and therefore also coastal fish populations. By the 1860s the early signs of overfishing had been noted across northern Europe causing alarm to small coastal communities that relied on inshore fishing with small boats.

Starting in 1863, the UK government appointed Royal Commissions to examine the allegations of overfishing in British waters. Despite gathering ample evidence to the contrary (including from Channel Island vessels), the Royal Commissioners famously concluded that European fish stocks were inexhaustible and that no amount of fishing effort could make an impact on them. Activities such as trawling and dredging were deemed to be beneficial to fish stocks by 'ploughing the seabed' in preparation for the next generation of fish.

Opposing the Royal Commissioners was the first generation of fishery scientists whose landing statistics and biological data suggested that fish stocks had been overfished for decades and that the bycatch and continual seabed disruption negatively affected fish stocks. By 1900 there were two opposite opinions on the issue of overfishing but it would be a few decades before the commercial fishing fleets, when faced with decreasing catches, would ask their governments for assistance with managing fish stocks.

This debate was repeated in Jersey at the turn of the twentieth century when the fisheries scientist James Hornell locked horns with his amateur naturalist father-in-law Joseph Sinel via a series of public lectures and newspaper letters. Hornell had been gathering local fisheries statistics since the 1890s and believed that management measures were needed to prevent stocks from being overfished. Sinel countered by adopting what he felt was a common sense attitude that, because fish are so numerous, no amount of fishing could dent their stocks. Eventually Sinel's opinion won through and it was not until the back half of the twentieth century that meaningful fisheries management started to operate locally.

The debate between Hornell and Sinel has been repeated ever since, not just locally but across the globe as governments attempt to balance often doom-laden statistical assessments from their fisheries scientists against the economic and political interests of commercial fishing fleets. The result has frequently been compromises that do not offer safeguards for fish stocks, the marine environment or the fishing industry itself. Consequently it is estimated that around 90% of current global fish stocks are either being exploited at their maximum sustainable limit or have gone beyond this point and are overfished.

The Channel Islands are situated on the edge of the English Channel which is one of the most heavily fished sea areas on Earth. This, in combination with the actions of local and EU vessels, means that overfishing is as much of a concern locally as anywhere else in Europe.

This book has looked at the available data for local fish species and has highlighted trends that may be due to natural causes, warming seas or historical overfishing. We have also included the IUCN threat assessments for each species which will give an indication of its global population status. However, we do not feel that in most instances there is enough data to provide a locally applicable threat assessment score

A single day's catch (in 1959) of at least 80 fish by a shore party at Icho Tower, Jersey. Recent fishing records suggest that hauls like like this are now a rarity.

although we have offered a 'CI Status' rating system based on probable commonality. This reflects several factors, such as habitat availability, breeding potential and geographic range, as well as probable abundance.

In the absence of detailed data for most fish species, we would request that readers do all they can to minimise their impact on local (and global) fish stocks. If you are an angler then please respect local regulations or guidelines and only take enough fish for your needs. Wherever possible return fish alive and use methods that will minimise damage to individual fish as well to general stock levels.

If you are a consumer then consider purchasing fish that are sustainably sourced by either looking for certification on packets or menus (e.g. the Marine Stewardship Council) or by consulting lists such as the Marine Conservation Society's online *Good Fish Guide*. Sustainability is the publicly stated aim of every international, national and regional fishery but it is only rarely being achieved. Sustainable fisheries are certainly possible but this requires everyone (governments, public and industry) to play their part, no matter how big or small that may be.

Bibliography

Below is a brief list of the more useful publications consulted during the writing of this book. Individual species' records relating to the Channel Islands from these and other sources have been computerised and a copy has been given to the Jersey Biodiveristy Centre.

* = useful identification guide
\+ = useful summary of local species

+Ansted and Latham, 1862. *The Channel Islands.* Allen and co.

+Chambers, P., Binney, F. and Jeffreys, G., 2016. *Les Minquiers: a natural history.* Charonia Media.

Couch, J., 1865. *A history of the fishes of the British Islands.* Groombridge and sons. 4 vols.

Culley, M., 1979. *An investigation into some aspects of the fisheries of Jersey.* Portsmouth Polytechynic.

Day, F., 1880. *The fishes of Great Britain and Ireland.* Williams and Norgate. 2 vols.

Daly, S., 1998, *Marine life of the Channel Islands.* Kingdom Books.

de Gruchy, C., 2015. *Marine spatial planning: an atlas and study of ecology and human activities in Jersey waters.* Unpublished MSc Dissertation, University of York.

+**Duncan, J.**, 1841. *The history of Guernsey with occasional notices of Jersey, Alderney and Sark.* Longman, Brown and Green.

+Gadeau de Kerville, H., 1897. *Faune de la Normandie: reptiles, batraciens et poissons.* Baillière et Fils. Vol. 4.

Gervais, P., 1876. *Les Poissons.* Rothschild. 3 volumes.

***Henderson, P.**, 2014. **Identification guide to the inshore fish of the British Isles.** Pisces Conservation.

Hornell, J., 1897. *The possibilities of fishery improvement in Jersey.* The Journal of Marine Zoology and Microscopy.

Jenkins, J., 1925. *The Fishes of the British Isles.* Warne and Co.

***Kay, P., and Dipper, F.**, 2009. *Marine fishes of Wales and adjacent waters.* Marine Wildlife.

+Le Mao, P., 2009. *Inventaire de la biodiversité marine dans le Golfe Normano-Breton: agnathes, condrichtyens et osteichtyens.* Ifremer.

+Le Page, L., 2009. *Angling in the Bailiwick of Guernsey*. Peterprint Limited.

+Le Sueur, R., 1967. *Marine fishes of Jersey*. Société Jersiaise.

***Louisy, P.**, 2015. *Europe and Mediterranean marine fish: identification guide*. Ulmer.

Marine Biology Section, 2014. *The Seashore Life of Jersey*. Société Jersiaise.

Marine Resources Research Unit, 1967. *The fishing industry of Jersey: a preliminary report*. Portsmouth College of Technology.

McIlwee, K., 2014. *The Jersey scuba explorers' guide*. Barnes Publishing.

Perrio, P., 2011. *Fishing in Jersey*. Jersey Evening Post.

Rodwell, W., 1996. *Les Écréhous*. Société Jersiaise.

+Sinel, J., 1905. The fishes of the Channel Islands. *Reports and Transactions of the Guernsey Society*. Vol. 5(1): 56:65.

Sinel, J., 1906. *An outline of the natural history of our shores*. Swan & Sonnenschein.

States of Jersey, 1982. *The fishing industry of Jersey*. States Greffe.

States of Jersey, 2017. *Non-native marine species in the Channel Islands*. Société Jersiaise.

***Teletchea, F.**, 2009. *Guides des Poissons de France: Côtes de l'Atlantique et de la Manche*. Belin.

Acknowledgements

We thank the following organisations for their assistance with the production of this guide: Alderney Wildllife Trust; CEFAS; Department of the Environment (States of Jersey; States of Guernsey); Guernsey Biological Records Centre; Ifremer (France); Jersey Biodiversity Centre; Jersey Seasearch; National Archives (UK); Société Jersiaise; Société Guernesiaise; West Coast Sea Angling Club (Guernsey).

We also thank the following individuals for their help with this and other marine biology projects: Lin Baldock; Rachel Baxter; Louise Bennett-Jones; Jonathan Billot; Francis Binney; Samantha Blampied; Darren Braby; Peter Crowther; Sabina Danzer; Chantelle de Gruchy; Denis de Gruchy; Andy Farmer; Daniel Ferguson; Sarah Fitz; Tim Froome; Simon Gavey; Derek Hairon; Tony Heart; Ed and Annie Hibbs; Charlotte Hooper; Courtney Huisman; Chris Isaacs; Gareth Jeffreys; Nicholas Jouault; Phillip Langlois; Dean Pitman; Paul Le Prevost; Roger Long; Richard Lord; Anya Martins; Kevin and Beverly McIlwee; Greg Morel; Leigh Mullins; Remi John Pinel; Jon Rault; Andrew Syvret; Bob and Jill Tompkins; Don Thompson; Jason Touzel; Trudie Trox-Hairon; Kirk Truscott; Stan Vaudin; Geoff Walker; Paul Wheaton; Chris Wood; David Yettram.

Picture Credits

Unless otherwise stated below the images used in this book are from the authors, from out-of-copyright works or from sources that have attributed the images as being publically usable under the Creative Commons licencing scheme. However, many of the angling and specimen photographs were contributed by individuals and we thank all those who gave permission for us to reproduce their work.

Photographs of angling specimens were kindly provided by: Darren Braby; Daniel Ferguson; Tim Froome; Simon Gavey; Tony Heart; Paul Le Prevost; Leigh Mullins; Steve Mullins; Jason Touzel; Stan Vaudin; and Paul Wheaton.

Other general fish and wildlife photographs were kindly provided by: Louise Bennett-Jones; Francis Binney; Samantha Blampied; Peter Crowther; Peter Gay; Chris Isaacs; Kevin McIlwee; Marine Resources (States of Jersey); Société Jersiaise; and David Yettram.

Index to Species

This is an index to the common and scientific names for the animal and plant species in this book. An asterisk denotes a main entry and/or illustration.

About the Authors

Born in Jersey, Alex Plaster grew up fishing and exploring local waters. His general interest in marine biology and fascination with fish led to a BSc in Marine Geography (Cardiff University) which included several months working with large apex predators in Bimini (Bahamas) using underwater video studies and elasmobranch tagging.

Alex is a lifelong recreational shore and boat angler but has also worked in Jersey's commercial fishing sector. He has also undertaken scientific studies projects around Jersey and is a specialist in using Baited Remote Underwater Video (BRUV) technology to look at the relationship between habitat type and fish assemblages. Alex is currently studying post release mortality rates within Jersey fish species.

Paul Chambers has over thirty years experience of studying the Channel Islands' marine life. He has an MSc and PhD from University College London and collects information about all aspects of local maritime natural history and culture.

www.ingramcontent.com/pod-product-compliance
Lightning Source LLC
Chambersburg PA
CBHW040139270326
41928CB00022B/3263
9780956065568